The Ghost Marriage

The Ghost Marriage

A Memoir

Kirsten Mickelwait

SHE WRITES PRESS

Published 2021
Printed in the United States of America
Print ISBN: 978-1-64742-030-7
E-ISBN: 978-1-64742-031-4
Library of Congress Control Number: 2020923322

For information, address:
She Writes Press
1569 Solano Ave #546
Berkeley, CA 94707

She Writes Press is a division of SparkPoint Studio, LLC.

For my parents, Kenneth and Helen Mickelwait,
who taught me to use my words

And for my children

Someone I loved once gave me a box full of darkness.
It took me years to understand that this, too, was a gift.

—Mary Oliver

CONTENTS

Part I

Prologue 1

Is This Hollywood? 3

A Charmed Life 17

Adaptation 22

My Problem Child 35

Fault Line 47

A Basket of Bells 55

Part II

Football Players 61

Au Revoir, Hooverville 71

Under House Arrest 83

Meshugaas 94

The Bearded Woman 101

Road Kill Café 113

Gimme Shelter 125

Broken Bones 133

Kangaroo Court 141

The Nuremberg Defense. 155

A Diploma of Virtue. 160

All the Bells and Whistles 165

How the Light Gets In 172

Fugue State. 179

Pyramid Scheme 189

Part III

Requiem and Raw Sewage 205

Indemnification. 219

A Shakespearean Tragedy 235

The Whole World in His Hands 251

Part IV

Earth Is Forgiveness School. 265

All the Things He Didn't Do 276

These Men Don't Like You. 283

O Magnum Mysterium. 289

Despair Is a Spiritual State. 298

A Meatball at the Mouth of a Cave. 305

Lifting the Veil. 312

Disembarkation. 318

Part I

Prologue

It was a fine day for a funeral. The January sky was clear, and the pale winter sun warmed our heads as we stood around the tiny grave. Who gets cremated *and* buried, anyway?

The family gathered under the awning facing the priest. I should have joined them there because, technically, I was family—my nearly adult daughter and son were the children of the deceased. But so much had happened between their dad and me, I stood instead off to the side by the small group of friends who had come to St. Helena for the funeral.

"Into your hands, O Lord, we humbly entrust our brother Stephen," the priest said. "In this life you embraced him with your tender love; deliver him now from every evil and bid him enter eternal rest."

Bronte wept quietly. Amory stood ashen-faced and fought back tears. He had been their father—of course they still loved him. But my eyes were dry.

"The old order has passed away," the priest said. "Welcome him, then, into paradise, where there will be no sorrow, no weeping or pain, but the fullness of peace and joy with your Son and the Holy Spirit for ever and ever."

The old order has passed away, I thought. *Has it? How can I know for sure?* Steve Beckwith and I had shared twenty-six years together. First there was the bliss of courtship, then the contentment of marriage and the love of parenthood. Then anger, spite, unforgivable damage. He had spent the last five years trying to destroy me. What I didn't yet know was that our relationship wasn't over. He still had things to say.

"In the name of the Father, and of the Son, and of the Holy Spirit," the priest intoned.

Everyone crossed themselves.

"Amen."

I didn't kill him. But he would have told you different.

Chapter 1

Is This Hollywood?

It was the fall of 1985 and I had just spent a year in Rome, working illegally as a tour guide and chasing *la dolce vita*. I'd managed, barely, to afford a crumbling apartment on the top floor of a *quattrocento* palazzo in the historic center. I'd had a decent boyfriend—someone with a real job, not one of those sweet-smelling lotharios who strutted the piazzas looking for female tourists to seduce. In my spare time I explored every wrinkle of the Eternal City, its heroic statues, its ancient stones. But after a year of living this fantasy, I finally understood that I'd never have a real life there. Rome, as it turned out, was for Romans. I was thirty and I wanted an adult's life. I needed to go home and start a legitimate career. And, after a lifetime of ambivalence about marriage and children, I realized that I genuinely wanted both. It was time to grow up.

I returned to California and my future loomed like an ominous cloud. After the year abroad I was starting from scratch, so I temporarily moved back into my parents' mid-century Eichler house in Palo Alto and hung my clothes in the closet of my childhood room. Then I spent my days looking for work and apartments in San Francisco and occasionally cooking an Italian meal for my mom and dad. On the heels of a year in Caput Mundi, this felt a bit humbling.

My parents had been incredibly patient with my wanderlust. They themselves had married late for their generation and didn't have children until they were thirty-five. In the days before my flight to Italy, they'd remained diplomatically silent about my finances, my professional future, and the mystery of whether they'd ever see me again. But now my father seemed to have reached the end of his tolerance. "You know, by the time your mother and I were your age, we were married," he blurted out one day. "You need to think about settling down before it's too late."

Your age? Too late? What had happened to my liberal parents, the original "what color is your parachute" thinkers? Suddenly I was living on the set of *Father Knows Best*. My twenties had been a festival of career building, international travel, and short-term relationships. It had been a decade defined by unfettered freedom and perpetual fun. Clearly, the party was over.

Helen and Ken Mickelwait had modeled a perfect marriage for me and my younger sister, Ingrid. Their relationship was built on shared interests—hiking in the high Sierras, folk dancing, intellectual pursuits—as well as mutual trust, respect, and affection. Looking back, I see what cool people they really were. There were always book clubs and discussion groups, dinner parties with ethnic foods, outreach-based church activities, dancing lessons. When my sister and I were well into elementary school, my mom earned her teaching credential and became the director of a nursery school, and Dad was fine with the fact that she no longer had dinner on the table by five o'clock. They seemed to adore each other and to understand what a good marriage required: patience, tolerance, flexibility, and communication.

They made it look so easy, I'd always assumed that I'd have a marriage like the one they had. But I was also dazzled by glamour and passion, and a year in Italy did nothing to disabuse me of wanting them. I decided that when I married, I'd have the comfort and stability of my parents' marriage, plus the dramatic sizzle of big romance.

Within a few months, I found a beautiful little second-floor flat in the outer Richmond district of San Francisco. I set myself up as a freelance publicist and marketing writer and was making ends meet, barely. By August, it had been eight months since I'd returned from Rome and, aside from a book club and an occasional meal out with female friends, my social life was dead. That wasn't all bad—since I'd left for Europe, the AIDS epidemic had hit the city hard. Suddenly life felt serious.

Later that month, I attended a friend's wedding at the Pavilion of Flowers in Golden Gate Park. The big white Victorian greenhouse looked like spun sugar, and the technicolor flora of orchids, lilies, and tuberous begonias was the perfect backdrop for Joyce and her handsome new husband, a former acting student, to say their vows.

I admired all the beautiful specimens—both floral and human— and piled my plate with canapés. The crowd was largely peopled with those I'd worked with at the American Conservatory Theater before I'd left for Europe: actors, acting students, and theater staff. Amanda, with whom I'd worked in the marketing and development office, sidled up to me, her plate equally loaded with food. Across the room she'd spotted Richard—a budding actor who had wooed her and then unceremoniously dumped her for someone else—and was strategically placing herself out of his line of sight.

"Remember this, my friend," Amanda said, surveying the room. "Men are dogs. There is no exception to this rule."

"I hear you," I said. "Not that I've tested that theory in the last eight months."

"Save yourself the aggravation," she said. "It's been proven. By me. Repeatedly." She wandered off to refill her champagne flute.

I scanned the crowd for another familiar face when a couple approached me. It was Esther Conway, one of ACT's board members, and a good-looking man of indeterminate age. Esther was in her fifties, with heavy blonde highlights and a bubbly Doris Day personality. "This is Kirsten," she beamed to said good-looking man. "She used to be the publicist at ACT. Isn't she bright-eyed and beautiful?"

I shook his hand. "Steve here noticed you from across the room," Esther said, "and I told him you were as lovely inside as out."

I did a kind of aw-shucks maneuver with my right foot and said thank you. "Of the two of us, Esther is obviously the better publicist," I said.

We all chuckled, and Steve asked what I was doing now. I explained the freelance work but quickly ran out of steam. The truth was, my world was suddenly shockingly simple and unburdened. I had no children, not even any pets. My time was my own. I read a lot and went to movies. Saying it out loud made it feel thin.

By now Esther had excused herself to freshen her drink. It was just this Steve guy and me. He was a partner in a small law firm in the city. He'd just bought a house in the East Bay. He loved to scuba dive. I still couldn't figure out how old he was—his face was fairly youthful, but he was graying at the temples. His tall frame looked great in a suit and tie. Must be divorced, I thought. And what was he doing with Esther? He grinned when he said he'd come with her but wasn't actually on the guest list.

Steve was purportedly fascinated by my career as a writer and my recent return from Italy. We quickly learned that, years before, we'd both taken the overnight ferry from Brindisi to Piraeus. Tell me more, his eyes said. He really listened. He had the swashbuckling charisma of a Kennedy or a Clinton, but I didn't trust it. "Men are dogs," Amanda had said. It was an easy way to sum up dating in the eighties.

As I felt myself running out of things to say, I made an excuse about getting back to a friend, and Steve asked for my business card. I watched him discreetly tuck it into the pile of cards he'd been collecting all evening—probably all from women, I thought. I escaped to the terrace with a fresh glass of champagne and stood looking at the night sky, an occasional star blinking through the fog. I suddenly remembered something my Roman boyfriend, Antonio, had said to me just before I'd left Rome: "Per le ultime due settimane, si parla quasi sempre in inglese." *For the past two weeks, you have spoken almost always in English.* I could hear sorrow in his voice.

"That's not true," I said, in English.

"I like you better in Italian," he said. "You are harder in English, *più nervosa.*" He said this without anger, just stating a fact. But the fact was this: I *was* softer, more childlike and vulnerable in Rome. And that wasn't who I really was. Now, back on American soil, I had returned to that harder self. I was jaded, skeptical, facing the world with my arms crossed. Still, it seemed like a better alternative than being disappointed all the time.

I didn't think about Steve again until a week later when I got an envelope in the mail. *Saw this and thought of you*, he'd written on a newspaper clipping about a writers' conference in Squaw Valley. I didn't write fiction or poetry, but I appreciated the effort. I didn't respond, though. What was I afraid of? Okay, even then I knew: Being an adult meant that saying yes to this man, even a little, would eventually lead to the hard stuff. Like compromise. Like accepting someone if they didn't meet my exacting fantasy of a boyfriend. Like working at a relationship.

Over the next two weeks, Steve bombarded me with notes and phone calls. "This is Steve Beckwith," he'd say, always using his full name like it was a business call. He did have a great, husky voice. I finally agreed to meet him for drinks—and drinks only—at Le Central, a classic French bistro in the financial district. When I walked in, Steve was seated at the barstool closest to the door, facing me with a broad grin on his face. I was suddenly charmed by his confidence, his lack of pretense at being so glad to see me.

We moved to a table and ordered drinks—a Manhattan for me, a dry martini for him. This was the eighties. People drank. After chit-chatting about work and his interest in scuba diving, I broached the question I'd been wondering since the wedding.

"So what's your relationship to Esther?" I asked. "She won't object to our meeting like this?"

Steve threw his head back and made a little laugh like a cough. "I don't know if you've noticed, but Esther is quite a bit older than me." He was thirty-eight, he revealed.

"Okay," I said.

"Our relationship is casual. We met through the alumni association at William and Mary. And I helped her with a few legal issues."

"So . . . nothing romantic?" I asked.

"Nothing serious," he replied. The laugh again. Subject over.

Drinks led to dinner at La Contadina, an old-school Italian place in North Beach. I showed off a little by speaking Italian with the waiter, who made my day by asking if I was from Rome. I could see the admiration in Steve's face, and I felt proud. Momentarily, I was the Continental femme fatale.

Our conversation wandered from the Contras—whom Steve called "freedom fighters"—to gun control, which he was against. We soon established that he was a registered Republican, while I was a bleeding-heart liberal. "This is clearly our last date," I said with conviction but also a little regret. He was so good-looking and unabashed.

Steve drove me back to my car. As we pulled up to my parking spot in his American-made SUV, I had my hand firmly on the door handle as we said goodnight. Then I glanced over my shoulder and saw a change of clothes hanging in the back seat. "I guess you were planning to get lucky tonight," I said, and he smiled sheepishly. This man was so handsome and charming, he must have felt that it was his natural right to assume that any date would last at least twenty-four hours.

I leaned over to peck him on the cheek, my hand still on the door handle, but he pulled me closer to turn it into a long, tender, toe-curling kiss that literally stole my breath. "I had no idea Republicans could kiss like that," I finally said. But I was suddenly confounded. This wouldn't be our last date after all.

Steve and I fell into bed on our third date—which, in 1986, showed restraint, I thought. In Italy, the men put on a good show during the seduction phase but were surprisingly traditional—one might say patriarchal—between the sheets. Sex with Steve reminded me how egalitarian American men could be. My pleasure had equal rights to his. I saluted my decision to return to Yankee soil.

Pros: Smart. Funny. Handsome. Employed. Thoughtful. Generous. Seemed to adore me.

Cons: Republican. Conservative. Lawyer. Just bought a house in Pittsburg, in the East Bay, a place I had no intention of visiting, let alone moving to. Liked to camp. Wore a digital dress watch and wingtip shoes.

After two more dates, I ran the pros and cons by my friends. I seemed to be the only woman I knew who didn't want to marry an attorney. Hadn't they heard all the lawyer jokes? Steve was not the man I thought I'd ordered. I'd always pictured myself with an architect or journalist, someone who wore corduroy and kept a journal. This guy had never even been to a foreign or vintage movie. He'd barely heard of *Citizen Kane*.

But Steve's charm and finesse were wearing me down. Women were attracted to him and men admired him. Dogs sniffed him out eagerly, then curled at his feet. He was affable and smart and kind. He brightened every party just by walking into the room in a crisp pink

Oxford shirt. In September, I arranged to introduce him to my closest girlfriends. We'd gathered in the bar at a downtown restaurant, and after about an hour Steve joined us—one man surrounded by five women who'd already been drinking. When the waiter arrived, Steve said, "Make mine a double. This is an emergency." Everybody laughed and gave me approving glances.

"He looks like a politician," Hope said later. "No, he looks like an actor *playing* a politician."

"He's got the goods, he really does," Ruby said. "Wit, personality, kind eyes. What are you waiting for?"

By the end of September, I'd begun to capitulate. Steve took me to dinner at a Moroccan restaurant by the beach, where we sat on the floor and ate tagine with our hands. We drank sweet white wine and then hot mint tea from a brass kettle poured into tiny cups from a height of three feet. A belly dancer undulated around the room, clanging little cymbals on her fingers. We were laughing and kissing and touching each other's faces, our fingers still smelling of cumin and lamb. No man had ever courted me like this. I began to forget about the politics and the digital watch.

Autumn. San Francisco is notorious for confusing its seasons. Fall is like summer in other cities—hotter days, less fog, everything steeped in sunlight and the faint smell of woodsmoke.

We were walking along Fillmore Street, our hands interlocked and our steps in sync. The sidewalk was full of women with big permed hair, heroic shoulder pads, stirrup pants.

"I have a favor to ask," Steve began solemnly. He always knew how to raise a subject with a little fanfare.

I smiled. "You can ask."

"I'd like you to call me by my full name," he said.

I was silent for a beat. Then, "You want me to call you Steve Beckwith all the time?" I pictured out loud a scene in bed, when I would cry out his name in the throes of passion. "Steve Beckwith! Oh, Steve Beckwith!"

We laughed.

"No, sweetheart. I'd like you to call me Stephen. The only other person who calls me that is my mother."

"Wow. That's quite the honorific." But I *was* honored. And thenceforth he became Stephen to me.

In October, Stephen and I joined my friends Ellen and Wes to celebrate Wes's thirty-fifth birthday. They were meeting Stephen for the first time, and I was hoping they'd like him. Ellen was one of my closest friends—we'd known each other since right after college, when we'd both worked in McGraw-Hill's local editorial bureau. The four of us took the ferry to Tiburon to have dinner at an upscale Mexican restaurant perched over the water.

"All I ask is no waiters singing 'Happy Birthday,'" Wes said. "No silly hats, no candles. This is an incognito event."

Got it, we said.

Toward the end of the meal, Stephen excused himself to go to the restroom, then came back in time to order dessert. About fifteen minutes later, we were serenaded with a parade of waiters and mariachis wearing big hats and singing "Happy birthday, dear Wes."

Wes smiled weakly. Stephen was grinning.

Wow, I thought. *That took some balls.* I swallowed any further thought of what had just happened.

We took the late ferry back to the city. When we returned to Ellen and Wes's apartment in the Marina, the men went inside to check out Wes's new wide-screen TV. Ellen and I remained in the car, talking.

"So?" I asked. "What do you think?"

"Well, he's definitely good-looking, I'll give you that," Ellen said.

I was silent, waiting. "I can hear there's a 'but' coming," I finally said. I thought back to the birthday cake incident, when Stephen had deliberately countered Wes's wishes.

Ellen chose her words carefully. "All I'm going to say is: This is a guy who gets what he wants. And right now, what he wants is you."

I laughed. I didn't hear the warning in her words. All I heard was flattery.

For my own birthday in mid-November, Stephen made plans to take me away for the weekend, telling me only what to pack. We drove up curvy Highway 1 to Mendocino, a cliff-hanging coastal village filled with cozy Victorian cottages and sparkling views of crashing waves. We checked into a sentimentally decorated bed and breakfast inn—lots of lace and bowls of potpourri—where Stephen had reserved us a suite with a brass bed and a fainting couch. My first stop was the bathroom and, when I emerged, Stephen had laid out a feast on the couch—Petrossian caviar, smoked salmon, and an icy bottle of Stolichnaya. He held up a glass. "Happy birthday to my best girl," he said.

The rest of the weekend followed suit. We parked in his SUV on a cliff to watch the sunset, and he pulled out a bottle of brandy and two crystal snifters. We arrived for dinner at the hotel's restaurant, where three friends awaited us. There were rich desserts with candles and massages booked for Sunday afternoon. As we snaked our way home along Highway 1, a cassette tape of Anita Baker sang "Caught Up in the Rapture," and by now it was true.

One night Stephen and I lay in bed giggling. From where I lay, I could see the fog whispering outside the window. He was perched on an elbow leaning over me, his face a few inches from mine. My fingers were stroking the hair at the back of his well-shaped skull.

"I love your hair," I said. He smiled.

"I love your eyes," I said. He kept smiling.

"I love your nose," I said. He really did have a beautiful nose, the bridge between his eyes narrower than normal.

"I love you," I said, and we both looked shocked. It had just slipped out, like a thread of drool. The only other man I had ever said the word "love" to had been my father, and that was a very different word.

"I love you too, Kirsten," Stephen said. Then we moved from saying the word love to making it.

Two days later, I received a card in the mail. Inside was scribbled an enormous *L* in script. Below it he'd written, *We said it: the L word.* We both knew there was no going back.

Deep down, though, I was still resisting something. My whole life, I had played it safe. Whenever I got bored or found a man too challenging, I had moved on, preferring solitude to being in a demanding relationship. Looking back on my short adult life, I felt like I'd achieved a lot so far—a career, financial independence, lots of travel. But I had never committed to something for a lifetime. Now I was thirty-one and Stephen was thirty-eight. This relationship was getting serious, and we both knew where it was going. The permanence of it terrified me.

Stephen had already been married once, for nineteen years. They'd been separated for about six months, and his divorce wasn't even final. He had four daughters, aged thirteen to nineteen. We talked only superficially about his first marriage to Beth, on whose apparent drinking problem Stephen blamed the dissolution of the relationship. Was it ignorance or fear that prevented me from asking deeper questions, demanding more details? No one's perfect, I told myself. Everything about Stephen was so bright and shiny and strong, why go looking for trouble?

There was also some odd background with Stephen's own family. His father had worked for the railroad on the East Coast and, among the four children, Stephen was the only success. Of his three siblings, one brother had died under suspicious circumstances in Thailand (family rumor was that it was a drug deal gone bad). His sister was living on welfare in Arkansas. And the youngest brother had done some time in prison for tax fraud. Stephen had been the golden child, the one who had made it out alive, who had gone on to succeed in an even bigger arena. Not only was he the only one who had attended college, but he'd gone on to law school on the G.I. Bill, served on the law review, and worked for the Judge Advocate General's office in the army before landing at a prestigious law firm.

It was a lot of baggage. But I told myself that love doesn't just show up on your doorstep, tied with a bow. There was so much right about this man, how could I possibly toss him back in the pond and keep fishing?

Amanda and I were picnicking on a bluff at the Marin Headlands, the Golden Gate Bridge laid out just below our feet. We were stretched out on a wool blanket, looking up at the impossibly clear sky, while I elaborated all the minute arguments against jumping into the future with Stephen Beckwith.

"It's always easier to say no," Amanda said. "For once, why don't you try saying yes?" Amanda was the author of the phrase *Men are dogs, there is no exception to this rule.* And yet here she was, talking me out of running away.

"Um, fear of failure?" I asked. It was so obvious, even to me. Until now, all my failures had been small ones, easily forgotten. My decisions reversible. But I had always succeeded at the big things. And I was willing to work hard to get what I wanted. But it had always been solely on me. I'd never had to depend on a man for anything. I had spent my entire adult life coming and going as I pleased, decorating my apartment exactly as I'd liked, cleaning up after only one person. What if my own effort wasn't enough to sustain a whole life together?

I had been in the ninth grade when the term "women's liberation" entered the public domain. I took several courses on feminism in college, and that perspective defined my adult life. At some point, I must have taken a vow of emotional and financial independence.

Now I was falling in love with a guy who seemed straight out of central casting as a traditional husband. I was conflicted and said so. And whenever I brought it up to Stephen, he assured me that he was looking for a new chapter with a smart, driven woman like me. I didn't try to talk him out of it. He was saying all the right things.

The following Wednesday, Stephen called from work. He had something important to discuss. No, it couldn't wait. I agreed to take a break from my pressing schedule as an underemployed freelance writer, and we met at Vicolo Pizza on the waterfront north of town, then strolled along the Aquatic Pier, the bay white-capping all around us. Stephen was chatting about this, joking about that. No urgency.

Finally, I broke. "Get to the point! What's so important that we're playing hooky from work?"

His business, it turned out, was that he wanted to move in together. On the one hand, this was a tempting offer: I was thirty-one, never married, and making about $500 a month as a freelancer. We'd said the "L" word. All systems were moving forward. On the other hand were the estranged wife, the four daughters (whom I had not yet met), the fact that things were moving incredibly quickly. What was the rush?

I took both of his hands in mine and locked eyes with him. There was a handful of men fishing off the pier, and I could smell the tang of their bait and hear their shouts on the wind.

"Until last year, I wasn't sure how I felt about marriage and children," I said. "But now I know I want them."

Stephen nodded.

"And you already have a family," I added.

There was a thick pause. Then Stephen said, "I was gone a lot when they were growing up. I was busy making partner, working all the time. I'd love to have another chance to do it right."

If I'd been older, or wiser, or had children of my own, I might have pointed out that Stephen still did have a chance to make it right with his teenage daughters. But I was young and naïve, and what did I know about kids? His words unlocked a gate in my heart. My lease would be up in January, and we giddily agreed to start apartment hunting in December.

Later that month, I called in sick to my family's annual Thanksgiving dinner, and Stephen and I spent the long weekend at an inn halfway up Mt. Tamalpais in Marin County. After an intimate holiday meal at the tiny restaurant, we wandered out onto the pitch-dark road, where we could look out over the twinkling lights of the entire San Francisco Bay. We stood in silence, his arms around my waist.

"Could this moment be any more perfect?" I asked, immediately chagrined at the words that could have hopped off a greeting card.

Stephen didn't say anything for a few minutes. And then he did. "Actually, there's one thing that could make it more perfect," he said. He turned me to face him.

Suddenly, everything seemed to be rushing forward, like I was falling down the mountain in a car with no brakes. I said nothing, willing the moment to stop while I gathered my thoughts and caught my breath. But Stephen kept talking. " . . . If you'd agree to marry me."

This was it. *Try saying yes*, Amanda had said. Why was that so hard?

"Um, okay," I finally said—perhaps the least eloquent proposal acceptance ever uttered by a woman. It felt like the bravest thing I'd ever done.

Stephen kissed me and I kissed him back. We pulled apart and, I am not kidding, we saw a shooting star. Was this Hollywood?

Chapter 2
A Charmed Life

My life had been a wide-open plain of possibilities. Now we were on a track, speeding forward into the future together. After Stephen's proposal, I didn't tell anyone for a week, just to make sure it was for real and that I didn't chicken out. But once I got used to the idea, I relaxed and started enjoying our new life together. We leased a two-bedroom flat on Lake Street with a view of the woodsy Presidio. Stephen moved his mother into his house in the East Bay. We bought a Vespa scooter and zipped around the city to movies and dinners and strolls along the Embarcadero.

By his early twenties, Stephen had already been married with several kids. He'd never tried Thai food or listened to live jazz, and I loved introducing him to all the things he had missed. For the fiftieth anniversary of the Golden Gate Bridge, we got takeout Cambodian and parked the SUV at Sea Cliff, where we had a front-row seat to the lighting of the bridge as we listened to the celebration on the car radio. For Christmas, we gave each other mountain bikes and rode together every weekend, from Ocean Beach to Marin County. It was a charmed life. I couldn't believe my luck. I now understood the cliché "I fell in love with my best friend."

There were also a few bumps, of course. With my previous aver-sion to commitment, I'd never actually spent more than a solid week with a man. And Stephen was still married; his divorce wouldn't be finalized until a few months before our wedding. We were both pretty strong-willed people, used to our own routines. Once we got over the scorched-earth period of moving our belongings into the same apartment (there was now a La-Z-Boy recliner in my living room), life settled into a fairly predictable routine—days of bliss punctuated by a few hours of conflict.

Conflict: Not our strong suit. I'd been raised by parents who talked everything through, and I thought that was how all families communicated. The biggest parental disagreement I could remember was the time my mother brought home a winter-white car coat with a belt slung low across the back. "What do you think, Ken?" she asked as she sashayed around the family room, simulating a fashion show runway.

My dad was a kind person, and diplomatic. "I like the color," he tried.

"Should I keep it?" Besides groceries, almost no purchase went undiscussed between them. It was rare for Mom to buy herself a new piece of clothing.

"I'm not sure about the belt in the back," my dad ventured care-fully. "It makes you look a little . . . " He searched for the ideal word. "Broad across the beam."

My mom stopped sashaying. "Oh, Ken," she whimpered, as if he'd just announced he was leaving her. She retreated to the bedroom in disappointment and humiliation.

Dad looked at me. "Well, I'll never do that again," he sighed.

Stephen was from a different school. Any occasion in which I expressed opposition to his wishes, he'd go mute. Indefinitely. We'd been talking about marriage vows—like those of every other couple married in the eighties, ours would include the promise to "never go to bed angry." I'd reminded him of this at bedtime on more than one occasion. But one time I decided to wait it out. I was tired of always being the one to offer reconciliation, a way forward. *This time,* I thought, *he can come to me.* I waited.

It didn't happen. After three days of being ignored and glared at and given his back in bed, I finally conceded.

"I give up," I said wearily, addressing his back. "You're thirty-eight years old. You've already been married once. Is this really how you resolve a disagreement, by going silent until you get your way?" I walked him through the life cycle of an argument. "Okay, first I tell you what I want. Now you tell me what you want. Now we offer rebuttals. Now we gradually meet each other halfway." It was like coaching a child on the basics of civilized behavior. But I could see the gratitude on his face for pulling him out of his standoff. And I realized that not everyone had been raised in the Walton family.

On the few occasions when we talked about his first marriage, Stephen gave a generic reason for its failure, like "we got married too young" or "we grew apart." He would cite his ex-wife's drinking problem or her irresponsibility with money. I reminded him—and myself—that there were two sides to every story, that no one person is entirely to blame for the failure of a marriage.

I eventually met the girls—Lisa, Samantha, Michaela, and Julie— who seemed delighted to meet me and thrilled about our engagement. Lisa was headed to college at UC San Diego, and the other three would continue living fulltime with their mother. Everything seemed hunky-dory on the surface. But in hindsight, I realize what a brave face they were putting on. I had no idea how to lift the old familial rug to see what was lurking under there, and there was a wide cultural gap between us. I was a National Public Radio–loving book reader who prided myself on my travel and basic grasp of several languages. The Beckwith daughters were more mainstream, with the pop-culture interests of most teenaged girls. And while I acknowledged this philosophical chasm, it wasn't anything I was prepared to worry about.

We'd see Lisa on college breaks and the younger girls every month or so when we'd take them out for a nice dinner and ask them about their high school lives. We'd celebrate Christmas and birthdays and check in occasionally by phone. It wasn't until years later, when I was a mother of teenagers myself, that I realized how inadequate this was.

My family, too, seemed an easy sell. My younger sister, Ingrid, and I hadn't been close for many years, so I didn't invite her opinion of my new fiancé, but her longtime boyfriend, Keith, and Stephen hit it off well. I think my parents were just relieved that I was finally going to settle down. Helen and Ken Mickelwait could get along with anyone, I'd learned, and they seemed as charmed by Stephen as everyone else. Looking back, I wonder if they'd had their own concerns about Stephen's larger-than-life personality. If they did, they didn't share them with me.

During our seven-month engagement, I had a recurring dream in which I found myself in a church, ready to be walked down the aisle. But no plans had been made. This was not the wedding I wanted. Someone else had picked out the flowers. Or I was wearing a ridiculous dress. Or there was horrible music playing. Every week, a new variation on the theme of being out of control. Finally, just a week before our actual wedding date, I had the dream for a final time. This time everything was perfect—the venue, the dress, the flowers, the music. Stephen waited for me at the altar. He was grinning. He was wearing lederhosen.

It was the morning of our actual wedding. Stephen had spent the night in a hotel downtown with his four best friends, after his bachelor party. I had suggested that the night before the wedding might not be the best time for the bachelor party, but it was the only date these four busy, middle-aged men could get together. At about eight in the morning, Stephen called me from a pay phone on the Embarcadero, where he was out for a morning run.

"Turn on KBLX," he said.

"What's happened?" I asked. Had there been an earthquake? How could I have missed the tremors?

"Just turn it on," Stephen said. "I love you. See you at two." I found the station. The disc jockey was wrapping up the weather report—an early marine layer that would burn off by noon. "Now here comes a tune, one of my personal favorites," he said, "and this one is dedicated to Kirsten from Stephen with all his love." It was Anita Baker's "Caught Up in the Rapture." Stephen was a master of the thoughtful, creative gesture.

Perhaps by now my fear and skepticism should have evaporated, so that I'd finally feel secure in my decision to marry this man. But as I got my makeup and nails done, as I did my own hair, as I loaded my dress into the car to drive to the wedding venue, I thought about brides left at the altar, none of whom ever saw it coming. *It could happen.* That was me—always hedging my bets.

We were married at two o'clock at the Ginsberg Collection—an antiques and furniture showroom in an industrial district of San Francisco. It was an old brick warehouse that had been reoutfitted as an elegant private home, with lots of Southwestern and Mexican folk art and large white sofas. My dress and headpiece were straight out of the 1920s—a dropped-waist cascade of creamy lace, a corona of tulle and flowers circling my hair—and I entered by a circular stucco staircase from the second floor. In his taupe Italian suit, Stephen still looked like an actor playing a politician, but better. He'd never looked so handsome—and there were no lederhosen in sight. In front of 125 guests, we were married by a judge who had gone to law school with Stephen, and after the ceremony there was a quesadilla bar and Tex-Mex food. We were happy and smiling and relieved that it all went off without a hitch. And so our future began.

Chapter 3
Adaptation

I could finally relax. The deed was done, and I didn't have to worry about the decision anymore. From our San Francisco flat, Stephen and I plotted the future, looking at houses for the time when we'd be ready to start a family of our own. Before long, I got a good job at UC Berkeley as a writer in the development office, and Stephen became a partner at a new, bigger firm. We became that happy married couple at Home Depot, loading up our cart with landscaping supplies for our new four-bedroom house in Orinda. We were the people taking weekend trips to Sea Ranch and Carmel with friends, sitting around a firepit telling stories of our still-young lives. For a couple of years, I published a quarterly newsletter on travel to Italy, which allowed us to travel there twice a year and write it off on our taxes.

After all my worrying, I had finally achieved what I'd feared for so long: a true partnership. A man who really seemed to know who I was and who loved me for being that person. For all of our differences—our politics, our pastimes, even our senses of humor—there was a core place where we came together. We were both eldest children—high-achievers, reliable, conscientious, cautious, and maybe just a teensy bit controlling. But we recognized it as a common trait.

It was our native language. "That's what I admire about you most," Stephen once told me. "You're always moving forward, always upping your game." In those moments, I felt truly seen. It felt as if we were playing from the same rule book.

There had been one little incident during our honeymoon, however, that had spooked me. We were staying in a beautiful hotel in London that occupied what had once been a series of row houses in South Kensington. The structure was probably about two hundred years old. On one of our last nights, I awoke to a bizarre sensation. I was being lifted up off the bed, about three or four feet, and dropped back down onto the mattress. Then lifted up again and dropped again, repeatedly. It felt nothing like a dream. It felt absolutely real. I looked over at Stephen, sleeping next to me, and could see a slice of light coming from under the bedroom door.

There was some kind of malevolent spirit taunting me, I felt sure of it. After the dropping stopped, I felt a pair of hands around my throat, tightening not enough to strangle me but enough to scare me. I looked into the face of this demon, and a man's face grinned back. It was Stephen's face.

The episode finally ended, and I drifted back to sleep. In the morning I told Stephen about the nightmare, but I didn't mention the part about his face. Perhaps it was some residual spirit, I thought, some restless, long-ago tenant of the historic property. Perhaps it was presenting the face of the person I loved most, just to be more threatening. I put the whole thing out of my mind.

Those first four years of married life were such fun, filled with good work, good friends, disposable income, lots of travel. But, after a few years, our married friends had begun reproducing, moving into the next chapter of coupledom. We still saw Stephen's daughters regularly if not frequently, but it was hardly the same as raising a family myself.

As reluctant as I was to give up our hedonistic lifestyle, I could feel my thirty-five-year-old body aging and my heart longing for a child. I finally brought up the subject.

"Remember that conversation we had before we moved in together?" I began. "The one about wanting a family?" We were sitting in the backyard, the sun filtering through the big oak tree.

"What conversation?" Stephen asked.

"You remember the one," I said. "When you told me how you'd love to have the chance to do it right this time?"

"Oh. *That* conversation." He was smiling as if he'd been caught with his hand on someone's wallet.

I cocked my head. "You were lying about that, weren't you?" I said. "You were just saying that to get me to move in with you."

His sheepish expression said, *Boys! What're you going to do?* "Kind of."

I shook my head. "A deal's a deal, Beckwith. I want a child. And I'm not getting any younger." In my gut I felt he'd be a great dad this time around, just as he'd become a great husband this time around. Then I reminded him of my vision of parenthood as a fifty-fifty division of labor, that I wanted a full partner in this endeavor. He'd already helped raise four daughters, so it sounded reasonable to both of us. Stephen never pushed back on the idea again. I started reading the books, planning the nursery, talking about our future as parents together. And he jumped on board.

Then we were the grim-looking couple sitting in the OB-GYN's office, the fertility specialist's office, and the emergency room as I suffered one miscarriage, then another, followed by a seemingly endless period of infertility. During the eight and a half weeks of my first pregnancy, I had excitedly purchased blue-and-white patterned fabrics and cut hundreds of triangles, which sat on the dining room table in neat little piles as I began to pin and stitch them together into what would become a baby quilt for our firstborn child. When it became obvious that I had lost the baby, I carefully put the unfinished stacks of fabric pieces into a box and placed it on a high shelf in the closet of the room that was no longer a nursery.

Finally, after three years, we were the happy parents of a beautiful, dark-haired daughter, whom we named Bronte and on whom the sun rose and set. During her first few months, Stephen stayed home as much as his work schedule allowed, and we actually raced each other to be the first to get her when she awoke in her crib. I retrieved the box of blue triangles from the shelf in the closet and finished the quilt.

Then, when Bronte was four months old, we hired a nanny and I returned to my Berkeley job part-time. For the next two years I felt more balance in my life than I ever had. It was the happiest we'd ever been together.

Bronte's birth brought out a tenderness in both of us. I had never been an overtly maternal woman, but now, with my own child, I could feel an invisible umbilicus connecting me to her at every moment. I felt my patience growing like an afternoon shadow. I was enchanted by her every mood and expression. And Stephen was besotted too. He played the kinds of games with her that only dads can play, swinging her above his head, making loud "raspberries" on her stomach. I frequently found them asleep together in Stephen's La-Z-Boy recliner, Bronte nestled into his shoulder. We lived in a fairytale castle under an oak tree.

The arrival of Bronte also heralded other family miracles. Stephen's daughters—now aged nineteen through twenty-five—were thrilled with their new half sister, and the baby gave us something to bond over. They cooed and laughed while holding her, brought sweet little gifts, and stopped by to spend time with Bronte.

Even more surprising, my sister, Ingrid—who'd never wanted children of her own—soon fell in love with her. She became a dream aunt. As Bronte grew older, Ingrid's fun sense of humor, energy, and fascination with the spontaneous hilarity of babies brought a whole new dimension to our relationship.

During our period of infertility and miscarriages, we had bought a run-down 1912 farmhouse in St. Helena, in the Napa Valley, which we spent a year renovating as a weekend home. On our very first weekend there, we stood gaping at the missing floorboards and uninsulated walls. All I could see were the months of renovation that lay before us.

"I could live here fulltime," Stephen said. He'd grown up in the woods of upstate New York and had always wanted to move back to the country.

"You work in the city, remember?" I said. "I work in Berkeley. That's two hours away."

"We could make it happen if we really wanted to."

"I don't want to," I said.

"We'll see."

Nearly four years and another miscarriage later, at forty-one, I was finally pregnant with our second child. Stephen and I both agreed that it was time to fire the nanny and for me to become a fulltime mother. It was an idea that terrified me, but now that Bronte was a toddler, I also knew that I was missing the fun stuff—the playdates and art classes and story time at the library. The idea of moving to the Napa Valley fulltime suddenly didn't seem quite as impossible as before—only one of us would have to commute to the Bay Area, and Stephen assured me that he could work part-time from home. Only one concern still haunted me.

"If something happened and I had to go back to work, there's nothing for me up there," I said. "I'm not a wine writer. All my potential employers are here in the Bay Area."

"That's not going to happen," Stephen said, fixing me with his litigator's gaze. "I'm not a risk-taker, Kirsten. Financial stability is really important to me."

As always, I believed him. Stephen had proven to be an excellent provider, bringing in a handsome law partner's salary, investing in stocks and real estate, creating retirement and college funds. Even with the child support he was paying to Beth, his ex-wife, for the two daughters who still remained at home, we were doing just fine.

We sold our 1912 fixer-upper—now beautifully fixed up—which was a great weekend house but no place to raise children, and rented a ramshackle three-bedroom house tucked away on a hidden acre just a few blocks from St. Helena's Main Street. There was a pool and rolling lawns and a few rows of grapevines. There was a tire swing hanging from a large elm tree. There was also a converted barn out back that Stephen quickly turned into a home office, so he had to go into the city only a few days a week. In February, amid the worst floods of the previous forty years, we welcomed our son, Amory. Of Stephen's six children, this was his first boy. Life felt miraculous and complete.

Several years earlier, before Bronte was born, Stephen had reactivated an old back injury that ultimately resulted in surgery to correct a herniated disk. He was in the hospital for several days, during which I visited daily, brought him mail and his favorite foods, and watched the Superbowl at his bedside. The night of the surgery I cried myself to sleep. When he came home, I created a makeshift hospital room, complete with an adjustable bed and his computer on a rolling table so he could work lying down. I waited on him hand and foot, taking a few days off from work until he could get up and around on his own.

"No one has ever taken such good care of me," he said, squeezing my hand. And I had never taken such good care of anyone, I realized.

I had never before put someone else's needs so far ahead of my own, because I'd never loved someone this fully.

Now, with a newborn and a toddler to care for, I was no longer the wife who created a hospital room at home. I was the mom who couldn't get the bed made before it was time to crawl back into it. I walked around in a half stupor carrying a ten-pound baby while trying to keep a toddler amused. And although Stephen was working part-time from home, he was still putting in long hours. He needed to be alert at his desk, and Amory woke up five times a night. We hired a nanny to help during the day, but I was so exhausted from the constant night feedings that I couldn't catch up on my rest.

I began to feel tiny tears in the fabric of our marriage. Stephen was being called into the San Francisco office more, and he would arrive home after the two-hour commute looking shell-shocked. We tried to recalibrate during the weekends, but by Sunday afternoon I could feel us girding our loins for the week ahead.

Any mother will remember the signs: You've been transformed from a woman who used to read a book a week to one whose every waking thought is about survival. Your brain is filled with logistical minutiae: shopping lists, baby-safe toys, worries about that rash, times of drop-offs and pick-ups. You're a kind of machine that operates in response to the needs and wants of others. You feel like you may be missing the point of parenthood—it's just one long form to be filled out, with vaccine dates and emergency contacts. In the car, at every stop sign or signal your right arm reflexively springs out to protect the cargo in the passenger seat, whether it's a child, a bag of groceries, or just your purse.

Then you smell the top of your baby's warm head, or your child says something that makes you laugh out loud, and in that instant, you become one giant, pulsing heartbeat.

Of course, for all its character-building, having children also comes at a price to the marriage. During our first few years together,

Stephen and I had had the robust physical intimacy typical of most newlyweds. There was romance and spontaneity and gazing into each other's eyes as we made love. There were gushy notes and surprise gifts and naughty talk. But as we went through the miscarriages and infertility, sex became utilitarian. For me in particular, there was an agenda, and lovemaking was scheduled according to timing and basal body temperatures.

Once we had the objects of our desire—"a boy for you, a girl for me" as the song goes—we could relax again. But by then we were both exhausted from the challenges of work and parenthood. Stephen, being a man, was predictably still interested in sex. I, on the other hand, had usually had my share of physical affection by the end of each day, after the cuddling and nursing and sitting with children on my lap. We began to negotiate the frequency of our conjugal visits, scheduling them a week in advance. That was normal for this time in our lives, right?

Meanwhile, I was still clinging to my ideal of marriage as an equal partnership. I understood that Stephen was our provider, and motherhood was my fulltime job, but I still wanted him to help with the kids in the frantic morning hours before getting Bronte off to preschool or to occasionally bathe Amory at night. I resisted the image of me as nothing more than a mother—my sense of self was at stake.

It was a normal Tuesday morning, with Bronte finishing her scrambled eggs in front of *Sesame Street* while Amory made an increasing fuss in his baby rocker.

"Can you please just get her dressed while I nurse him?" I asked, the teensiest note of irritation in my voice. "I can't do both."

Stephen was sitting at the kitchen counter, his back toward me. He didn't move. He didn't say anything.

"Stephen, I'm talking to you." And then I noticed his shoulders shaking, his head bent. I walked around to face him and saw his tearful, crumpled face. It was the first time I'd seen him cry.

"I can't do this anymore," he said. "You can't expect me to be on parent duty every morning and also be the only breadwinner." I could almost hear the sound of glass shattering on pavement. It was my feminist ideals. Stephen truly did adore his children, I knew that, and he was a loving, engaged father when he wanted to be, which was often. But I was finally realizing that my idealized version of new age motherhood was bartered off the day I gave up my career and moved to the hinterlands. I watched him sobbing and sniffling and considered my options.

"Okay," I said finally.

"'Okay?' What does that mean?"

"Okay. I get it. You're the traditional dad and I'm the traditional mom. It's not what I wanted, but it's what I got."

Stephen was cautious. "Are you mocking me?" He wasn't used to getting his way so easily.

"Nope. Go do your thing. I'll get the kids ready." I was on my own now during the work week. Despite my feminist ideals, I had agreed to be Donna Reed. I would make the best of it.

A year after our move to St. Helena, we bought a house of our own on Mee Lane, two miles south of town. The 3,400-square-foot modern Mediterranean split-level had an acre of landscaped yard, a lap pool, a hot tub, and vineyard views in three directions. A flock of geese flew over the house twice a day, and jackrabbits hopped in the yard. On weekends, up to a dozen hot air balloons drifted overhead, their silk colors taking on the light and shadow of the early morning sky. I had to pinch myself daily; it was so far beyond what I'd ever expected for myself or my children.

But it wasn't all raindrops on roses and whiskers on kittens. Stephen continued to commute to the city, and it continued to wear on him. He'd moved to a new law firm that wanted him to put in more face time at the office. He returned home every evening, dragging himself through the door with an expression of exhaustion and a hint of residual road rage. He was losing his enchantment with the profession and the constant stress to rack up billable hours. There were a few periods when he was in trial preparation and had to live in a San Francisco hotel for several weeks straight. The plan to live in the country was beginning to shred a little at the seams.

I had an idea.

"You're paying about fifteen hundred dollars a month on hotels," I said. "That's as much as a mortgage. What if we bought a condo down there for you to stay in during the week?"

Buying real estate was one of Stephen's favorite things to do. So after several weekends spent touring apartments in the Bay Area, we purchased a cool two-bedroom conversion loft near Jack London Square in Oakland, just a few blocks from a BART station. The idea was that Stephen could use it during the week, and we'd also have a weekend place in the Bay Area whenever we wanted to visit.

Now he was gone Monday through Friday almost every week. He called each evening after the kids were in bed. As we talked, we tried to bridge the widening gap in our daily lives.

As the months passed, I started making friends among the other preschool moms. We'd sit with our feet in the kiddie pool at the country club or in the sand at the playground and talk—first only about things like viruses and breastfeeding, then about science fair projects and birthday parties. As the kids grew older, there was the occasional mention of a book or movie or even a trip to the city. Also, there may have been a teensy bit of gossip.

Bronte was growing into an animal-loving girl who also liked ballet and dressing up. By the age of nine, she was an avowed vegetarian, and we leased her an old Arabian horse at a nearby lesson barn. Amory was becoming a typical boy, all Legos and trucks and knights and warriors.

After preschool, we enrolled both kids in a small, one-room private school that was like a little liberal arts college. The parents were a group of smart, creative people who quickly became like my own extended family. In the interest of finding something to do as a couple, I formed a bocce team, which strengthened those friendships even more. Every Friday night all summer we met to play and eat and laugh, with the children running wild in the neighboring park. It reminded me of the best times of my own childhood.

Both Stephen and I were infatuated with our children, on most days, and spent our weekends happily focused on kid-centered activities. When he was with them, his voice took on a softer, more playful timbre, and I think in those moments he became the man he'd always wanted to be. Our former travels to Italy and Asia were replaced with trips to Yosemite, Disneyland, Club Med. It was working, this precarious arrangement. For now.

But as one decade slid into another, moth holes appeared in the fabric of our marriage. We seemed to be reading from two separate survival manuals. Beyond the weekends and annual vacation, we became increasingly focused on carving out time for our individual interests. I started working on an ambitious novel and applying to writers' conferences. I began to remember who I'd been before the earth shifted and I became a wife and mother.

Meanwhile, Stephen moved through a series of expensive hobbies—from scuba diving to motorcycles to three-week trips to Alaska with a group of buddies every summer. Each hobby required a full complement of equipment and attire. For the camping phase, he bought every available item in a camouflage pattern. This morphed into a fascination with the great outdoorsmen of history. He began wearing pioneer-style shirts and leather pants. Then whole suits of buckskin, with leather lacing and lots of fringe. He carried a huge buck knife in a leather scabbard on his belt. At the annual school camping trip, he made several costume changes each day, showing off his full Daniel Boone repertoire. Amory, now six, still thought it was cool to have a dad impersonating Grizzly Adams, but Bronte and I were mortified. I could hear the other parents snickering in the background. How, I wondered, had my conservative lawyer husband turned into a caricature?

I tried to maintain a sense of humor about the whole thing, but it was becoming bizarre. "How would you feel if I started dressing up like Laura Ingalls Wilder?" I finally asked. "People are starting to stare at you."

"What do you care, if it gives me pleasure?" Stephen snapped. "You were only happy when you were dressing me from J. Crew. You're so controlling!"

This was an increasingly common refrain: I was so controlling. I wanted him to be something he wasn't. He was "busting his hump" at a job he hated, and it was going to kill him—sooner rather than later. He deserved to act out his fantasies in his off hours, he said. I'd listen with pursed lips, then return to my computer and throw myself back into my fictional life.

It wasn't until many years later that I wondered: Had my own upbringing in such a calm, rational family left me ill-equipped to deal with people who weren't always reasonable? I expected people to play fair, to do the right thing. Here was a man who played by completely different rules.

The buckskin gradually gave way to black leather when Stephen bought a motorcycle, then two, then three. One afternoon at a back-to-school picnic in the local park, I heard a roar in the distance and watched with growing dread as he pulled up looking like a Hell's Angel from Oakland. He was riding his black-and-chrome Harley, dressed head-to-toe in black fringed leather with lavish beading on the back. It didn't help that he'd put on weight—a lot of weight. The crowd of genteel, middle-aged parents turned and smiled graciously as he dismounted and strolled proudly into the picnic area, taking off his Kaiser-style helmet and tossing his gloves inside. I'd seen the bike before but never the full outfit. He walked up to me and grinned, knowing I wouldn't choose this moment for an argument.

"New look?" I asked.

"Oh, this old thing?" he said, smiling.

Long pause. "Well, I guess it's official. You've now been every member of the Village People except the Native American."

"Hmmm. A Native American!" He was clearly enjoying himself. I couldn't tell if the source of his pleasure was the act itself or my pained reaction.

I suddenly remembered the year after we were married. Stephen had been born on a leap year, and this was both his fortieth and tenth birthday. I threw a surprise party for him at a small diner in San Francisco and had decorated the place with all the accoutrements of a young boy's life. I asked his mother to send photos of Stephen as a little boy, which I'd had enlarged, framed, and hung around the room. In each photo, he was dressed up as a boyhood icon: A policeman. A fireman. A cowboy. A superhero. Now, looking at his cartoonish getup, I wondered, did he not finish fulfilling those aspirations?

Chapter 4
My Problem Child

The boat had been so comfortable, I didn't want to rock it. I'll admit that now. And there were others to consider—Bronte and Amory. The man I'd married was turning into someone I didn't recognize and, if not for our two kids, this might have been the time I started to think about moving on.

What I should have done was to immediately drag us both into therapy to ponder the deep questions: Why are we growing apart? How can we realign ourselves? And why are you dressing like a weird character from a B movie? But therapy felt out of reach—Stephen was still gone almost every weekday, so scheduling an appointment seemed impossible. I made a point never to argue with him in front of the kids, and by the time we were alone at the end of the day, I was too tired to fight about something that had already passed.

Meanwhile, Stephen's compulsions were becoming even more obvious. He bought several big plastic sheds and lined them along the side of the house to store his increasing collection of sports parapher-nalia. I called it Hooverville. He had three motorcycles lined up in the driveway next to his big black truck. He wasn't a big drinker, but he started smoking up to two cigars a day when he was home. And he managed to shop and eat in a parallel universe to mine, despite my efforts to keep only healthy foods in our pantry.

On weekends, he would grill himself massive cuts of red meat for lunch, washed down with a beer or two. On a couple of occasions, I went into his truck to borrow a CD and found the floor littered with fast food and candy wrappers. Another time I walked into the kitchen to see him spraying a big shot of whipped cream into his mouth straight from the can. Over our eighteen-year marriage, he had gained about eighty pounds. He complained about his expanding girth but usually reacted fiercely to any suggestion of help.

By the summer of 2004, I was escaping into my writing as often as motherhood allowed. Having written not a single short story in my life, I pursued an ambitious high-concept novel set in six historical periods. It was pure folly, but it was also a much-needed creative outlet. I took online courses. I attended summer writers' conferences. And I kept a daily writing log, working while the kids were at school or after they'd gone to bed. When, after four years, I completed a first draft, I worked with a professional editor to help me refine the manuscript.

At first, Stephen was supportive. Just as he'd always had his hobbies, now I finally had one of my own. And when, after a long search, I signed with a New York agent, he proudly shared the news with our family and friends, toasting my success.

But he gradually soured on the idea. When I asked him to read the final manuscript, he didn't get past page thirty. He began to view my writing as an extramarital affair, seducing me away from my duties as a wife and mother. "You just want to hang out with your writer friends," he said when I signed up for yet another workshop. I wondered if he pictured us gathered in smoky rooms, wearing berets and drinking absinthe.

Now when Stephen called from the Oakland loft for our nightly check-in, he was demanding and greedy for my attention. If I was interrupted by the kids or another call, he exploded. "This is *my* time," he complained. "I don't see you all week, and now you hardly have the time to talk to *me*."

It was futile to point out that I was still on duty with our kids, that there were nights when I didn't feel like talking at all.

Every extreme hobby, every argument, every rationale always led back to Stephen's deep unhappiness in his job. He had once been an accomplished, even brilliant, trial attorney. But, as civil lawsuits were increasingly settled out of court, he found himself less interested in the profession. He faulted the adversarial nature of the legal field, although I couldn't help noticing that he had no problem being adversarial at home. "This job is killing me" was a frequent refrain. "While you're here living the life of leisure in the Napa Valley, I'm busting my hump at a job I can't stand. This job is taking *years* off my life, Kirsten. But I guess you don't mind, as long as my life insurance policy is paid up, right?"

The objective viewer would probably suspect depression or even bipolar syndrome. I think I was too afraid to look under the moldy rock of our marriage to see what crawled beneath. It felt like my hands were already so full, an official diagnosis would have been too much to bear.

Instead, I challenged him to give it all up. "Let's scale down and buy a smaller place," I'd say. "Let's sell the other properties and get out from under all this overhead. You can find another kind of work if we don't have to maintain this lavish empire." He'd grumble and evade but finally admit that he was the one who wasn't ready to give up the fancy lifestyle. So I worked hard to maintain the status quo, hoping that things would work themselves out if everything stayed in balance at home.

Some women find they become invisible to their husbands as the marriage ages. Mine was the opposite problem: I became magnified in Stephen's mind—I was both the beloved mother of his children (on the good days) and public enemy number one (on all the other days). I was the lightning rod for his anger and depression, the first point of contact for all the things wrong with his life. I found myself anticipating his return home each weekend with a growing sense of dread. From the moment he walked in the door, he seemed to be looking to find fault, to find someone to blame. And his crosshairs usually landed directly on me. There was never any physical violence, but the emotional violence felt bad enough.

On Friday afternoons I would scan the house looking for vulnerable spots. I straightened up, stocked the fridge, put my writing things away. Some weeks, he would come home and everything would be fine. But I never knew which mood would walk in the door. So every week, I prepared for the worst.

I was spending increasing amounts of time managing Stephen's moods, his impulses. About the time he tired of the camo-wearing phase but had yet to discover the Davy Crockett phase, he became obsessed with the idea of buying a weekend property with a "water feature."

"We need a place in the country," he said. "We need to get out of town."

"But we already live in the country," I said, surveying our landscaped acre surrounded by vineyards, mountain views, and raised vegetable beds.

"No, the *real* country," he said. "Not this tourist trap. A real weekend place with lots of acres. A tractor. Near a lake or a river. Or maybe a pond."

The idea of buying yet another property made me anxious and tired.

"I need this, Kirsten. I need to have a fun project, to really get away from work."

"I get it that you're burned out, Stephen," I said. "I support the idea of your finding a different line of work."

Now I tried weakly: "If you're planning an exit strategy, this isn't the time to buy another property."

"This is just the thing I need to keep my spirits up," he said. "If we buy a country place, I won't feel the need to leave the firm." As an added incentive, he agreed that we could downscale our house in St. Helena, maybe move back into town. "Okay," I said. "We'll look."

Two weeks later, after several days of touring homes in California's foothills, we made an offer on a place just outside Nevada City. Twenty acres of manzanita and scrub oaks, apple and pear orchards, a small horse facility, a potentially charming farmhouse. And a pond. Stephen quickly crunched some numbers to prove that, with a simple refinancing of our primary home, we could afford the place. We'd practically be losing money if we didn't invest in it.

"I'm not a risk-taker, Kirsten," he assured me. "I value financial security as much as you do." This had been a frequent refrain in our marriage and, as always, I believed it.

He was so good at this, convincing us both that what he wanted was the best thing for everyone. With resignation, I climbed on board. If this was what it would take to make Stephen happy again, then sign me up. We named the place Pear Tree Hill. And although it didn't (yet) have animals or crops, we casually called it "the farm."

Stephen instantly returned to his old self—buoyant, enthusiastic, full of plans and great ideas. I congratulated myself on making a compromise that would save our family. We embarked on a year-long renovation project—me as Secretary of the Interior, Stephen as Sovereign of the Outer Realms. We worked hard. We lived for days on end amid paint cans, contractor dust, and remnants of fiberglass insulation. Every Friday we would leave our beautiful, comfortable home in the Napa Valley to dwell in construction chaos, never losing sight of the bucolic paradise that we knew awaited us. I focused on cabinet refacing and carpet fibers and paint colors that were "found in nature." The kids ran around exploring and throwing fallen pears, thrilled with their new rural empire—which Amory had been overheard at school calling his "retirement property." We'd come home Sunday nights with dried sweat on our brows, red dirt under our fingernails. Soon, we said, we would sit in our Adirondack chairs on the porch and sip margaritas as we watched the sun set over the rust-colored hills.

By the time the major construction was complete, we'd spent about fifty percent more on it than the cost to purchase our primary home in St. Helena. But Stephen wasn't done. He now subscribed to *Pond* magazine and was undertaking a full renovation—draining it, lining it, building pipe systems, and researching fish. Every trip to the local hardware store yielded another truckload of landscaping supplies and equipment. It wasn't long before he returned from the Kubota dealer in Roseville with a bright orange tractor, which he delighted in teaching seven-year-old Amory to drive. Within six months, he'd traded it in on a bigger tractor. In neither case did Stephen discuss it with me first.

I remembered Ellen's warning to me upon first meeting Stephen twenty years before: *This is a man who's used to getting what he wants.* How quickly she had seen through him. Saying no to Stephen Beckwith now was to invite a man-sized tantrum. And, as he always liked to remind me, he was the one earning the money.

I also did my share of spending, of course, furnishing the three-bedroom house and two-bedroom guest cottage. There was original artwork on the walls and antiques from the Alameda Flea Market. There was wool sisal carpet on the floors and black slate counters in the kitchen. When we were finished, we had a wonderful place to share with friends and family, which we did. We floated on the pond during the hotter months, and in winter, the ski resorts were just an hour away.

Meanwhile, I'd started looking at smaller houses in St. Helena.

When we'd moved to Mee Lane, Stephen had been the one to push for a place outside of town. But now that the kids were older, I was spending a couple of hours each day chauffeuring them to school and activities—moving into town would make everyone's lives easier. I took Stephen to see a couple of places, but he found something wrong with each of them. "I wouldn't consider living on a corner," he'd say. Or "Have you seen all that junk in the neighbor's yard?"

Finally, I burst. "You're never going to agree to moving into a smaller place, are you?"

He invoked a maxim that I'd heard him use many times before: "I've never regretted the houses I've bought, only the ones I've sold." Then he added: "I didn't mean we'd actually *sell* our house. Maybe we could rent it out."

"You lied to me again, Stephen," I said.

"You must have misunderstood."

That fall, I turned fifty. *It's not so bad,* I thought. I lived in one of the most gorgeous places on earth. Two beautiful, healthy children. A difficult marriage, but still intact. I'd written a novel and gotten an agent. I was still fit, and I had every material achievement a woman could reasonably want.

Stephen had me convinced that Pear Tree Hill would be just the ticket to get him out of his doldrums at work. And, for a while, it was. But at about the time we finished the renovations—and long before we'd finished paying for them—he crashed again. Irritable. Critical. Looking for the next distraction, the next vacation, or the next purchase. Sometimes he would go for days without speaking to me—looming like a shadow in my peripheral vision, a cloud of dread about what might come next. One morning I snapped. I had awoken to find him sitting across the bedroom, glaring at me. I didn't even know what the cause was this time, what minor crime had prompted this display of hostility.

I got up and walked over to him, my hands on my hips. It felt like a cliché posture, but I was loaded for bear.

"What the *hell* is wrong with you?" I yelled.

"I don't know," he mumbled, and gave me a look of misery. He was a pissy, moping child, looking to his mother to make it better.

"You don't know? So *you* don't even know what's wrong, but your default plan is to go around not speaking to me for a week?"

No answer.

Finally he said, "You don't love me anymore."

I laughed. "So this is *my* fault? Because I don't love you enough? Seriously? How about trying to be *lovable*, Stephen? Don't act like an asshole for three years and then wonder why I don't love you enough." I was wrapped in my fury. And now that I'd started, I couldn't stop.

"You're a grown man. You're a goddamned *grown-up*!" I paced the room a little, choosing my next angle. He was silent, and for once I'd taken the floor. It felt good, even though I knew there would be consequences later. Gradually, I calmed down a little and my voice softened.

"Guess what? Happiness is a *choice*." I was sitting on the bed now, staring at him. "It's a choice you make every day. You think I just wake up every morning, bright and cheerful, because my life is perfect and your life sucks? No. Every day I *choose* to be happy. Even when you're impossible to live with and make me feel guilty every time I turn around. I am *trying* to be happy!" But now I was crying. Was it possible that I wasn't capable of fixing him? The one question I avoided asking was whether I did, in fact, love him anymore. I was afraid of what the answer might be.

Things improved for a while. I could tell that Stephen was trying to be more pleasant. But in the fall of 2005, he visited the doctor for a routine checkup and returned in a black mood. The news was not good. Five morbidity factors: diabetes, fatty heart, hypertension, high blood pressure, and fatty liver. He had brought this on himself, and he knew it, with his unhealthy eating and lack of exercise. But wait! There was a silver bullet! His doctor had suggested gastric bypass surgery, a procedure not usually recommended for someone at his weight, but all the morbidity factors deemed him a candidate.

"Dr. Dunham says it might even eliminate the diabetes," Stephen told me. We were sitting in the small alcove that served as my writing studio, Stephen slung over the armchair. "If I'm totally honest with myself, I have to admit that I have an addiction to food," he said. "A bad one."

Then, with a sparkle in his eye, he told me the details of the surgery, pulling out a glossy brochure describing the latest laparoscopic techniques and technology. This was so typical of him, I thought. Rather than do the hard work of dieting and exercising, he was happy to pay someone else to fix the problem for him. No matter that there were some unpleasant, often permanent side effects to the surgery—weakness, dizziness, dental problems, dysphasia, gallstones, kidney stones. "My self-esteem and my moods have been so low," he was saying. "This could really bring me back to my old self." Wearily, I conceded and agreed to invest in the $25,000 procedure, which would only partially be covered by our health insurance.

I tried telling myself that perhaps this was indeed the solution we needed. But inside me, a rage was building. Stephen's health wasn't just about him—it also affected me and Bronte and Amory. Where would it end? I could see myself in ten or twenty years as the still-fit wife of a prematurely aged and sickly husband. I was beginning to see that he was driving the family bus over a cliff.

Stephen had the laparoscopic surgery at St. Mary's Medical Center in San Francisco. As Dr. Dunham had predicted, he awoke from the procedure without diabetes—a medical outcome I still don't understand. He came home with a stack of pamphlets on how to manage his new lifestyle; he now had a four-ounce stomach, we were told, the size of a fist—and he must eat accordingly. I wondered how that was going to work, but Stephen was full of zesty optimism. Everything would be different now, he assured me. He'd reclaim his former physique, along with his positive attitude, his self-esteem, and his interest in work. He'd start running again. I nodded. I really wanted to believe it too.

And the pounds did come off. Within a couple of months, Stephen was fitting into his clothes of years before. He was feeling better, looking better. He was thrilled with his get-out-of-jail-free solution. But gradually, the dark moods returned, along with the criticism. I started thinking of him as a silverback gorilla, the bellicose alpha male. I was back in defensive mode.

Stephen came home from work early one night with a look of utter defeat. "We'll talk after the kids are in bed," he said and, as I cleaned up the dinner dishes, I tried to guess if this was just his latest woe-is-me ploy or if there was real danger in the air. Two hours later we sat on the couch—it seemed we never used the living room anymore except for the conveyance of bad news.

"International Paper called today to tell me they've decided to change counsel," he said, his silver head falling into his hands. International Paper was a Fortune 100 company, the producer of Masonite, Stephen's only major client since I had known him. It had kept him and a staff of ten employed fulltime for several years. "They've also fired Mulligan." John Mulligan was IP's in-house counsel.

"What happened?" I asked, afraid of the answer. My stomach felt like it was working its way up to my throat.

"They found out that I was working with Mulligan on a scheme that was a little too creative for them," he said.

It took me a minute to find any words. "But why?" My husband—the brilliant, strategic, successful lawyer.

"It would have totally benefited them in the long run," he said. "But in the short run, we had to do some work-arounds that were"—he paused—"a little legally questionable."

"But you were working with Mulligan!" I protested. "You were just following his orders."

He said nothing.

"Right?"

"Well," he stalled. "It was actually my idea." A small smile broke through the sad mask of his face.

"Tell me everything," I said. "Please. Now."

There had been a time when he'd been called his firm's "rain-maker." Now he would be an outcast. I could see his lingering pride as he explained the doomed scheme. There was a long silence as I processed this new damage to our crumbling enterprise. *I am not a risk-taker, Kirsten.* And yet it seemed that Stephen never met a risk he didn't like.

We sat there for a few minutes in silence, marinating in our shame and despair. "So," I finally said. "What now?"

"Well, you know my partnership at the firm requires a pretty high level of billings every month."

I immediately started thinking of how he might source new clients. With whom could he network to generate some quick new business? I started throwing out some names.

"Kirsten," he said. "I'm done with that. If someone brings me business, I'll work on it. But I'm not going out pounding the pavement looking for new work. I refuse to do it."

I stared at him in bewilderment. Bronte was twelve and Amory was eight. "So we're just going to sit here and wait for the financial apocalypse?" I asked. "You would really do that to your family?"

"I'm not doing anything to our family, sweetheart. I can stay at the firm for at least another six months and get a regular paycheck. There are a few small projects I'll work on for some other partners. In the meantime, I have an idea for a business I want to start. If it goes well, it could more than replace my income from the firm."

He went on to describe his idea—a claims administration business that would cash in on the product liability class-action suits he'd been working on for the past several years. There were models elsewhere in the country. He'd start working on it immediately.

"It sounds like it's time for me to start looking for work," I offered. But we quickly assessed that any local job I could find—pouring wine at a tasting room, working for a local nonprofit—would pay less than the cost of babysitting. I remembered the conversation we had before we moved to this charming valley: "If something happened and I had to go back to work, there's nothing for me up there," I had said.

"That's not going to happen," Stephen had said. "I'm not a risk-taker, remember? Financial stability is really important to me."

Chapter 5
Fault Line

There had been flooding in the new year, and by May 2006 the vineyards were still puddled, causing the grape growers to talk about delayed bud-break. The soggy landscape was fitting; even I could no longer ignore the fact that my marriage was in trouble and I was deeply unhappy. Stephen was home fulltime now. It's not that he was a tyrant every hour of the day, or even every day. But my anticipation of his black moods made me recede into myself. I struggled to be cheerful and competent around the kids. I chose my words carefully around Stephen, trying to stay upbeat and agreeable. But it was like living on a fault line—the prospect of a massive earthquake was never far from my mind.

One weeknight, when he was out for the evening, I found myself sitting on our king-sized bed thinking back to 1985, the year I'd spent in Rome working as a tour guide. I was such a happy, curious, passionate young woman then. I could clearly remember the heat of the rosy ancient stones and the cooking smells escaping from kitchen windows. I closed my eyes and recalled the euphoric feeling of riding on the back of Antonio's Vespa, zipping around corners and speeding through narrow alleyways. Complete freedom. Life seemed to stretch before me with such adventure and possibility. Then I married Stephen Beckwith, and for a long time it *was* a wonderful adventure. When, exactly, had it turned from genuine love to this painful regret? How had I allowed this to happen? How had I become a victim of someone else's dysfunction?

The tears started slowly at first, then spilled down my cheeks. Then came the sobs, the runny nose, the utter feeling of devastation over what I'd done with my life. I thought about how I might leave, what that would mean for Bronte and Amory. How Stephen would react. The scenario just didn't seem possible. The repercussions would be too great. *I'm trapped*, I thought. *I'm a hostage.* In that moment, I heard a single sentence in my head: *Your soul is dying.* Years later I would read a line in a travel article by Andrew McCarthy that made me remember this moment: *That was when I located myself.*

At my urging, Stephen agreed to couple's therapy.

We settled on Patricia Hirsch, a local psychotherapist with an unfailingly calm and empathetic manner. She also saw a lot of other couples in St. Helena and, as I waited outside her door, I was always a little afraid of what familiar face might emerge from the previous appointment. "We're just in for a tune-up," one friend said quickly when I bumped into her with her husband in the hallway.

I started the process by meeting with Patricia by myself for a one-hour session, then a second, then a third. Once I started talking about our marriage, I couldn't stop.

When I told her about the hobbies, the costumes, the motorcycles, and Stephen's massive knife collection, she asked, "Do you think perhaps there's some undiagnosed mental illness here?"

I laughed. Somehow, even then, I still couldn't see the severity of it. "Maybe I've overstated the case," I said. "Midlife crisis, yes. But mental illness? That sounds a little drastic." In the back of my mind, though, I remembered Stephen's siblings, a family of ne'er-do-wells.

Was there something there that was now playing out in his own behavior?

"Regardless of the cause," Patricia said, "Stephen is clearly a bottomless pit of need. It's not your job to fill it. And you couldn't fill it if you tried."

A bottomless pit of need. That phrase rang a clear bell in my head. In that moment, I realized that my marriage would never improve, despite what palliative measures we took. Stephen would always need more. Leaving his job, buying the farm, having gastric bypass surgery, purchasing more vehicles and knives and houses—none of it would ever be enough. My tearful scene on the bed was the moment I realized that I would never again be happy with this man. For years, I'd felt trapped—by my worry about the kids' welfare and by my own fear of Stephen's anger. I wanted out.

I could let everything go except the children. For their sake I had clung to the fantasy that somehow I could salvage the marriage. Now I saw past that myopic vision. I had to save myself in order to save my kids.

A few days later, I was talking in hushed tones over coffee to Martha, my closest St. Helena friend. Until now, I had shared the usual complaints about my quirky husband in a joking manner. But I'd never confessed how serious my concerns had become.

"That's called the hungry ghost," she said now, matter-of-factly.

"The what?"

"It's a concept of Chinese Buddhism, referring to people who are driven by addictions and other intense emotional needs. Stephen is a perfect example of that."

The hungry ghost. It felt good to have a name for it, a diagnosis of the thing that was eating our marriage alive. It was the jealous mistress who would not quietly walk away. An actual mistress would have been easier to heal from; ours was a condition from which there would be no escape.

—

"Sit down, Stephen. I need to talk to you." It was June, and we were back in the living room, the waiting room for disaster. The kids were in bed. Stephen had yet to meet with Patricia, but after my third session with her, I'd gotten a level of clarity I'd never had before. I was sitting stiffly on the sofa; Stephen was sprawled opposite me in the armchair. The light in the windows was fading quickly. I could find no more excuses to avoid this conversation.

"I'm ready to leave this marriage," I began.

Without missing a beat, he said, "So am I." He looked at me blankly.

"Really?" This was a turn I hadn't expected. If this decision was mutual, we could move forward with less anger, less blame. We could both make a clean break, and everybody would win. Then I remembered Patricia's advice.

"But Patricia says that if we split immediately, without doing more work, it would be too sudden, with too much misunderstanding," I continued. "She says even if we do decide to split, we should work on our relationship for a few months so we can do it in a way that's best for the whole family." For a moment, I had seen the door open wide, my escape route clearly marked. But not so fast, the fates seemed to say.

"That makes sense," Stephen said. For someone who was ready to leave the marriage himself, he was awfully accommodating on this point. We agreed to see Patricia together every week for three months and, at the end of the summer, we'd decide what to do.

August arrived, wilting hot, and the third month of our three-month probation. Our weekly sessions often brought us back into the ring, fighting over the same issues, with the same results. But at home, I could see Stephen was trying to be nice. He actually acknowledged his history of anger and criticism and admitted that, of the two of us, he had the most work to do. In return, he seemed to expect me to forgive all, immediately. He'd come up behind me and wrap his arms around my waist. I tried to respond. I was struggling to keep my heart open and to love him in this moment, free of all the bad memories. But most days I couldn't do it. "You'll need to give me a little time," I'd say. And he'd stomp off, then punish me with silence for the rest of the day.

At the end of the summer, the annual family vacation loomed— plans we'd made back in the spring, before things officially fell apart. Traditionally, we'd alternated who got to choose the destination, the rule being that it must be a trip that had something for every family member. The previous year, I had planned a canal tour in England and Wales. After a week in London—one of Stephen's favorite cities— we'd chartered our own narrowboat through the historic canals net- working the countryside, past villages and locks and pastoral views that seemed plucked from a Beatrix Potter book. All four of us agreed it was the best vacation we'd ever taken as a family.

This year, it was Stephen's turn, and he had chosen Alaska—his most beloved place in the world. It had no appeal for me, and even the kids seemed less than enthusiastic.

"That's your fault," Stephen said. "Kids are sensitive. They're just following your lead." But Alaska it must be. "It's really important to me to share this with all of you," he said. "This really means a lot to me." No matter that he'd spent three weeks in Alaska every summer for the past seven years. We were going in August. I tried to summon some sense of adventure. Maybe we'd love it. At the very least, there would be plenty of time to read.

Meanwhile, Stephen had been giving the kids chores from which they could earn money for the trip. He bought them each a nylon travel wallet to carry their bounty. One of his favorite things to do in Anchorage was to spend a day wandering the streets of gift shops, and every summer he would return bearing bags of Inuit handicrafts, caribou-themed clothing, and gold jewelry. He wanted to share this experience with Bronte and Amory.

But the week in Alaska didn't go well. Stephen was trying hard to be easygoing and upbeat, but every time there was a decision on how to spend the day or where to eat, he bargained and cajoled until the rest of us conceded. The natural scenery was breathtaking, but it felt forced on us. "Look, there's an eagle!" "Wow, did you see the size of that moose?" By the end of the trip, we were all tired and anxious for home.

In Anchorage, on the morning of our flight back, we were packing our suitcases in our suite at the Captain Cook Hotel. As usual, I was supervising the kids, surveying the room for stray toys and shoes. Bronte, thirteen, was sprawled on the bed reading a book. Amory, nine, was playing with one of the plush toys he'd bought at a gift shop.

"Amory, where's your wallet?" Stephen asked.

Amory had carried his red nylon travel pouch throughout the week but had barely spent any of the $300 it contained. Now a search began for the missing wallet.

We looked everywhere. In every drawer, under every bed, we even stripped the sheets. I unpacked Amory's suitcase, where he said he'd last seen it. It was gone. Stephen's muttering grew louder. He began tossing clothes on the floor as he pored through everyone's suitcase yet again.

And then, the volcano erupted. He was suddenly yelling and throwing things like an angry god. The room began to vibrate with his fury.

"Why do I have to do goddamn *everything* around here?" he shouted. He was storming between our two rooms in a rage, sweeping things off of counters, throwing sofa cushions. The pressure of trying to be so nice all summer had blown the valve wide open.

"I give you *one* thing to be responsible for. One thing! And you can't even do that. You're nothing but a bunch of selfish, lazy children!" It was clear that he included me in this accusation.

By now both Bronte and Amory were facedown on their beds, sobbing. I'd been on the receiving end of Stephen's anger many times, but I had never seen him treat the kids this way.

"Stephen," I said, forcing calm into my voice. I followed him around the room, trying to make eye contact. "It's just money. It doesn't matter. Look at your kids. You're scaring them."

But the storm continued. More yelling, more throwing things. It was like trying to chase a tornado. Finally, I grabbed his arm. "Stop it!" I screamed. "Look at what you're doing to your family!"

He stopped. He scanned the room, a look of disgust still hanging on his face. "Get your bags," he said finally. "We're going to be late."

Stephen was sullen for the whole trip home. He lost his temper once again at the Anchorage airport when I found us a place in the wrong security line and he stomped off to find the right one. As I waited with the kids, Bronte said, "At least he could say he's sorry."

I squeezed her hand. "He *is* sorry, sweetie. He just can't say it." But I didn't believe it. Everything felt like a lie now. The love I had felt for this man had once blazed at 120 watts. In the last few years, it had dwindled to the flickering flame of a bad scented candle. And this morning I had felt it blow out entirely.

Back in San Francisco, we stood at the curb in the chilly dark, waiting for the airport shuttle bus that would take us to Napa. As the bus approached, Stephen rummaged through his backpack to retrieve our tickets. I saw a look of exasperation come over his face— he rolled his eyes and shook his head. I wondered what we'd done now to aggravate him. We mounted the bus and took our seats—with Stephen and me in one seat, the kids directly behind us. Once the bus was underway, Stephen turned around to Amory.

"Ammo," he said in his fun dad voice, "Daddy feels kind of silly now." He pulled the red wallet out of his own backpack.

"You found it?" Amory's eyes were wide with wonder and relief, and Stephen smiled and nodded sheepishly. *Isn't that funny? It was in my backpack all along.* I waited to hear the words "I'm sorry," but they didn't come.

Then he turned to me with a glare. "Weren't you the one who checked my backpack?" When he saw my expression, he pretended to be joking.

It was done. Lights out.

Chapter 6
A Basket of Bells

I planned to break the news to Stephen during our upcoming appointment with Patricia. I wanted a witness. I couldn't risk the possibility of him going on the attack or twisting the truth or trying to talk me out of it.

During those two days before our session, I observed our life as if through a one-way window. I looked at the expansive views over the vineyards, understanding that they would not be mine for much longer. I watched the kids in their moments of daily innocence, so ignorant of how their lives were about to change, and silently asked their forgiveness for what I was about to do. I took the dog for her usual morning walks, and by the time we returned home, my face was usually wet with tears. It was enormous, this decision. I was about to alter everyone's lives.

Yet there was also a kind of thrill, knowing that I was about to jump out of the airplane. I had been unhappy for so long, and now I was about to do something drastic to change it. My heart raced thinking about it. Was my parachute packed correctly? I had no idea.

On Tuesday, in Patricia's office, we sat several feet apart on the leather sofa. Patricia asked how we were this week. We fell into our usual offensive positions—Stephen blaming me for my selfishness and my imperfect performance as a wife and mother, me blaming him for his constant anger and criticism. I kept waiting for the right moment to announce that I had reached my breaking point.

How typical that I was still concerned with conversational etiquette, that I was trying to avoid an awkward juncture as I announced my intention to leave. I watched the clock wind down toward the end of our fifty minutes. It felt like I was standing on the top of a steep cliff, looking down at the ground hundreds of feet below. But the idea of waiting a whole week until our next appointment was out of the question.

Stephen had just finished his latest salvo against me (I had selfishly ruined the Alaska vacation because I was so controlling and rigid in my interests), and Patricia asked, "Kirsten, can you meet Stephen halfway on this point? Can you agree to accept fifty percent of the responsibility for this standoff?"

The room was mute as I considered the question. Then I said, "No, I can't accept fifty percent."

"What about thirty percent?" she asked, her voice a straight line.

"I can't accept thirty percent," I said. "I can't accept one percent." The tears were sliding down my cheeks, gathering at my jawline.

Patricia was puzzled. "Kirsten," she said in her monotone. "What is it you want to do?"

Months passed as I considered my words. "I want to separate," I finally said. "I *need* to separate."

And there it was, out in the daylight, for everyone to hear. My nose was running, but I didn't reach for a Kleenex. I didn't dare look at Stephen. He was silent.

"I see," Patricia said. Then, before she had a chance to recalibrate, Stephen got up and walked out, slamming the door behind him. Patricia and I sat there for a moment, absorbing the sound. I realized that the rest of this conversation would have to be held back at the house, without Patricia's intervention or protection. I hurriedly wrote her a check as she said something about next steps, but I couldn't hear her words. All I could think about was what the damage would look like when I got home.

By the time I pulled into the garage, Stephen's pickup was in the driveway, the truck bed already partly loaded with his things. I quietly entered the house—saying a prayer of thanks that the kids were still out—and found him in the bedroom, slamming drawers and pulling hangers. I walked into the room and watched him for a moment. "Do you want to keep talking?" I finally asked.

"There's nothing more to say," he said. "You've already decided what you want. Which will affect this entire family, by the way. Have you even thought about what this will do to the kids? Have you thought about anyone but yourself, Kirsten? No, you haven't. As usual, you've only thought about yourself." He brushed by me, his arms loaded with buckskin and camo and combat boots. I was tired of fighting. The deed was done. I knew him well enough to know that he wouldn't be leaving without launching a few more blame grenades.

"Where do you plan to go?" I asked, but I already knew.

"I'll be at the farm," he said. "I'll call later to talk to the kids."

I walked to my little office alcove across from the kitchen and sat at my computer, pretending to occupy myself with email while he finished his departure scene. Now that I'd finally launched the thing I'd been imagining for weeks, I couldn't fully absorb it. Then I heard him gun his truck as loudly as he could and screech back down the driveway. He was gone.

I sat, frozen, stunned by what I'd just done. We hadn't discussed how or what we'd tell the kids, so what was I supposed to say to them when they returned? A whole family had now been broken apart, because of me.

I walked through our bedroom and into the bathroom, looking around to see what he'd taken. And there, next to the toilet, was something that made me laugh out loud. A set of small brass bells on a silk rope—the bells that Stephen had taken every Christmas Eve night and shaken outside the living room window, while inside I worked the kids into a state of near hysteria as we heard "Santa's sleigh bells." He'd done it every year until Bronte and Amory were both too old to believe—about three years earlier. Now, as a dramatic gesture to show me exactly what damage I'd wrought, he'd thrown the bells into the trash. And, just in case I wouldn't notice them at the bottom of the wastebasket, he'd carefully draped them over the edge—a touching tableau of good times now ruined. *Good one, Stephen*, I thought. *Let the games begin.*

Part II

Chapter 7
Football Players

It was a week before the kids even noticed that Stephen was gone. We were so used to his absences that at first nothing seemed amiss. When they finally asked where he was, I told them that Daddy was staying up at the farm for a while and, with Bronte approaching the eighth grade and Amory the fifth, they readily accepted that explanation. Meanwhile, I walked around with a heart full of grief mixed with profound relief at his absence. And dread about the conversation that would eventually have to involve the children.

When Stephen returned to St. Helena a week later to pick up some more things, we agreed to sit down and explain things to Bronte and Amory. Only much later did I realize what a terrible idea this was, to blithely tell them—with no notice whatsoever—that we were separating. Yes, kids are sensitive and smart, and surely they had sensed the tension between us. But they had no inkling that it would come to this. We had kept our loudest arguments for when they were at school or asleep. Why hadn't we let them know how bad things were over the summer, when we were spending an hour a week yelling at each other in Patricia's office?

—

My friend Harriet called. Roughly ten years older than me, she had recently married for the second time, after several bouts of cold feet. Ironically, I'd been the one to counsel her toward marriage. I'd repeated the words of my friend Amanda from twenty years before: "It's a lot harder to say yes than to say no. Be brave and say yes."

Harriet had taken my advice and was now a mostly happily married woman. Today it was her turn to counsel me about divorce. "When men are rejected, they turn into football players," she said. "They'll do anything to hurt you. And they usually use money to do it." She ended the conversation by advising me to clear out all our joint accounts. "Take the money now, ask questions later," she said.

I was sitting on the swing on our long back porch overlooking the vineyards to the eastern hills. The leaves were turning, and I could smell the vinegary odor of discarded grape skins after the crush of winemaking. It was a smell that always made me feel wistful.

"As tempting as that is," I said, "I just can't do it. I need to be the adult and not throw the first grenade. Stephen would go ballistic."

"Don't say I didn't warn you," Harriet said.

Over the next few months, Stephen vacillated dramatically. In one phone conversation, he was contrite and sad. He told me that his first wife, Beth, had said that she'd always wished they'd made more of an effort to get back together. "We shouldn't throw away twenty years of marriage just because of one bad summer," he pleaded.

The next time we talked, he said, "Except for the births of our two children, the last twenty years have been a complete waste of my time." In another phone conversation: "If I lose you, it'll be the greatest regret of my life." We both cried.

Then there was the conversation in which Stephen revealed something that explained so much about the previous five years. "I've been addicted to Vicodin since my last back surgery," he confessed. "They say it can cause irritability."

He said it as if he were admitting to a weakness for French fries. And blaming his black tempers on something other than himself. Here was one more glaring symptom of dysfunction that I'd completely missed. My husband had been addicted for years to an opiate narcotic that often leads to much harder drugs, and I hadn't even rummaged through his bathroom drawers.

"I guess the time to have told me about that would have been years ago, Stephen," I said. "It's really too late now." I hung up the phone in a fog of disbelief.

With each interaction, I realized a few things. Stephen loved me, I knew that—as much as he could love anyone beyond himself. And he would always be a master manipulator. And I would survive this better than he would. With every thrust and parry, I was more certain that I wanted out of the marriage permanently. I started calling him "Steve" again. The honorific of using his full given name, as his mother had, was something I no longer deserved or wanted. The first time I said it, Steve gave me a sharp look. He knew exactly what it meant.

A few weeks after we'd separated, Steve announced that he was going back to Alaska to "find himself." "I've never just taken time off, with no strings attached," he said.

I guess the previous six years of three-week Alaska trips don't count, I didn't say.

"I've been supporting other people since I was nineteen years old," he said, retreating to his favorite role—the victim of everyone else's bad behavior. I didn't point out that this was because he had married his high school girlfriend after she'd gotten pregnant, and that they'd had four children in six years. He didn't say where he'd be staying or when he'd be back. So I continued with the status quo, caring for the kids and keeping the house as if everything were normal. But I felt like a fraud.

—

It was autumn of 2006. Turn on any news channel and you'd hear that we were heading toward the worst financial crisis since the Great Depression. The residential housing boom had come to an abrupt end. Job growth had dropped, houses were no longer flying off the market, consumer debt was soaring, and mortgage delinquencies and credit card defaults were on the rise. It was a bad time to consider divorce.

Steve had made some preliminary efforts to start his new business, Western Pacific, but apparently that was on hold until he found himself in Alaska. We had no income and were now living off of savings. In fact, we were investing several thousand dollars each month to get his fledgling business off the ground. In the meantime, we were spending money at our usual rate—six mortgages, two cars, utilities, food, a gardener, a pool service, and more. Our familial enterprise was so big, I had no idea where to stop the bleeding. I was the one paying the bills from our joint checking account, so I could see where it was going, and how fast. But every time I told Steve the bad news, he was shocked and accusatory. How could I be spending our money so quickly? I started sending him itemized reports, and the accusations stopped.

One day I came home to a message on our answering machine from a Harley-Davidson dealer in Roseville. At first I figured it was a wrong number, until the man's voice asked how Steve was liking his "new wheels." He'd apparently bought the new motorcycle about a week after he moved up to the farm. He and I were still splitting expenses from the rapidly dwindling checking and savings accounts we shared. Now he was engaging in more retail therapy to offset the unhappiness I had caused him. The term "sinking ship" sailed around my brain constantly. I had been poor before, but I had never been headed for a financial disaster like this one.

Harriet's words chimed in my head like a bad doorbell. She'd been right. If he couldn't have our marriage back, Steve would set it aflame and take us all down with him. I could almost smell the odor of burning wood, carpets, clothing. Experience had taught me that confronting him about his wild spending would achieve nothing but his fury. So I decided to fight fire with fire. Every time I learned of an unnecessary purchase he'd made, I'd take that same amount and deposit it into a secret account in my own name. He was so oblivious to our finances that he'd never even notice.

"I'm calling it my Italy fund," I boasted in an email to Victoria, a writer friend in Mill Valley. No, I didn't think I'd actually save enough to go to Italy, especially when I was actually worried about where I'd be living in the years ahead. But the idea of escaping back to my life before Steve Beckwith was one of the few thoughts that gave me comfort in those days of anxious uncertainty.

We continued to see Patricia for mediation, and in our weekly meetings we managed to broker an uneasy agreement about who would live where and how we'd share the kids. Now that Steve had found himself in Alaska and had nursed his wounds at the farm, he was back, and he wanted equal custody of our children. When he announced this fact during one of our therapy sessions, it took my breath away. He had missed more than half of their childhoods while he was working in the Bay Area and traveling, and now he was starting a new business.

I didn't blame Steve for wanting to see more of the kids, but I was suspicious of his motives and nervous about his parenting choices. If we shared the kids equally, he would owe me no child support. In fact, if I went back to work, I might end up supporting him. More than that, the idea of losing Bronte and Amory for half the month made my heart feel hollow and panicky—I honestly hadn't seen this one coming. But it was too late to turn back now. I had made this messy, complicated bed.

We had heard about an estranged couple who used two

houses—the children stayed in one while the parents rotated between the two places week to week. It did sound like a good arrangement for the kids, and Steve loved the idea. But I knew down to my very fiber that it would drive me insane. Not just one house to clean up after Steve, but two. Still sleeping in the same beds, with just the ghost of the other person on the other side. I simply couldn't do it. I knew that his unspoken agenda was that I would still be maintaining his house and his life, just as I had been doing for twenty years.

But that's not what he said. "It's just like you to put yourself first, ahead of your children" is what he said. "Once again, only thinking of yourself."

"What are your concerns, Kirsten?" Patricia asked in her always calm, nonjudgmental voice.

I tried to explain that I no longer had the patience or the strength to share a physical space with Steve, but I ended up in tears instead.

Patricia turned to him. "Steve, how long would you envision this arrangement continuing?" she asked.

He assumed a look of exasperation, as if this should be obvious to everyone. "Well, until they go to college, of course." Patricia and I both gasped audibly. "What's wrong with that?" he asked. Amory would leave for college in nine years.

No, I said. Just no. One of us would stay at Mee Lane and one of us would find a rental. The kids could rotate between the two. Most split families did it this way. Since the house would soon be up for sale, and since Steve couldn't clean a house to save his life, I should be the one to stay at Mee Lane. I would stage it and take responsibility for cleaning it up before every showing. Otherwise, it would never sell. He finally agreed reluctantly, and I offered to help him find a rental.

Within a couple of weeks, I'd found a large rental house on Pratt Avenue, a tree-lined road just a few blocks north of downtown St. Helena. It was an unrenovated sixties ranch style, but nicely furnished with three bedrooms and two baths. Best of all, it sat on a half acre with big lawns front and back. It had a country feel, a woodburning fireplace, and a lot of privacy, all of which were essential to Steve. He grudgingly looked around and made it clear that he would be living in reduced circumstances, while I would continue living like royalty at Mee Lane. I reminded him that living in a house on the market was no picnic, and that I would be responsible for keeping it presentable. He finally agreed to take the Pratt house.

"Just one condition," he said. There was always a condition. "I also get to keep the farm. I'll live there on the weeks I don't have the kids."

The mortgage on the farm was nearly as much as the mortgage at Mee Lane, and it was still in both our names. I had assumed we'd rent it until we decided what to do with it. But I agreed, for now. Stephen always had to feel like he'd won something.

Bronte and Amory started school in September 2006 from the launchpad of two homes, not one. Bronte was entering the eighth grade, Amory the fifth. Each Sunday they would either leave or arrive with their brightly colored duffel bags, their school backpacks, their stuffed animals. We told them they should keep clothes at both houses, but the idea didn't appeal to them. When they were home with me, all seemed normal. But I knew that this sudden new arrangement had to be taxing them.

I'd begun pacing a lot. The dog's two-mile walk every morning wasn't enough—my subconscious mind seemed to think that, if I kept walking, I might ultimately gain some distance from the problems that were piling up on my doorstep like yellowed old newspapers. Today I was pacing the length of our long back porch, scanning the horizon for answers, zipping and unzipping the front of my sweatshirt like a tiny metal mantra as I marched back and forth.

With us hemorrhaging money and Steve bringing in nothing, it had become obvious that I needed to find some kind of job. I'd spent the past week talking to several employment counselors, trying to figure out what I was now qualified to do, given the past twelve years of fulltime motherhood. They all advised me that women in my situation had up to a year to figure out their job situations. One advised me to go back to school to get my doctorate to teach at the university level. "You're clearly intelligent," he'd said. "You need to take this time to reenter the workforce in a meaningful way."

Steve had a different idea. "You need to find a job *tomorrow*!" he said. And with the way we were losing money, I knew he was right.

When Bronte was two, I'd left my last real job, as an editor and writer at UC Berkeley's Office of University Relations. It had been a great career position, and I'd been good at it. But that had been twelve years before—I now had a gaping hole in my résumé from the time I had invested in homework supervision, school fundraisers, the care and feeding of four people and a dog. All the writing courses and conferences, the agent I'd found for my novel, and the hours spent learning the craft of fiction had done little to restore my confidence about actually earning a living again.

One day I steeled myself, picked up the phone, and called Elizabeth Sullivan, my former supervisor at Berkeley, who still worked in University Relations. "I'm back in the game," I said. "Do you know of anyone who needs some freelance help?" I waited for the nervous laugh, the awkward pause, the sorry tone in her voice.

"In fact, I do," she said. "We need to create a fundraising brochure for the College of Letters and Sciences, and the whole department is overbooked at the moment. When can you start?" It was as simple as that. It wasn't a fulltime job, but it was enough to get me going.

"I've found some work," I proudly told Steve that night.

His skepticism was evident even through the phone cable.

"Really," he said. "Doing what?"

"Well, it's just one project for now, but it's a good project," I said. "It could be the beginning of something regular. It's a start, anyway."

"Freelancing from home? That sounds like the kind of la-dee-da arrangement you'd come up with. You need a *real* job, Kirsten. You need to go to work like the rest of the world."

"So tell me all about *your* new job, Steve," I said, and that shut him up. His new job was a fledgling business that not only was not yet earning a profit but was costing us tens of thousands of dollars to get off the ground.

"Besides," I reasoned, "what about the kids? They're not old enough to drive, and we live three miles from town. Who's going to shuttle them back and forth to school and sports? I can't get a real job as long as we're in this house." And so my freelance career began.

The life of sharing Bronte and Amory equally with Steve was breaking my heart. I felt as if I had tended this garden so lovingly and vigilantly, and now it was being turned over to someone who promised that they'd water and weed and fertilize, but whose attempts would be sloppy and half-hearted. I knew he loved them; there was no doubt of that. But I also knew that he wasn't used to devoting the same passion and rigor and commitment that I had for so many years. Our standards were so drastically different. I thought of the times that Steve had taken them for an afternoon to let me write, and they'd returned with half-gallon bottles of soda or giant milkshakes. I knew I needed to let go, to allow everyone to learn their own lessons. But I also felt responsible, like I was sending the kids to a well-meaning but slipshod foster home.

God or fate or my fairy godmother had always led me in the right direction before. I was trying to trust my own inner guidance, the same voice that had told me to get out of this marriage. But the kids— they were enough to make me want to capitulate. Was I modeling good behavior by leaving a life that was making me unhappy? Or was I ruining their lives in pursuit of my own happiness? Such were the questions that wrote themselves on my bedroom ceiling each night.

—

Within two months of my beginning to work for UC Berkeley again, I got a referral to a second client, a small creative agency that did fundraising collateral pieces for organizations in the arts and higher education. They promptly put me to work on a capital campaign for San Francisco's Academy of Sciences that was building a new state-of-the-art museum, aquarium, and planetarium. I couldn't believe that the arc of my new career had so quickly brought me to such a fun assignment. I gushed a little to my friends.

While others toil away for years suffering rejections and hear the sound of the wind whistling bleakly through their folder of freelance clips, you've managed to succeed at an impressive rate in your newly resurrected career, wrote my friend Rita. She was an attorney in the Bay Area but should have been a fulltime writer herself. *Interviewing penguins indeed. Why, you got to jump right to extraordinarily cute birds rather than having to start with some lesser species, say, for instance, moths, who are known to eschew answering questions and continue glumly chewing cashmere sweaters.*

I had to admit that, on the surface, my new life did appear pretty magical. I was still living in the Mee Lane house and driving a Lexus SUV. It must have looked like I was enjoying myself. But the day-to-day experience was anything but easy. Between scrambling to meet freelance deadlines and keeping up an appearance of cheerful normalcy with the kids, I was starting to fall apart. I was pulled over for speeding three times in four months—then received a letter from the DMV telling me that, with the next offense, my license would be suspended. I lost my phone, keys, and glasses on a nearly daily basis. And I was prone to burst into tears or snap in anger with the slightest provocation. I could feel my psyche becoming as brittle as a dried wishbone. I was holding our life together with spit and glue, but there was no way I could fall apart now—I couldn't do it to the kids, and I couldn't show Steve my weakness.

Chapter 8
Au Revoir, Hooverville

October arrived. Now when I swam in the afternoons, the sun had already ducked behind the oak trees to the west. Soon it would be too cold to swim at all. My heels were dry and cracked from all the chlorine and hot pavement of the summer weekends by the pool. I felt old.

But that month, I joined the St. Helena Chamber Singers. I had been raised singing in groups—Christmas caroling, campfires, and family gatherings. Suddenly, here was a group of more than sixty people who met weekly to rehearse a major classical work as well as selected carols, culminating in two performances just before Christmas. I showed up nervously for the first night of rehearsal. I hadn't read music or sung in front of others since I was a child. It felt like the first day of seventh grade.

As I sat there following along with the more seasoned altos, though, I could hear the cobwebs clearing from my shaky voice. "You're either a leader or a leaner," the choral director was fond of saying, and I definitely leaned on the voices of the other, more experienced women who surrounded me. Each week I listened to the practice CD and plunked out my part on the grand piano that had sat unused for years in our living room. With each rehearsal I became more confident of my sound. And soon I had fostered some lovely friendships, particularly with the older women—many of whom had been through divorces or widowhood or other misfortunes, and all of whom had landed safely, happily, on the other side. To myself, I called them the aunties.

I began to scrutinize our financial statements more closely. Of our several checking accounts, we had one that we'd used only for real estate transactions. Recently Steve had told me to ignore this account—we should just use the main checking account from now on, he advised. So I was now paying all our monthly bills out of the main account, and we were each taking a draw of several thousand dollars a month for our own personal expenses. It seemed more than adequate even though, financially, we were headed into oncoming traffic.

One Monday morning I took a deep breath and opened the bank statements that had been piling up on my desk, to try and impose some order on the chaos. I hate looking at bank statements. I hate even talking about money. But I put on my big-girl pants and my glasses and got to work. There, in the "don't use anymore" account, I saw some regular deposits and withdrawals I didn't recognize. Nearly $5,600 each month, deposited from Nossaman, Guthner, Knox, and Elliot—Steve's old law firm. Apparently these were the dividends from his partnership—money we'd paid into the firm when he'd become a partner, which were now being refunded to us over a period of months. And each month, that same amount was being quickly transferred—usually within a day—to an account at another bank I didn't recognize.

Steve was apparently taking his dividend payments and siphoning them off to his own account so he wouldn't have to declare them as shared income. Harriet had been right, again. He was in football player mode, and he was using money to play offense.

Dear Steve, went my email the next day. *Reviewing our recent statements from B of A account 2596, I've noticed some undeclared deposits and withdrawals in the amount of approximately $5,600/month from Nossaman to your personal account at Bank of the West. Can you shed some light on this? According to my math, to date the deposits total approximately $22,568.*

He didn't respond for a few days. I sent him a refresher email on the subject. Finally, he responded: *Apparently my automatic deposits have become confused. This was an oversight. Obviously, if your interpretation is correct, I may owe you some money. I'll send you a check shortly.*

That would be great, I wrote. The things I *didn't* say to this man could fill a book.

For Thanksgiving, Steve and I took the kids to Safari West, a local wild animal preserve that offered a buffet turkey dinner within the park. I just couldn't see cooking and serving the whole dinner at home—too much work and too much time for what had become a charade. We strolled along fenced savannahs with prides of grazing lions. We fed giraffes and chimpanzees. Then we lined up for the buffet with other families who didn't want to cook that day.

After Steve's gastric bypass surgery, the doctor had explained how he now had a tiny stomach and should eat only fist-sized portions. Now I watched as he piled ten or twelve fists of turkey, mashed potatoes, stuffing, and cranberry sauce onto his plate. Then I watched as he ate all of it.

He finally pushed back from the table. "I don't feel so well," he said.

"I'm not surprised," I didn't say. It wasn't my problem anymore.

In early December I called and asked Steve for his help in getting the heavy Christmas boxes down from their high perch in the garage. His dramatic sigh told me that this was a task he was not eager to perform. Such was the extent of my Stockholm syndrome, it didn't occur to me to ask anyone else. I was still in denial that there were certain areas in which I was helpless without a man. As days and then weeks passed, I gazed up at the piles of boxes marked *Tree Stand and Lights, Ornaments,* and *Crêche & Angels* and wondered if it would happen at all. Each time Steve came over, he had some excuse; it was never a good time. I imagined myself a Dickensian orphan child, gazing at those boxes with big sad eyes: *Please, Sir, won't the Beckwiths be having a Christmas this year?*

Finally, two Sundays before Christmas, he showed up with an extension ladder and without a word began stacking the boxes in the hall. Only then did I realize that we'd be out every night that week. The kids would be at his house for the weekend, then I'd take them skiing all the next week before Christmas Eve. This was the only night before the day itself to decorate the tree with them. He'd be dropping them off at my house that evening.

It was three thirty. I raced to Up Valley Nursery, which sold and delivered trees. I paced the lot and found a small, full spruce that would do fine. It could have been a cactus, for all I cared—as long as I could get it home in time. But the flannel-shirted young nurseryman shook his head. "Sorry, ma'am," he told me, "we're only open till five, and the delivery truck is full."

I actually clasped my hands together in the official manner and leaned forward in supplication. "Please," I begged. "I have no husband! I'm all alone!" Even I was annoyed by my lack of self-respect, but I didn't care.

"He's the guy you need to talk to," the young man said, cocking his thumb at an older man standing near the counter. Brian Byrne: the weathered local hero, St. Helena's fire chief and also owner of the nursery. I'd barely even spoken to Chief Brian before, and then only at the fire department open houses I used to take Amory to when he was little. Now I threw myself at his mercy, apologizing for my lack of foresight, admitting my weakness, my vulnerability, my abject stupidity for being separated during the holiday season.

He gave me a wry smile and said simply, "Address?"

I told him.

"Be there between now and five to let us in."

I thanked him profusely and nearly curtseyed. Then I rushed home to straighten up and clear a path for the tree.

Brian showed up before five, as promised. There had been a bad accident that morning in town, and as he sawed off the tree's lower branches, he told me about it. There were three fire trucks, two ambulances, even the Life Flight helicopter. The driver had died.

I gasped, hands to my face, watching him tighten up the bolts on the tree stand.

"Yeah, after we finally got him out with the 'jaws,' we lost the pulse. We called the chopper and told it not to bother landing." Here was this man, setting up my Christmas tree, and he'd tried to save a life that morning.

Chief Brian picked up the discarded branches and stood back, admiring his work. "That should do you okay," he said.

I assumed the position of clasped hands again, this time in copious gratitude, and began to thank him in the names of my children and my future grandchildren.

"Don't forget to put your saw away," he said, nodding toward the hacksaw on my floor. "And Happy Holidays to you and yours." Then he was gone, backing out of my driveway with the speed and confidence of one who has driven his share of fire trucks.

Within five minutes, Steve showed up to drop off the kids. Bronte and Amory rushed inside with their usual fanfare and were immediately hit with the smell of fresh evergreen.

"A tree!" Amory cried. "Can we decorate it tonight?"

"Well, sure, I don't see why not," I said, ever so casually, as if the thought hadn't occurred to me before that moment.

Steve said nothing and didn't bother going into the living room to admire the spruce with the kids. Had I asked him to help me get a tree, I knew he would have refused. But now I could see his displeasure at the fact that I'd somehow done it without him. "I can't believe you actually bought a tree without them," he said, shaking his head. I gave him a fake smile.

After dinner, the kids and I put up the lights and ornaments in record speed. By their bedtime, the tree twinkled and glimmered in full splendor. I stood and looked at it with a special awe. It felt like a little holiday miracle. And next year the boxes would be stored within easy reach. Never again would I be dependent on Steve.

In mid-December, our chamber chorus performed Mozart's *Coronation Mass in C Major* in the town's lovely little Catholic church, accompanied by a twenty-piece orchestra, which gave me a joy I hadn't felt in years. By then, the group had become an extended family of friends, and after the concert I hosted a party that included karaoke and singing show tunes around the piano. Bronte and Amory peeked shyly into the living room, watching the hijinks of all the tipsy adults. Until that night, they'd thought *I* was the most ridiculous person on the planet. How wrong they were.

As our first post-separation Christmas approached, I tried to assuage my guilt for breaking up the family. I was also trying to offset Steve's anger whenever possible. But the flare-ups were frequent—I felt like a teenager trying to avoid the wrath of her bad-tempered dad. I'd been having Steve over for dinner once a week, just to keep things friendly in front of the kids. I made little gestures of goodwill, like bringing his mail over and saving him the Sunday paper. I even invited him to my family's annual Christmas dinner, which he refused and then, three days before the holiday, asked if the invitation was still extended. Yes, I lied.

Ever since the separation in August, my mother—struggling with mild dementia—had asked me repeatedly, "Are you sure you two can't work things out?"

"Yes, Mom," I'd say. "It's really for the best this way."

She'd shake her head and look worried. "But are you really sure?"

"I'm sure," I'd say.

As always, Christmas dinner was held at Ingrid and Keith's small house in Menlo Park, with Keith's grown children mingling with my own much younger kids, and many large dogs roaming around in every spare pocket of space. Steve showed up and parked himself on a kitchen barstool, chatting with Keith, with whom he'd spent many summers camping in Alaska. We all pretended nothing was wrong. But Steve didn't make the slightest effort to talk to anyone else. My widowed mother, for whom moving without assistance was virtually impossible, was planted in a chair in the living room.

The next day on the phone, Mom's memory was unusually sharp. "Steve didn't even come over to say hello to me," she said. "Not once."

Now it was my turn to say, "Are you sure?"

"Oh, I'm sure," she said. "You can go ahead and divorce him now."

As I went through my days—straightening the house, dropping off the kids, unloading the groceries—a switch went on and off inside me. I swung from a feeling of giddy escape to a fear of what Steve might do next to exact revenge. Ever since our separation, his moods had ricocheted between civil and vindictive. I never knew who I'd encounter on any given day. And I didn't know how this was going to end—it would either be a complete victory of independence, or he would make me suffer until the end of my days.

My dreams were water-based, every night a different scenario: It was raining, then flooding. Or I drove my car into the ocean and couldn't get out of the vehicle. Or I was going over a waterfall, feeling the earth drop out from under me as I plunged into a froth of white water far below. Or I was in the ocean, deep underwater, frantically searching for the surface. My book of dream symbolism explained that water dreams represented emotional energy. *Whether clean, murky, still or choppy, water indicates your emotional state*, it said. No kidding.

One morning in January, I did something I'd never done: I called an attorney. I'd never done this because I'd been married to an attorney. I wished I could just call Steve instead and let him handle this little legal matter for free, but I couldn't because I was divorcing him. We each needed our own divorce lawyer, and the idea terrified me. Steve wasn't a divorce lawyer, but he was a fierce litigator. He had the killer instinct. I knew I'd have to find someone just as fierce. This part was going to get ugly.

Steve and I had continued to see Patricia, the therapist, each week, in an attempt to keep things civilized. In one session, we discussed the possibility of mediation, which sounded so civilized and humane and really, why wouldn't you do it? But I knew that Steve would easily and skillfully manipulate the situation so that, once again, we'd all be his dancing puppets. I felt like I'd been doing his bidding, often without even realizing it, for twenty years. He was that good.

So I called every friend I knew who'd been divorced and asked for recommendations. One name kept coming up: Glen Fisher. "He's simply the best in the valley" is pretty much what everyone said. I made an appointment for a consultation.

One week later, I was sitting in his elegantly appointed office in downtown Napa. Glen was a small and tastefully dressed man in his sixties, not a big smiler, very taciturn and businesslike. As I sat across from him at the round conference table, I noticed a box of Kleenex stationed at the center. The Kleenex box seemed to have become a talisman for this chapter of my life. The phrase "vale of tears" entered my head and stayed there for the next year.

—

February. We'd been separated for six months. We'd been calling it a "trial separation," but for me the verdict had been written a long time ago: I wanted a divorce.

"I thought we were going to work on things," Steve was saying. "But apparently you've already made up your mind. You've decided what's right for Kirsten, not what's right for the whole family."

I was so sick of this room, with its bad miniblinds and tissue boxes on every surface. "Something has died for me," I said, as if we were talking about a pet rabbit. I was sitting on Patricia's soft, ratty sofa, a wad of Kleenex balled in my fist. I still couldn't say the words *I don't love you anymore.* Not because I didn't mean them, but because I knew it would hurl Steve into a new level of angry behavior. "Let's move forward," I said. "Let's just put this behind us."

I still could say these things only in Patricia's office. I needed to have an impartial third person present—maybe at least one person in the room would agree with me, or at least not tell me how selfish I was. With that one word—*divorce*—I could see the possibility of reclaiming my life down the road. It would take a long time, I already knew that, and the next few years would be horrible and painful and aggravating. But I was no longer on Steve's bus, watching him drive us over a cliff. Instead, I was looking up at that cliff, watching bonfires burning along the ridge. Orange flames, flying ashes. The sky clotted with black smoke.

The following weekend, I watched out the window as Steve made trip after trip with a hand truck between the backyard and the driveway. All the stuff he'd accumulated and stashed in the growing rows of storage sheds I'd called Hooverville—scuba equipment, camping supplies, old legal files, carpentry tools, and who knew what else—now rolling away, slowly but steadily, out of my life for good.

It was a pathetic scene: Stephen's anger and sadness gathered in his hunched shoulders as he wheeled the hand truck back and forth. And yet, it was the happiest I'd felt in months—maybe years. His spending and hoarding, his growing piles of *stuff*, had weighed on me more heavily than I'd ever admitted to myself. I wanted a lighter, more flexible life. And I'd been buried alive with things I didn't want.

After a few weekends of this, Steve's things were finally, completely gone, leaving a filthy residue of dust and spiderwebs and mouse shit in the garage. He had cleared out the things he wanted but left the rest—and the dirt—for me to clean up. I saw a few old receipts lying on the floor and walked over to throw them away before I began sweeping. As I turned the yellowing slips of paper over in my hands, I noticed that one of them was a gift certificate for an hour massage at a local spa, with no expiration date. I'd probably given it to him for Father's Day years before. I swept the whole floor, dusted all the surfaces, swatted at the remaining cobwebs, and went inside. Then I picked up the phone and booked myself a massage appointment.

On my morning walks with the dog, I would head east on our rural road, acorns rolling and crunching underfoot. I looked up to the ridge—amid the thick growth of firs at the summit, there was a break in the foliage where I could see the sky on the other side. For some reason, this made me happy. I could actually see the top edge of the ridge, and the blue sky through the trees. But, as I continued walking, I looked more closely. It could just as well be the reflection off an aluminum roof. Which was it? It seemed desperately important to know.

Things had been fairly quiet between us for a week or two when Steve called one night, loaded for bear. "So you're lawyering up, I hear," he said, his voice already rising. "I wanted to try mediation and do this thing in a calm and civilized way, but no, you needed to go out and hire the *best attorney in the county*!" He spit the words out like venom.

I held the receiver a few inches from my ear. I gazed out the kitchen window, but it was dark and all I could see was the reflection of a tired, anxious woman staring back at me. Sure, I probably should have told him first. But fear makes you do irrational things.

"I know. But I just don't think mediation is going to work," I tried. "You're a seasoned attorney and I'm not. It puts you at a real advantage, and I feel like I need an advocate of my own."

"Oh, you've got an advocate, all right," he said. "And now I need to go out and hire an attorney too. Do you have any idea how much this is going to end up costing us? Why didn't you talk to me before you ran out and hired the most expensive lawyer in the valley? Did it ever occur to you to discuss it with me first?"

"I didn't discuss it with you first because I knew you'd talk me out of it," I said. "I'm sorry you don't like it, but it's what I feel I need to do."

"Yeah, what you feel you need to do is take all my money," Steve seethed. "That's *my* money, Kirsten. I earned *everything* in this marriage. And now you're going to spend it all on your fucking attorney."

"It's *our* money, Steve. California is a community property state. I gave up my career to be a fulltime mother to our children. You liked that idea at the time."

Steve knew the law far better than I did. But this was the first time I realized that he really did view our assets as rightfully his. All the time I had put into raising our children, maintaining our homes, volunteering at the schools, and being his administrative assistant and accountant counted for nothing now, since I hadn't been contributing to the bank balance.

"You know what I think? I think you came back to California from Italy to find a sucker like me to marry you so you could then take everything I own," he said. "Well, I fell for it. I stupidly fell in love with you. I walked right into it. Congratulations, Kirsten. Well played."

It took me a minute to find my voice again. "Let me get this straight. You're suggesting that I came back to California—where I was raised and where my family still lives—just to find someone like you to marry me, then have two children and stay married for twenty years, all just to use the community property laws to take your money?"

"That's right."

I laughed. "You're delusional, Steve. You're rewriting history. You're conveniently forgetting about all the years we shared when we were both perfectly happy."

"And you used sex to get me to marry you."

"I beg your pardon?"

"You heard me. You just manipulated me into falling in love with you. And now you want to get rid of me as easily as if you were firing the pool boy."

When I finally hung up the phone, I was rattled. Not about the hurtful things Steve had said, or even the fantastical lengths to which he'd taken his arguments. I was upset because I hadn't yet told Steve about hiring a lawyer. How could he possibly know? He didn't have close enough relationships with any of my friends to have learned it from them. I began to worry that he'd had my phone tapped. I called Glen to ask what to do, then spent a long time talking to the phone company, but it was an arduous, expensive procedure to have one's line monitored and swept for bugs. It was usually only done for businesses or in the cases of criminal investigations.

So began a period of paranoia, watching what I said on the phone to my friends. He had definitely gotten inside my head. Which is exactly where, I suspect, he wanted to be.

But I'd said it out loud: I wanted a divorce. Steve was more angry, vindictive, and manipulative, but we were moving forward, and there was nothing he could do about it.

Chapter 9
Under House Arrest

N ow that we'd said the *D* word, we both acknowledged the next hurdle: selling our primary asset on Mee Lane. Of course, what we hadn't anticipated was the massive financial crisis and Great Recession of 2008 just around the corner—the major worldwide economic downturn that would devastate our country for more than two years. As news began to emerge of the banking fiasco and its impact on the real estate industry, we told ourselves that the St. Helena market—which had been rising for several consecutive years—would somehow be insulated from what was going on all over the country. We were wrong.

But back then, our hopes were still high, and I fantasized about soon moving to town, walking and biking everywhere, and having higher speed internet. As we anticipated putting our home of eleven years up for sale, we embarked on three painful months of renovations. We hired contractors to replace windows, to rebuild some rotten framing under the house, and to completely retile the pavers on the porch. We had the exterior repainted, the yard relandscaped.

The thing about big houses is that, at some point, you stop owning them and they start owning you. This home that had witnessed so many happy moments, childhood firsts, and celebrations was now just a weight around my neck. I felt trapped, like I was under house arrest.

I was still working from home as a freelance copywriter, interviewing scientists and students and professors by phone while in the background buzzsaws screamed and hammers pounded. During the ten days of painting, the entire structure was swathed in translucent Visqueen, casting a dull pall over the whole house. It was like living in an embryonic sac, but with television and phone service. It was a minor war zone.

Amid the chaos and the noise, I soldiered on, trying to be both a breadwinner and a mom. But despite my incredible good luck in landing two new excellent clients, I began to recognize a self-destructive quality in myself. I'd always been rigorously self-critical, a perfectionist about my work, which carried over into my sense of personal esteem. As a fulltime mother, away from the workplace, I'd felt that I'd overcome this judgmental streak. Motherhood had softened and matured me, I thought. I was happier in my own skin, as the saying goes.

But now the old demons rose up as if they'd never been away. As a freelancer, I had to knock every project out of the park, to ensure that my clients would hire me again. I had to look at everything I wrote with an unforgiving eye, missing no typo or dangling modifier. I was constantly envisioning worst-case scenarios and worrying that my work wasn't good enough. What I thought had been growth was only a temporary reprieve as I'd dealt with children instead of colleagues and employers. Now I was back to the old, self-critical routine.

Bronte was in middle school now. American Girl dolls and Breyer horses had been replaced by brands like Juicy and American Eagle. She was wearing makeup and styling her hair and reigning supreme over the bathroom she shared with Amory. She attended the Congressional Youth Leadership Conference in the fall and was proud of being "one of the smart girls" (her words). And she was as horse-crazy as ever. My sister, Ingrid, another equestrienne, had arranged for Bronte to care for a retired A-circuit hunter-jumper Arabian gelding, and she spent every possible afternoon out at Oakville Farms, a local riding barn.

Amory was having a banner ninth year, even if he wouldn't admit to it. He was becoming a strong player on his Little League and soccer teams, and his project won first place at his school's science fair. He also went semi-pro with his acting and musical talents, as Macavity in his school's production of *Cats*. But at home he was still the sword-loving, Lego-building kid he'd always been. And he was as funny as ever. "Hello, strange creature," he said one day when he saw a deer outside our car window. "By what name do the natives call you?"

I was more grateful than ever now when he could get me to laugh. I kept looking for subtle signs of trauma or grief from his and Bronte's new living arrangements, bouncing between Steve's house and mine, but I could see none.

When the family health insurance provided by Steve's law firm ended, I spent several long hours on the phone applying for new insurance in my name for myself and the kids. I didn't trust Steve to pay attention to the details of something so tedious.

"We can split the cost for the kids' insurance," I told him. "I'll make sure the premiums are paid each month." He was only too happy to let me take care of this. "But be sure to get your own policy," I added. I gave him the contact information for Blue Shield.

Back when I was a fulltime mother, my days had easily rolled one into the other. Now I had to fit life at home with the kids into half the time—or less—than I'd been used to. My first concern was meeting work deadlines, proving myself in a world that, just the year before, had been unfamiliar and unnecessary. Now I needed that world more than ever. And I didn't want Bronte and Amory to notice the difference.

Amory's tenth birthday fell on a Friday. His school allowed birthday treats to be brought at two forty-five on the afternoon of the child's birthday to share with classmates before the kids were let out at three. I'd achieved some local renown for my original cupcakes—coconut flavored with cream cheese frosting and toasted coconut on top, or lemon with tiny slices of candied orange, or maybe chocolate with a surprise peppermint filling. I had always loved bringing some new delight to school events, and as Amory got older, I could see the look of pride on his face when the other kids gathered around to see what came out of my Rubbermaid cupcake carrier.

Today, however, the ingredients lay untouched on the kitchen counter as I fielded phone calls, finished a deadline, answered emails about yet another round of revisions. By one o'clock, I was mentally calculating cooking times, cooling periods, and decorating. I'd have to have them in the car by two twenty-five if I were to get to the school in time. It was already too late. My reputation would have to take a hit: I'd swing by Safeway and pick up three dozen ready-made cupcakes—the hideous kind with lard frosting in Day-Glo colors.

I continued working until two o'clock. Then I remembered the packet of proofs that had to be dropped off at the Fed Ex box by two forty latest. I grabbed the package and my purse and hopped into the car for the twenty-minute drive into town. Traffic. A short line at the Fed Ex office. By the time I got to Safeway, it was two fifty. I found four plastic containers of Valentine's Day–themed cupcakes and raced to the express checkout.

The checker was a pale-faced young woman with whom I had often chatted and laughed as I went through the line. Her nametag said "Devon." Today I had no time for any of that. I handed her my debit card as she tried to scan the four packages.

"Price check," she called into the intercom. "Ma'am, these don't have a bar code on them," she explained.

"I'm in an awful hurry," I said. I glanced at the big clock on the wall, which said two fifty-eight.

"I'm so sorry," she said. "I can't ring you up without a bar code."

"How much do you *think* they are?" I opened my wallet. "Can I just pay cash?"

"Price check, please," she repeated into the intercom, a bit more loudly. My stress was contagious, and she'd clearly caught it.

"Here's thirty dollars," I said, plunking down two bills on the counter. "Surely that's more than enough?"

"I'm sorry, ma'am," she said again. "I have to ring them up with the right bar code. Let me just run to the bakery department." She turned to leave.

The clock now said three-oh-five. School was already out. The cars were lining up in the parking lot, children piling into backseats.

I grabbed the bills and shoved them into my purse. "It's too late!" I cried. "School's out! Can't you people ever do anything without your fucking corporate protocol?"

The young woman stared at me, her mouth open in a little aperture of hurt. I could feel the eyes of other customers on me too, heads turning to see what the commotion was about as I ran from the store. I might not be shopping there for a while.

I pulled up in front of the school at three fifteen—at three twenty, they started charging a dollar for every minute you were late. The last of the other parents were pulling out of the lot. And there stood Amory on the curb, head hung in shame. When he saw me, his chin started quivering, and I felt my own eyes start to water. He made no move to open the back door but just stood there glaring at me. I rolled down the window.

"Where were you?" he said. I saw a shiny tear roll south on his left cheek.

Suddenly, I was crying too. Until now, one of the most important things I had given my children was the understanding that if I'd said I would do something, I would do it. It was a simple but essential credo. Now it was no longer true. "Ammo, I'm so, so sorry," I sobbed.

He looked at me with alarm, but the anger remained. "I told all the kids you were bringing homemade cupcakes," he said. "You made me look like a liar. And an idiot. A lying idiot."

"Honey, I just got overwhelmed with work today. I didn't have time to make them, so I ran to Safeway and got held up in line. . . ."

"It doesn't matter," he said, climbing into the car. "I don't care. Just take me home. I *hate* this school." But I heard the subtext: I hate *you*.

"You know what?" I tried, wiping the tears from my own cheeks. "Sunday night we can make whatever kind of cupcakes you want, and we'll bring them in on Monday. How about that?"

"It's too late," Amory said. "I don't want them anymore." We drove home in silence, the stink of failure filling the car.

"Be good to yourself," everyone said. "Take time to heal." Every day seemed to be filled with new land mines, and right now I felt like I was missing a few psychic limbs. I was *trying* to be good to myself. I was walking every morning, writing in my journal, continuing to see Patricia, and working on my own creative writing whenever I could squeeze it in. But the writing wasn't going well. I felt completely stopped up.

If only I could go back to my happy place and write well, I thought, all else would feel manageable. Wasn't it ironic that all that time I'd been coping in an unhappy marriage, I was able to write with abandon? According to Patricia, that was because I'd been putting up an emotional wall, and my writing was the bricks and mortar of that wall. Now that I should be feeling free and able to write whenever, however, and whatever I wanted, I was paralyzed. That was probably the fear and the chaos at work, Patricia said. But how could I make it stop?

One morning as I was trying to get a basic grasp of astrophysics to prepare for an interview with a Berkeley professor, the phone rang. It was my friend, Mitzi Muehling, who had just earned her realtor's license and was trying to build her local business.

"Have you thought about what you'll do once you sell your house?" she asked, none too subtly.

"Well, I'd love to buy something smaller in town," I said. "But I haven't really thought it through yet. I'm not sure how much I'll have to spend."

"I go to brokers' open houses every Wednesday to see the new listings," she said. "If you ever feel like coming along, you could see what's on the market."

"Sure," I said. "That's so nice of you!"

"Hey, friends do that for each other."

I already understood that when we decided to list our house, Mitzi would expect to represent us. I decided to cross that bridge when I came to it. I was optimistic—tragically overoptimistic, it would later be revealed—about the future.

Mitzi and I had been friends since our kids were in preschool together, about eight years before. Her daughter, Brooke, and son, Easton, were exactly the same ages as Bronte and Amory. We'd ended up doing a lot of playdates together for the kids and going out ourselves for lunch or a movie. Mitzi was not a typical choice as a friend for me. She had the vibe of a former cheerleader—a twinkly smile of perfect teeth, a baby voice as sugary as candy corn. Still, there was a gumption I liked about her. She and her husband, Dirk, had run a local bed and breakfast but, outside of that, Dirk had never held a real job. Now Mitzi was supporting the whole family by going back to work in real estate. Despite her breathy demeanor, she seemed like a hard worker with a good heart. I liked her.

Wednesday mornings became a weekly date. Armed with fresh coffee and scones, Mitzi expertly pointed out all the ingenious ways I could make each home uniquely mine. Knock out a wall here. Put in an extra half bath there. She could absolutely see me in this house. Or that one. I couldn't deny that I enjoyed it. I loved the fantasy, the idea that a new house would bring me a new life. That I could put Mee Lane and everything that had happened there behind me. I was on an outbound flight, and Mitzi was my friendly flight attendant. She even dressed the part, all perky scarves and fitted blazers. I was inhaling her optimism like the oxygen masks that drop from the overhead compartments.

Finally, after months of noise and construction dust and me jettisoning half our possessions to stage the house for future buyers, we were ready to put it on the market.

I cautiously broached the subject of hiring an agent with Steve. But, as in everything else, he had his own plans. He wanted us to sell it ourselves. "I'm not going to pay six percent to some stranger when we can do it just as well," he said. "Do you know how much money that is?" By "we," he meant me. I was the one living in the house. I'd be the one marketing it and showing it and, really, handling the whole thing. I put my foot down, and after much argument he finally agreed to hire an agent.

Step two: I proposed that we hire Mitzi, which met with the expected response.

"Oh, no you don't! First you talk me into using an agent, then suddenly you want to hire your friend? I see where you're going with this. Do you really think I'm such a sucker?"

I calmly pointed out that we had socialized for years with Mitzi and Dirk, and that he had always liked them both. I told him how generous Mitzi had been with her time, coaching me on how to prepare the house for sale. Finally, I told him that she would discount her commission for us, from six to four percent of the sale price. That was the magic bullet.

I called Mitzi and told her the good news. "I hope it won't be too awkward for you representing both of us when we're not really getting along," I said.

In her chirpy, upbeat voice, Mitzi assured me that she was good with difficult situations. "If at any point our relationship is at risk, I'll resign the business," she said. "Our friendship is way more important to me than any sale."

I hung up feeling excited and relieved. We were on our way.

In February, the cloudy skies turned the hills black, but pink blossoms were beginning to peek from the limbs of the plum trees lining our driveway. I had driven the dog down to Rutherford, where we walked the long drive to Rubicon Estates winery. This road, too, was lined with flowering fruit trees and the intoxicating, musty odor that meant spring had to be around the corner. That smell always took me right back to childhood, walking to school, a feeling of hope and possibility and safety.

I hadn't been home an hour when the phone rang. The telephone was rarely a friend these days. And sure enough, today Steve was calling to report that his Aunt Mildred had died after a long battle with cancer. I had met her on a couple of occasions—the youngest of Steve's mother's ten siblings, Mildred was a spitfire who had become a nun. I liked her odd combination of spirituality and spunk. While her death wasn't a surprise, it was still a sad shock that the family's youngest child was gone. To compound the grief, Mildred's grand-nephew—the son of the niece who had cared for her in her final months—had been killed in a motorcycle accident on his way home from her deathbed. There would be two funerals now—in Hartford, Connecticut.

"Of course you should go," I said. Steve knew that I was swamped with freelance work. For the first time in my career, I was writing content for a website, and it was a steep learning curve. Suddenly every page accordioned out to countless other pages. The number of text "buckets" seemed to change daily. And though the client kept adding more pages, the deadline remained the same. I was completely unhinged by stress. I couldn't afford to fail on this one.

The funeral fell on a week when Steve would normally have taken the kids, which meant that a week I was counting on working long hours would now be largely devoted to ferrying Bronte and Amory to school, sports, and the horse barn. It meant spending half my days being a mom, when I needed a stretch of time to focus solely on work.

"I'll be gone for five days," Steve said. "I'm leaving Saturday, and I'll take the kids as soon as I fly home on Wednesday night."

"I know you'd do the same for me," I said, wondering, *Would he?* But I was still determined to be flawless in my record with him. My Stockholm syndrome had me convinced that one day he would look back and thank me for my impeccable behavior in the face of his tyranny. Or maybe it was just that I didn't want to lower myself to his level of behavior. Either way, I was still trying to be the Girl Scout.

By Monday, with my deadline closer and my stress level higher, I received an email from Steve. *Have to alter my plans a bit*, he wrote. *Aunt Louise is cleaning out the garage of the old house and said I can take a bunch of my grandparents' stuff. So I'm renting a van and driving back, should take about three days. I'll be home sometime Friday.*

Was he kidding? Rather than respond with an email, I picked up the phone.

"My deadline is next Monday and I'm not even close to finishing," I said. "I need every possible day. You just can't extend your trip like this. You told me you'd be back on Wednesday."

"This is really important to me, Kirsten," Steve said. "There's all kinds of farm tools and even my grandfather's homemade still." Steve had always talked fondly of his Hungarian grandfather's legendary still, how the man would disappear into the barn to drunkenly play his violin for hours.

"So go back and get them later," I said now. "Have them shipped. Just get home. I simply can't miss this deadline, and I'm exhausted."

"Sorry, I'm not going to do that. This is too important to me. I'll call you when I get back." He hung up.

I slammed the phone down. He called *me* selfish? He said *I* was a poor parent? Not for the first time, and certainly not the last, I cursed him to hell and wished him a nice trip.

That Friday, Steve called after dinner. "I'm back, I'm just going to drive straight to the farm for the weekend. I'll pick up the kids at our usual time on Sunday."

Had the man not been listening to our last five phone conversations about my workload, my deadline, my stress? Was he trying to get back at me for being gainfully employed? Or was he merely insane?

I began to weep. "I cannot do this anymore!" I sobbed. "I need some backup here! I agreed to take the kids so you could go to your funerals, but you've totally taken advantage of my kindness."

"I just thought because it was the weekend . . ."

"Yes! The weekend! The last two days before my deadline. When I'll be working around the clock because I've had the kids for ten *fucking* days straight!" I blew my nose. "I need you back here. Now."

There was a brief silence, then Steve sighed. "I'll turn around at the next exit," he said.

Chapter 10
Meshugaas

I had never been a big fan of uncertainty. I liked nothing better than to see my days (or years) stretched out in front of me with plans and routines and things to look forward to. Now the uncertainty of my future—and the futures of my children—translated into a pulsing beat of fear, fatigue, and frustration.

Each day I forced myself to look out the window and see mustard in the vineyards, voluptuous clouds overhead, blue mountains. I reminded myself that I had a roof over my head, I had plenty to eat, my children were healthy and safe, and I couldn't, at that moment, ask for anything more. That became my spiritual practice. It wasn't easy.

Steve and I had been meeting with Mitzi to prepare the house for market, discussing the price, remaining repairs, staging, and guidelines for showings. But Mitzi was still a close friend, and I'd also been confiding in her about my struggles with Steve. She'd been friendly and upbeat during our meetings with him, but afterward she said things like *I can't believe how he treats you like his secretary.* Or *I'm going to let you deal with him on that one.* She was very supportive about my decision to divorce—she'd seen firsthand what Steve was like at home.

It had been eight months since we'd separated, and I began to consider the idea of dating again. The last time I'd dated was in the dark ages of the 1980s, when people actually had to meet each other at parties and bars and weddings. Now there was online dating, and I couldn't wait to try it. *How civilized*, I thought. That's how naïve I was. *First you meet through writing, so you really get to know each other.* I created my profile and username—Wordygirl!—and posted some recent photos. I eagerly awaited the eligible men who would beat a path to my door. This would be easy and fun.

I went on a few dates. I had long correspondences with men who seemed interesting but then vanished for no apparent reason. I soon realized that dating at fifty was no better than dating at twenty. The vast anonymity of the internet allowed people to present their ideal selves, which often bore little resemblance to their actual identities. My sense of adventure was soon replaced by ennui.

I found that my single friends fell into two groups. There were those who were also on Match or some other online dating site. And then there were those, like my friend Judith, who saw only the stigma of it.

"I could never do that," she said, mimicking a shudder. "It just makes you look pathetic. And going on a date with someone you've never met? What if they're a sex offender?" Judith was my age—early fifties, with a broad Long Island accent.

"You mean like a blind date?" I asked. "You mean like meeting someone in a bar or at a party? Just because you meet someone face-to-face doesn't mean they don't have a sordid past."

"I know, I know. But I'm not going there. I'd rather meet someone the old-fashioned way. Like at a dinner party."

"And how's that working out for you?" I asked. "When was the last time you were even invited to a dinner party?"

"Good point," Judith said. "But I'd rather be single the rest of my days than go through that *meshugaas*."

There were times when I saw her point. The real drawback to online dating, I learned, was buying into the ideal that smiled out at you from the profile—the self-described congenial, successful, romantic guy—only to meet him and be disappointed. Men would often use the term "easygoing" in their profiles. What was that code for? Passivity? Apathy? "Live and let live" was another popular phrase. If they were so easygoing, why weren't they already in relationships? Then I realized the same question could be asked of me.

Ted seemed interesting. His profile included several photos of a boyish-looking guy with long strawberry-blond hair swept back off his face. He did something in the maritime industry, but he was vague on the details. He lived in Napa, so we agreed to meet for coffee in Yountville, the halfway point between us.

I'd arrived five minutes early and sat in my parked car across from Bouchon Bakery. When Ted walked up the block, my heart sank. The hair was the same, but this guy looked like he could have been the father of the man in the photo. I would soon learn that this kind of misrepresentation is common in the online dating world.

I was so angry, I considered turning the key and driving away, but I couldn't do it. *I'll give him one hour*, I told myself. This would become my approach to all first dates. One hour. Coffee or a glass of wine, no full meals. Easy in, easy out.

I walked across the street, and we made our awkward hellos. We bought our coffees and sat in the pretty courtyard as tourists gaped at the French pastries behind the counter inside. Ted was a licensed ship pilot who made a lucrative living taking large ships into and out of San Francisco Bay. He also had a successful charter boat business out of Sausalito. He'd also been a music producer. The stories went on and on. If I'd been attracted to him, or not so angry about the photo fraud, I might have tried to balance the conversation with information about myself.

But fifty-nine minutes into our date, I looked at my watch and said, "I'm afraid my time's up, I've got to run."

"Hey, I feel bad, I did all the talking!" Ted said.

I smiled wanly and beat a hasty retreat. He tried a few more times to get together, and I always had a lame excuse at the ready. If I couldn't see myself kissing a guy, there was no second date.

And then, one night as I was reviewing the "Who's Viewed Your Profile" section of my Match.com account, a familiar face popped out at me. It was Steve. My heart raced. This meant that not only was he also on Match but that he'd seen me online as well. I clicked his profile. Among the usual hyperbolic statements ("Funny, smart, sincere, great physical condition, romantic, easygoing"), he said he was looking for his soul mate. *I know you're out there and the stars will bring us together,* he wrote. *It's just a matter of time.* As a gesture of what I intended as good-humored acknowledgment, I sent him a virtual wink. *Look at us, here we both are getting on with our lives* is what I meant to say.

The next day, I received a chilling email. *Dear Wordygirl,* it began. *(See? I've found you out.)* He wrote that I had betrayed him—first in our marriage, and now this. How I'd been "trawling for men on the internet." How I'd gotten rid of him as easily as if I'd just fired the gardener.

Although I now see that it is best for me to be where I am now, he wrote, *I have to admit that for some reason I was really shocked to find you casting for dates on the internet.*

We'd been separated for nearly nine months. And he was shocked that I wanted to date again? Once again, Steve would judge me by a glaring double standard.

I ask myself, "If this woman cared for me the way she said she did for so many years, how can she just up and wash her hands of the relationship, almost with glee?"

This man, who had financially abandoned his family and been verbally abusive for several years, was now the victim.

So now I am coming out of my shell and opening up to new relation-ships, to a completely new life and path of my journey. I am saddened that the choices I have made have resulted in that journey not being one with you. I really, really thought you were the one. But I'll get over that, so they tell me.

You'll find no one who cared for you as much as I did, Kirsten. I hope I can find someone who will care for me that much.

That person is waiting for me. Steve

I read the whole message on the phone to my friend Sammy. Sammy was one of the kindest, most Christian people I knew. Her heart was enormous, and she always tried to think twice before she spoke ill of people.

"That's bullshit," she said. "When he says, 'You'll find no one who cared for you as much as I did,' it sounds like a declaration of love. But read it again, and it's a threat. It's like saying, 'I'm as good as it gets. You'll never do better than me.'"

She was right. Clearly I'd hurt him. But this was the same man who'd happily left his first wife and four daughters, never to look back. This was the man who, for the past five plus years, had been an angry, bitter husband, who had blamed me for everything from his weight to the weather. Our separation hadn't clarified anything for him—it just gave him more fodder for his blame.

The next day I wrote him back.

There were two people in this marriage, and for many years that marriage was happy and good, I wrote. *Then it wasn't good any-more, and whatever attempts we each made weren't enough to save it. There were still two people in that marriage, and I am one of those people.*

I went on to explain my own feelings of abandonment and fury, knowing it would fall on deaf ears. *I know there are still rocky times ahead, but I hope we can minimize the hurt and emerge friendly or at least decent, for the sake of our kids.*

I do wish you well, Steve. And I will never forget the good times.
Kirsten

That last sentence turned out to be a lie. It would be a long, long time before I could remember any good times at all. Looking back, though, I wondered why I was still trying to earn his approval.

"You're never going to believe who I saw last night at the Rotary Club's lobster feed," Judith told me on the phone a week later. Her voice had a conspiratorial hush.

I offered the names of a few famous people.

"Uh, no," Judith said.

"Aileen Russo?" I finally guessed. Aileen and I sang together in the St. Helena Chamber Singers.

"Bingo," she said. "And guess who she brought as her date?"

"Wait," I said. "You don't mean . . ."

"Yep," she said. "They were all over each other."

What galled me was not Steve's behavior—I already knew that he wasn't the least bit interested in making ethical choices. But Aileen was somewhat of a friend. She'd been to my house—and stayed long into the wee hours—when I hosted the party after our holiday concert. I expected more from a woman. Steve and I weren't even officially divorced yet. I felt humiliated that she was privy to the mess of our marriage and would probably share what she learned with our mutual friends.

When she heard the story, Mitzi, my friend and now real estate agent, said, "I can't believe she would crap like that in her own backyard."

A week or two later, I heard another chapter from Amory. Steve had invited Aileen and her son, Douglas, up to the farm with our kids for the weekend.

The next week at therapy, I threw down the gauntlet. "You're having an affair with someone I *know*? You had Aileen and her son up to the farm with our *kids*? Do you think of no one's needs but your own?"

Steve was clearly pleased. "It's none of your business whom I date, Kirsten."

"But, of all the women you could date, you choose someone I know. Someone who's been to my house. Someone I see every week."

Steve just smiled sheepishly and shrugged. He was loving this.

I went on a few more Match dates. There was the real estate mogul who talked with false modesty about his savvy investments. We seemed to be getting along well until he started asking me questions about the value of my own assets. When he heard the generous asking price of our house, he quickly ended the conversation and never called again. On paper, at least, I was worth more than he was. That was apparently a problem.

There was the sixty-year-old graphic artist who had given everything to his ex-wife in his divorce, including his two teenaged children. He came out to California from Maine with only his professional tools and nothing else—no savings, no insurance, no retirement funds. He was living in his second-floor studio until he made enough to rent an apartment. "It has a kitchenette and a half bath," he told me. "It's all exposed brick, quite charming."

"Wait . . . half bath?" I asked. "That means no shower or bathtub?"

"Right." He grinned.

"So how exactly do you keep clean?"

"Well, the B&B next door occasionally lets me use its swimming pool or hot tub," he said. "Or sometimes I can duck into one of their empty guest rooms."

I nodded and smiled as if this were the most reasonable thing in the world, then made an excuse to find my way back to my car.

Chapter 11
The Bearded Woman

Several months before, my sister, Ingrid, had called me from the car, breathless. "I've just been to see a psychic," she said. "Kirsten, you wouldn't believe all the things she got right. Dad was there. He had a message for you."

Our dad had died two years before. Sometimes I thought I felt his presence.

"At one point, the psychic said, do you have a writer in the family? I told her about you, and Karen said, 'Your dad wants you to tell your sister how proud he is of her writing. That she should keep it up.'"

That was enough. I was ready to believe. I asked for Karen's number and called to make an appointment. I couldn't wait to hear what she'd have to say about my current period of fear and loathing.

On the day of my appointment, I wasn't prepared for the woman who answered the door. Karen Peterson was pretty, stylishly dressed, and glowing with youth—the kind of woman you'd expect to see shopping at Nordstrom, not giving psychic readings in a Santa Rosa industrial park.

As we sat down, she said, "There's been a whole crowd of people waiting here for you all day." She explained that her particular gift was to channel spirits from the afterlife—a talent she'd had since she was a child—and she focused most of her work on those who had lost children, or loved ones to suicide. They were the ones who were suffering the most. I liked her immediately.

"I guess I'm really here for some reassurance," I began. "I'm so full of fear and anxiety right now."

Karen sat still for a few minutes, eyes closed. "There's an energy that's coming around you that's a father, grandfather, or father-in-law," she said. "Normally I don't see them in this way, but he's standing very clearly in front of me. He has a mustache and is wearing glasses, with a very sweet nature. There are other people coming in, so he wanted to make it very clear that he's here." She went on to name several close family friends who had also died.

"They're coming in together," she said. "And I just have to say that you've got a tremendous amount of support, Kirsten. I want to reassure you that you are *absolutely* on the right track. She laughed. "Your dad is such a sweetie. Were you really close with him?"

"Yeah." I nodded.

"Because he's really huggy and touchy-feely. He's holding your hand, and he's right here guiding you, Kirsten."

I nodded again, tears rolling down my face.

"One thing the spirits can't do is take away our lessons. I firmly believe that everything is knocked out before we're born. We pick the time that we're born, the time we go home, our life lessons, our relationships, our children—every single step is already mapped out."

I tried to imagine my dad there in the room with us. She had described him perfectly.

"Unfortunately, the only way we can appreciate the wisdom of it is to go over to the other side," she was saying. "Because when we're with God—which to me is a place of light, not a man with a beard, or a woman with a beard!" Karen started laughing. "Your dad told me to say that. He's trying to make you laugh."

I was beginning to see how this worked: It was like a divine game of charades. The spirits would present props and symbols or act things out, and Karen had to figure out how to interpret them accurately.

"When we're on the other side, after our death, most of us don't appreciate the lightness of it. In order to appreciate it, we have to have something to compare it to, which is darkness. There's a good reason why you're going through this. You need to try to look at the bigger picture, the common denominator in your whole life. Are you trying to learn acceptance and forgiveness?" She paused again and listened to her invisible guides.

I laughed quietly. *You could say that*, I thought.

"Another thing I'm hearing for you is patience," she said. "And this is the biggest message that your dad is giving me right now: Don't question that you're meant to go through this. You're not going to get the answers in your time, but in divine time. Everything happens when it's meant to happen."

I had thought that the reading would last an hour, maybe ninety minutes. But Karen was unaware of time. She just kept talking as long as the spirits guided her to.

"I'm also seeing something about selling a house," she said. "Whose house is being sold?"

"My husband and I are going through a divorce, and we can't get divorced until we sell the house. But in the current market, we can't sell it. Financial issues are a big deal right now. I'm very concerned about my ability to support myself."

Karen replied, "You're not going to be on the street without a place to live. That's not in the cards for you. So don't worry about that."

She went on about my need for creativity, Bronte's sensitivity to the divorce, my writing, my mother, several family friends.

Suddenly she said, "I'm feeling your mother. No, your ex's mother."

"What does she have to say?" I asked. "I can't imagine I'm in her good graces right now."

"She's doing this," Karen said, placing both hands over her heart. "Which means she's taking responsibility for her son's actions."

"Oh my God." My voice broke, and the tears were flowing again.

"She just wants you to know, Kirsten. She wants to apologize to you for that."

"Oh my God." I was crying hard now. I'd barely thought about Gloria since her death, and here she was, apologizing to me.

Karen continued, "She's taking a lot of the responsibility for the choices her son's making. She's saying that it has to do with things he went through while he was growing up."

"Wow." I knew that Steve had been the favored child, but I didn't know details.

"She's asking me to tell you: When you see Steve's face in your mind's eye, see a white light around him. In order to release the negativity from your body, send positive thoughts to him. And it'll help him get on his feet too. She's asking for your forgiveness. She has a tremendous amount of love for you and wishes you two could have had a different relationship. Does that make sense?"

"It does," I said, wiping my eyes.

Nearly four hours after I'd walked through her door, Karen gave me a hug and sent me on my way with a recording of the entire reading. I drove home in a fog of wonder and gratitude for the clear messages I'd been given and the knowledge that my dad and Steve's mom and so many others were close by. I'd always believed in life after death, but the veil between the two was much thinner than I'd ever imagined. Life took on a new dimension for me that day. I felt for the first time that a higher power was within my reach.

A few days later, just as Karen had predicted, I received an incredible writing assignment with a top design firm in San Francisco, and soon I was in a meeting with a major San Francisco graphic designer and his staff. The client was a sensory-testing firm that wanted a flashy new corporate identity campaign. I was the only writer on the project—me, a freelancer who until about six months before had been a stay-at-home mom of twelve years.

We were sitting in a concrete loft office sleekly decorated in black, white, and Chinese red. I was surrounded by people as smart as any I'd ever met, all speaking a language completely foreign to my hayseed ears. "Ideate and iterate." "Scaling data." "Design thinking." At the end of the meeting, after the client left, the designer pointed to me and said, "I'd like ten creative concepts that we can build the design around. Say, by Friday?" It was Tuesday. I was exactly where I'd asked to be—surrounded by smart, creative people who were going to pay me well for my words and big ideas. Only I had no big ideas. I was terrified.

Later that week, I was furiously trying to pack lunches and find backpacks when Steve asked to come over. "Something I have to talk to you about," he said.

How much more bad news? I wondered.

He arrived with a hangdog look about him, his face drawn, his shoulders drooping. The tension hung in the room like an unpleasant smell.

"As you know," he began, "we've been working hard to make Western Pacific a viable business. We apparently missed the window for lawsuits—a lot of states have shut down their class-action programs. We're going to have to pack up our tent."

"Pack up our tent?" I asked, stupidly.

"Shut down the business," he said. Over the past couple of years, we'd poured $200,000 into getting this business running.

"Shut it down," I repeated.

"We've given it our best shot. It's nobody's fault."

For months Steve had been telling me that once Western Pacific started getting some claims settled, the money would start pouring in. Our bank accounts that were now drying up would soon be replenished, and we could reach a divorce settlement with cash in our pockets. Everyone would be fine. I thought again of Steve's refrain, "I am not a risk-taker." The temptation to yell was strong, but once again I thought better of it. He could always outyell me.

I felt the tears burning, then dripping slowly down the sides of my nose. "So what now, Steve?" I asked. "What's the next big plan? Bankruptcy?"

He shook his head and pressed his lips together, as if he found himself in these trying circumstances through some great mystery. "I'm going to start looking for work again with law firms. I guess that's where I belong after all."

"Huh," I said. *Imagine that.* I showed him out and watched his defeated figure shuffle down the driveway.

I'd never felt so afraid or so alone.

No one told me how much work divorce is. The paperwork is horrendous: assets, expenses, appraisals, projected incomes, tax returns, escrow papers, and contracts. It feels like a fulltime job, a job made more miserable when the spouse does his best to hide assets and sabotage you.

One afternoon, I was talking to Jacqueline, the director of the private elementary school that Bronte and Amory had attended. Jacqueline and I had become good friends, but she'd also stayed in touch with Steve. She and her partner, Vince, had recently hosted Steve for dinner, and he'd brought a selection of knives from his extensive collection to show Vince, a sculptor and toolmaker. Now I was complaining to Jacqueline about the arduous task of evaluating assets accumulated over twenty years.

"Well, whatever you do, you need to get that knife collection appraised," Jacqueline said.

"The knife collection?" I knew about it, but Steve had always been tight-lipped on the subject. I did know that he went to the Atlanta blade show every spring. I often saw him viewing knives online, the way some men look at porn.

"Oh my God, yes!" Jacqueline said. "The few knives he brought to show Vince were showstoppers. I think one of them had a handle made of mastodon bone, or something equally outrageous. That collection must be worth a fortune."

"He told me it was valued at only a few thousand dollars," I said.

"Ha. I'll bet he's got single knives worth that much."

I suddenly remembered one day, years before, when Steve was out of town and he'd called to ask me to retrieve something for him in the garage. At his direction, I opened a padlocked metal cabinet. He told me to find a file on the top shelf. But as I was looking, I spotted a wooden case of drawers and opened it.

"Well, well, what's this?" I joked as I pulled open one felt-lined drawer after another, each displaying several knives of incredible workmanship.

"Not that! Stay out of there!" Steve was suddenly testy and agitated. He redirected my attention to the needed file, and we ended our phone conversation. If I'd had an ounce of cunning, I would have taken photos of the knives while he was gone, or at least written down the combination to the padlock. I should have had them appraised while I still had the chance. But this was years before I knew what was coming.

Now I was kicking myself. I realized that Steve must have had a private credit card and at least one secret bank account, because I hadn't seen any charges or withdrawals that could have explained all those expensive knives.

Ingrid had a similar reaction. Her husband, Keith, had gone to Alaska every year with Steve and had also seen a portion of the prized collection.

"Keith says you need to get everything appraised," she told me now. "That collection is worth a *lot* of money. And knowing Steve, he's not going to declare it of his own free will."

I became obsessed with the idea of finding Steve's records of knife purchases and sales. I knew that, as a collector, he'd be meticulous about this. He'd taken all his cabinets and files with him when he moved out, so there was only one option. I chose a day when Steve had dropped the kids off at school and was headed immediately back to the farm—when he didn't have them, he got out of town as fast as possible. Because we shared custody, we allowed each other to have access to our respective houses, in case one of the kids left something behind. A little naïve, in hindsight, but then, naïveté was my strong suit. Now I was going to be the devious, untrustworthy one.

I let myself into Steve's house by the back door. There was a sense of shame at what I was about to do, and anger at Steve for forcing me to sink to this level. I stood in the living room and inhaled the air of a house I had no supervision over. The woodsmoke smell of frequent fires in the fireplace. The clingy odor of fried foods. The sad, mildewy fragrance of bed sheets not washed every week. It broke my heart that Bronte and Amory were spending half their month living like this. And it also broke my heart that they really didn't seem to mind. Had all those years of healthy meals, educational toys, art and music classes, handmade Halloween costumes, and fresh flowers been for nothing? Would they have been just as happy being raised by hillbillies?

I walked through the house, seeing it as if for the first time. Hanging on the walls were the cheap posters and photos that Steve had owned when he met me—things he'd bought at big-box stores or from street vendors. Underfoot was a hodgepodge of floor coverings we'd had in storage—the pastel rug his mother had hand-braided for our wedding gift alongside the blue-and-white stenciled throw rug we'd bought for Bronte's nursery. It was a sorry patchwork of our history together. I thought back to how meticulously I'd decorated our homes—the original art, the custom-made window treatments—and realized that, although they might have been appreciated at the time, the only one who truly cared about them was me.

I wandered into the kitchen—dirty dishes and unopened mail everywhere. Counters not wiped with a lavender-scented spray, as they were every day *chez* Kirsten. I opened the refrigerator and surveyed the shelves of half-gallon soda bottles and bacon and unhealthy leftovers.

I walked down the hallway and poked my head into the bedrooms—beds unmade, clothes everywhere. Then I walked into Steve's bedroom and surveyed the room. The closet door was already open, showing hangers with plaid flannel shirts, fringed leather vests, buckskin pants. On the shelf above: cowboy hats, farmers' hats, motorcycle helmets. The last time I'd arrived to pick up the kids, I'd found Steve at the stove cooking grits in a pair of overalls. With no shirt underneath. He had officially entered his Li'l Abner period.

Who was this stranger? How had I lost the man I thought I'd married—that suit-wearing, scuba-diving, funny, smart, attractive, loving man? When had his body been invaded by this different person, this mad—or at least slightly crazy—man?

When I came out of my fugue state, I returned to the living room and started going through Steve's desk drawers, looking for a file label with the word "knife" on it. Nothing. I went through the many piles of papers on top of the desk. Nothing. I found some accordion folders on a shelf near the floor and rifled through them. Nothing. And then I found a file labeled "Correspondence" and flipped through that. Inside were copies of printed emails. Emails that sounded a bit familiar. I looked at the "To" and "From" lines at the top—they were all to or from me.

It took a minute to sink in. Then I got it: Steve had been reading my personal emails, all of them, which is how he knew about my hiring Glen Fisher as my attorney. He'd also been reading all my correspondence to my closest friends, venting in angry detail about my feelings toward him. He'd read every Match.com email I'd written to or received from other men. Everything.

I checked the date on the earliest email. It was dated September 17, 2006—a full year before. He'd been reading my personal email every day for at least a year. *A year.* I sank into the desk chair. The room was swirling a little, and I could feel the vomit rising in my throat. I had relied heavily on my friends, sharing each ugly, slimy detail as I negotiated my separation and divorce. The idea that Steve had been privy to my every thought and emotion, that he had been spying on me so intimately for so long, made me weak with anger and humiliation.

I thought back on the year since we'd separated, how I had struggled to act civil and even kind toward Steve, just to keep him from becoming vindictive. I'd thought I was containing the situation when, once again, I was living in a fool's paradise. Once again, I could see that my entire marriage had been built on the whims of a man who, at his core, had no sense of right or wrong. You know that feeling when you're standing on the shore and the surf pulls out the wet sand from under your feet? That was happening somewhere between my stomach and my heart.

I pulled all the emails from the folder and stuffed them in my purse. He could figure it out. When I got home, I immediately signed onto my accounts and changed every one of my passwords. Then I drove to the office supply store and bought a locking file box. If I could break and enter into Steve's house, he had probably already done it to me.

The following week in therapy, I confronted him. "You've been reading my personal emails? For a *year*? You *hacked* into my account?"

"I didn't hack into your account, Kirsten." He was using his calm, I'll-be-the-mature-one-in-the-face-of-your-hysteria tone of voice.

"Then how have you been able to read all my emails?"

"You *gave* me your password, Kirsten. When I needed to get into the joint bank account last year." He smiled at me smugly. "Maybe you should change your passwords more often." I looked over at Patricia, whose mouth hung slightly ajar. I didn't know whom I wanted to kill more: Steve or myself. Had there been a gun handy, a murder-suicide would surely have been in the headlines the next day.

This, then, was my own pathology: What I had thought was self-control and maturity had been borne of myopia, of denial, of dishonesty to myself. I'd allowed myself to be surprised every time Steve betrayed me. I'd been so busy trying to keep things normal for the kids, I didn't feel I had the time to go on the offensive, to anticipate Steve's next devious move. Despite all behavior to the contrary, I kept hoping and expecting him to grow up and play fair.

Now, beyond my blind rage at the invasion of my privacy, another curtain had been lifted. I stopped caring about the rules or what Steve's reaction would be. As long as we shared the care of Bronte and Amory, I would have to maintain a certain level of rational behavior. But I also had to stop thinking that Steve would come around and start behaving as an adult. I needed to stop playing defense and start playing offense. The thought exhausted me.

After our hour was up, Steve and I found ourselves outside the therapist's office together as we headed to our cars. I looked him fully in the eye. And suddenly I found the words that had escaped me in Patricia's office.

"I thought we could try getting through this like civil adults," I said. "But obviously you don't possess one ounce of integrity. You simply have no moral compass."

He stared at me blankly.

"Let me be clear, Steve," I continued. "I don't trust you. I don't respect you. I don't like you. You disgust me. I cannot believe I spent twenty years being married to you."

In the course of our marriage, Steve had often said things with the intention of wounding me. He said horrible, hurtful things the way he spent money—freely and lavishly. I, on the other hand, had always been so careful with my words around Steve. Knowing how quickly his anger could ignite, I saved them up for special occasions. As these words stumbled out of my mouth, my heart was beating fast. I knew they were the harshest things I had ever said to him. And I meant them. But Steve just shrugged and walked to his truck. Just another day at the office. Maybe he simply didn't care anymore. I know I didn't.

Chapter 12
Road Kill Café

A week after my showdown, we had our monthly meeting with the lawyers. Taylor Addison, Steve's attorney, was a big, matronly woman, equal parts intelligence and common sense. I'd been surprised and pleased that Steve had hired a woman. She and Glen Fisher had worked together for years and shared an easy understanding that we hoped would save us hours of negotiations.

This time, as Glen and I were sitting in Taylor's reception area waiting to be ushered into the conference room, I changed my tack. "It's time to take the gloves off," I said. "Until now, I've been bending over backward to play nice. But I just found out that Steve's been reading my personal emails for a year."

Glen nodded. "Got it" was all he said. Apparently this happened all the time in his line of work.

We entered the conference room, where Taylor and Steve were already at the table, and took our seats. After a bare minimum of small talk—we were all way past that—Taylor began.

"My client has been looking for work in good faith for six months now," she said. "And, unfortunately, we've had to reach the disappointing conclusion that, at his age and without a portfolio of business, his chances of finding substantial work in the legal profession are extremely low. Therefore, he'll be unable to pay any spousal support whatsoever for the foreseeable future, or for the purposes of this marital dissolution."

I looked across the table at Steve. He didn't look back at me. But he was nodding and grimacing, his poor-me, the-cards-are-always-stacked-against-me look.

"Oh, really?" Glen said. I could almost hear him loading and cocking his linguistic rifle.

"We agree, it's extremely unfortunate, this turn of events," Taylor continued, but Glen cut her off.

"So, let me ask, Steve, what exactly have you been doing to find work?" he said.

"Well, I've been checking Craigslist every single day," Steve said. "I've probably sent my résumé out to at least six firms a week. . . ."

"Craigslist? I would think that, at your professional level, you'd be beyond Craigslist," Glen said. "You were a senior partner in a sizable law firm. If I were in your shoes, I'd be calling everyone I knew. I'd be taking people to lunch. I'd be working every possible angle to get my foot in that door."

"Everyone knows I don't have a book of business," Steve said. "They're not exactly returning my calls."

"Well, maybe you're not trying hard enough."

I looked over at Glen and watched him transform into a pit bull before my eyes. "If you ask me, you're just sitting on your sad ass feeling sorry for yourself so you don't have to pay a cent of support to your wife! You know what *she* did? She immediately started making calls to old employers and colleagues. She started *working* it. Your wife is now working fulltime to support herself and your kids, while you sit around feeling sorry for yourself."

Glen's pit bull was suddenly countered by Steve's impersonation of a rabid bear. "You watch your mouth, you son of a bitch!" he bellowed.

"I'm not going to take this bullshit from a pissant, small-town lawyer like you!"

I watched in horror. Steve—the renowned trial attorney, the seasoned litigator, the veteran of hundreds of fractious depositions—was now yelling like a grade-school bully. I had thought that Glen would ultimately be outplayed by him when things got serious. But Steve was deteriorating before my eyes. He was making a complete fool of himself, not just in front of me but in front of his peers.

Taylor leaned forward to intervene, and I momentarily relished having another woman be the referee for a change. "Okay, okay, both of you, settle down," she said. "There's no need to get so heated. We're all adults here."

But Glen wasn't done. "Sorry, Taylor, I just can't sit here and watch this pathetic clown try to evade his responsibilities as a husband," he said. "This is ridiculous."

Steve stood up so fast his chair fell over. "Fuck you, you asshole!" He stomped toward the door. "We're finished here. These negotiations are over." *Slam.*

The three of us sat for a moment in awkward silence. Finally, I turned to Glen and said, "I guess when I said, 'gloves off,' I didn't exactly envision being quite that aggressive."

"Something needed to give," he said. "I'm so tired of being played by that fool." Taylor was shaking her head while Glen packed his briefcase. "That guy's an asshole, Kirsten. You've made the right decision, in my book." But I wondered if we'd ever reconcile long enough to actually get divorced. Now it would take months to get Steve back to the table.

In the meantime, our house had been on the market for over a year. There had been plenty of showings. Each time, I'd frantically straightened up and vacuumed, then taken the dog into town, and just as I'd gotten my laptop set up at a café, Mitzi would call to say, "They were in and out in five minutes. It wasn't really their style."

I started to get annoyed with all the bad news. Now when Mitzi called, she'd begin by saying things like "Don't shoot the messenger." I insisted that she host a couple of open houses on weekends, which she dutifully did, but her regular advice on how to improve our prospects was to drop the price. We dropped it, and then we dropped it again. Finally, in late November, we decided to take it off the market altogether for the holidays and try our luck again in the new year.

Meanwhile, the divorce was proceeding at a glacial pace, and I was still determined to find evidence of the value of Steve's knife collection. I decided that he had taken all his files—and probably the collection itself—to the farm. So, one weekend when I knew he had to stay in town for one of Amory's Little League games, I drove the 135 miles to Nevada City to take a look around. I was now an old hand at this breaking-and-entering business. But as I drove up the steep road and pulled into the unpaved drive, I felt ill. Seeing the farm again—after all the sweat and money we had thrown at it, after all the weekends and ski vacations we had spent there—made me feel sad and a little stupid. How had I agreed to such a lavish scheme? Why had I spent so many days here, when the place really held no attraction for me?

As I fiddled with the padlock at the front gate, a sign greeted me that had not been there before: *Warning—No Trespassing! Violators will be shot—survivors will be shot again.* This was Steve's idea of high humor. I pulled around to the rear of the house and let myself in by the back door. As I entered the kitchen, another sign: *Steve's Road Kill Café—you kill it, we grill it!* Steve had been so pleased with the way I'd renovated and decorated this house—a pewter-gray paint on the walls, creamy vanilla cabinets with brushed nickel hardware, subway tiles, black slate countertops. Now he was turning it into the set of

Dukes of Hazzard. I took a deep breath and reminded myself that I really didn't want this house anymore anyway.

I wandered into Steve's office behind the laundry room and started looking for files (yet another sign: *No Working During Drinking Hours*). I could find nothing related to knives. I walked into the garage and looked through cabinets and shelves, but still found nothing. Perhaps he carried all things blade-related with him at all times? For someone who could be so sloppy, he was apparently fastidious when it came to this.

I finally gave up and wandered through the house, assuming this would be the last time I'd see it. I knew that Steve and the kids had been up just the weekend before, and the rooms showed the expected chaos. Dishes piled in the sink. Sheets twisted on the beds. Damp towels on the floors. I inhaled deeply and kept moving.

And then I walked into the dining room and stopped. There, on the floor next to the sliding glass door, was a row of small flower pots. I walked closer and crouched over the familiar seven serrated leaves of *cannabis.* Each plant was about eight inches tall, the pots clearly positioned to get maximum sunlight while Steve was away. I tried to envision the scenario to make sense of it. Had the plants been here the whole weekend, while Bronte and Amory were in the house? Had Steve placed them here once the kids were in the car? Either way, it seemed foolishly risky to have them on the premises while the kids visited. Steve used to claim that he'd tried marijuana once in the early seventies but hadn't liked it. And now here he was, growing his own. It was as if he was determined to become the teenager he'd never had the chance to be before.

Stunned, I walked through the house again, looking for other misdemeanors. In closets, the kitchen, Steve's bedroom, and Amory's room, I found three rifles and fourteen lethal-looking swords or knives that he had probably bought at the Atlanta blade show for Amory. I lined them up against a wall and took a photo with my phone, then circled back to the dining room and took a shot of the marijuana plants.

I mutely climbed back into the car and drove the whole way home without even turning on the radio. I hadn't found any evidence of Steve's knife collection, but what I'd seen proved that Steve was on a bender of self-absorbed behavior. Getting full custody of the kids would mean an endless dogfight in court, even with my photographic evidence of Steve's misdeeds. And how much worse would his behavior become by the time Amory went to college? At a stoplight, I closed my eyes and rested my forehead on the steering wheel. All my problems would disappear if Steve would only die. That would make life so much simpler.

The following week, we were back on Patricia's well-worn sofa. Steve had balked at coming, but I had refused to tell him what I wanted to discuss unless he showed up, and amazingly, he did. Now I confronted him with what I'd seen at the farm, even though it meant a confession that I'd broken in when he wasn't there. I'd printed out the photos of the plants and the guns and laid them on the coffee table in front of us.

"Really? You're now growing weed inside the house where you take our children?" I began.

"I put those plants out after they were in the car," he said, as if this made everything okay.

"And you really think that, while we're trying to teach our kids not to use drugs, it's a good idea for you to be using them? You don't think this might be a bad example, breaking the law yourself?"

"I'm not breaking the law," Steve said, in that irritatingly calm voice he'd get. "I have a medical marijuana license."

"Of course you do. What's your medical reason?"

"I have chronic back pain. It helps a little, but I'm thinking of giving it up."

I shook my head and looked at Patricia, whose face was impassive. What would it take to get her excited about any of this?

"Okay, what about all the guns and knives?" I tried again. "You know how I feel about gun control, which is probably why you're deliberately exposing our kids to them. Do you really think it's worth the risk?"

"They're BB guns," Steve said. "They're perfectly legal too." He smiled. I shook my head some more. "You know, Kirsten, you can't control every minute of the kids' lives anymore. This was your choice to split up, and now I'm going to raise them my way. They really enjoy target and skeet shooting. They're actually good shots."

"I don't think I can express how much I hate you," I said. Once again, he'd gotten what he wanted.

It was spring. Again.

We'd put the Mee Lane house back on the market and received a couple of offers, which quickly fell through. Until we sold this house, we'd continue to bleed thousands of dollars each month and couldn't finalize our divorce. My fate rested in the hands of strangers.

One day, Mitzi called to ask if she could bring a couple over to see the house. But today her usually perky voice was subdued. She sounded as defeated as I had begun to feel.

A few months before, Mitzi had confided that she and Dirk were having more marital problems. He was depressed, he hadn't worked in years, and Mitzi was understandably getting fed up with the status quo.

"You really need to get some counseling," I'd advised. "Don't wait too long, like we did."

"I'm afraid to," she'd confessed.

"Why? Don't you want to fix your marriage?"

"I'm afraid it's already too late and we'll get divorced." She gave a sad little laugh. "Denial is so much easier!" I could almost hear her pouty expression over the phone.

Now I asked, "Everything okay?"

Mitzi sighed. I waited.

"Dirk tried to kill himself yesterday," she finally said.

"Are you joking?"

"The police found him in the minivan up on an abandoned property in Angwin with his wrists slit. He's lost a lot of blood. You should see the minivan. It's like a crime scene."

"Mitzi, oh my God! Was it a cry for help?" I felt silly using such a cliché, but the alternative was even worse.

"He wasn't fooling around. He cut himself from the wrist to the elbow, almost down to the bone."

"Do you have any idea why?"

Long pause. "Three days ago I told him I thought we should try separating."

"Wow."

"Yeah. Over the last couple of months, I realized that nothing's going to change. And I'm really better off without him, you know? I thought if we split up, he'd finally have to go out and find a job. But now he's in the ICU, and they don't know what he'll be like when he comes to. The blood loss might have caused some brain damage."

I took a long, deep breath. "Let's forget about the showing," I said. "Forget about selling this house at all until Dirk is okay and you can think straight again."

"But I need the money," Mitzi said, a whine creeping into her voice. "I need to sell something to get out of this, this shithole I'm in!"

I hung up the phone, the room spinning a little. It turned out my life wasn't the worst one in St. Helena.

My life had taken on a sort of numb quality in which I blindly tended to Bronte and Amory, worried about too much work or not enough work, walked long walks, and watched a lot of Netflix. I'd never felt so trapped. Each night, after the kids were in bed, I made a roaring fire in the fireplace and pulled up the big armchair and ottoman right next to it. Then I'd lie on the ottoman with my feet draped over the back of the chair, my head a few feet from the open flame, and doze off. The crack of the logs and the burning heat on my face was like a drug. I would awaken hours later, the room cold, the fire out, and shuffle back to the bedroom. Only later did it occur to me that a single spark from a flame that close could have ignited my hair or clothing. Maybe Steve's risk-taking was contagious.

In May Mitzi called out of the blue. Her voice had its old twinkly quality again.

"I have something I want to run by you," she said.

"Okay?"

"It's totally up to you, of course."

"Uh-huh?"

She took a breath. "Well, Steve invited me and the kids up to the farm next weekend, and if you have no objection, I'm thinking of going."

I was standing on the back porch overlooking the pool, the morning sun burning through the fog. I slowly tried to make sense of these words. Crows screeching from a row of distant trees. The rumbling of trucks on Highway 29. I had shared with Mitzi my growing hatred for Steve and the many reasons he had given me to feel that way. She'd been extremely sympathetic.

"Why would he do that?" I asked.

"I don't know." She giggled. "Just feeling social, I guess."

"But you're *my* friend," I said. "He doesn't even really like you. Or you him. Why would you want to go?"

"Oh, he's not so bad. And the kids and I could really use a weekend away. But it's entirely up to you. Of course it would be completely platonic."

"I would hope so!" I was so puzzled by the very idea I couldn't make sense of it. Was I overreacting? "I don't know, Mitzi," I finally said. "It's really your call. I'm just so surprised that this is even coming up."

"I know," she said, "but after all I've been through with Dirk, I think Steve is just trying to be nice."

"Well, that would be a first," I said.

That afternoon, I called Mitzi back.

"I've been thinking about it," I said. "There's just no way I feel comfortable with the idea of your going away for the weekend with Steve."

"But it's not like that!" she said.

"Even so, it doesn't feel appropriate. You're *my* friend. I brought you into this contract. It just doesn't sit right that you would be socializing with him when you're representing both of us."

She sighed. "You're probably right. I just thought . . ."

"I *am* right," I said, and hung up.

In the weeks that followed, I struggled to decide if Mitzi was as stupid as she now seemed. Her pragmatism—and what I had interpreted as basic goodness—were qualities I'd always admired. But now I saw that her judgment was flawed. I just couldn't determine how deep that flaw ran.

As the weather warmed, I started hosting an occasional songfest with members of my chamber choir. People would show up with plates of food, bottles of wine, and all kinds of instruments. We would end up on my back porch singing to the rising moon—everything from old English ballads to hits by the Weavers and the Kingston Trio to Bob Dylan. It felt healing and serendipitous. And it didn't cost anything.

On one of these occasions, I wandered into the kitchen to refill my wine glass and found Mike—a new group member I recognized from around town—looking at some family photos on the kitchen counter. "Cute kids," he said. "How old?"

"Fourteen and ten," I said. "Not always cute."

"I hear you," he said. "I have a daughter, Libby, who's ten going on twenty-five."

The small talk came easily. He had a friendly, stable quality to him, a few extra pounds, and a full head of brown hair. When he told me he was a CPA in Santa Rosa, I asked if he could recommend a good financial planner. "I could use some sound advice right now."

"Well, I can get you started for free," Mike said. "The principles are pretty simple. You don't need to pay someone right away. How about meeting for dinner, and we can talk about it then?"

And it was that simple. I suddenly had a financial adviser *and* a date.

My exchanges with Steve had shrunk to the language of business transactions, financial negotiations, and custody logistics, except for the occasional testy remark that would ignite anger about past transgressions on both sides. He still hadn't found a job. We still traded the kids every Sunday afternoon, ostensibly at five o'clock. Steve had started dropping them off at four, then two thirty, then one thirty. He also stopped by with the kids unannounced during the week because Bronte had forgotten her homework or Amory needed his baseball shoes. The result was that I never felt completely free of my parental role. I was never able to live a single life knowing that they might drop in at any time. Now that I was about to start dating again, how would that work?

I finally called Steve on it, with the expected result.

"You wanted them fifty percent of the time," I said. "You need to keep them until the appointed hour. And you need to call first before just dropping by."

"That's so typical of you, Kirsten," he said in his deadly calm voice. "You're too rigid. When are you going to learn to lighten up?"

The racing heart. The sweaty palms. "I've been more than flexible,

Steve. But you're completely disregarding my privacy and my time alone. When they're with you, their home needs to be with you. I feel like I'm the primary parent even when you have them."

"I get it," he said. "I'll be sure to let the kids know they're not welcome at your house except during approved hours. I'll tell them it's not their home except when you say it is. That'll make them feel good." *Click.*

I met Mike at a small café in town where the locals ate. He arrived straight from work, his Oxford shirt a little sweaty. We sat at a small table near the front and ordered white wine and some kind of pasta with spicy Andouille sausage.

"So," he said, "what's your story?"

I gave him the short version: two kids, ugly divorce. He told me about his own two failed marriages, both of which, in his telling, were the fault of his crazy wives. His daughter, Libby, was the light of his life and lived with him every other week. Besides being a successful CPA, he had started a chapter of Habitat for Humanity in Napa and had personally helped build four homes for low-income families.

We discussed the basics of financial investment, and Mike drew a few simple graphs on the paper tablecloth. Smart, stable, pragmatic, good with money. He was rapidly becoming more attractive, and then he hit a final home run: He was a Democrat. Now I officially liked him.

Mike gave me a big bear hug as we said goodnight on the sidewalk in front of the restaurant. His sweaty patches had dried by now, but he still had an earthy smell about him. I liked his forthright nature, and he brimmed with optimism. I wrote my number on a scrap of paper and shoved it into his pocket, then walked to my car with a smile.

Chapter 13
Gimme Shelter

And then, the day after the Fourth of July, after roughly eighteen months on the market and several false alarms, our house sold. We had lowered the price by an amount that could buy two homes in any other part of the country, but by now both Steve and I just jumped at the prospect of finally moving on. We signed, agreeing to everything the buyers asked for, including a sixty-day escrow.

In two months, I would be free of this old life. I also had just sixty days to find a new place to live and to move there with the kids. There wasn't time to buy anything. I had to find a rental immediately.

I searched Craigslist and the local classifieds. I called every realtor I knew. I drove around town looking for rental signs. I looked at several places a week, but in a town like St. Helena, the market is very small. Most of the places I saw were dreary and depressing, or were lavish homes far beyond our budget.

Finally, after a month of constant looking, I heard about a newly renovated little house on Pope Street. Three bedrooms, small yard, walkable or bikeable to school and everything else. The rent was as much as the mortgage on Mee Lane, but I filled out an application. I didn't hear back from the rental agent for about two weeks. And then, just one week before our close of escrow, she called to say that the owners had chosen another tenant.

I hung up the phone and looked around at the rooms of our house, now filled with boxes and packing supplies. The movers would be here on September 5, and we had no place to go. Sitting at my desk, I laid my head on my arms and closed my eyes. This nightmare would never end. My lifelong philosophy of work hard and prosper had turned out to be a joke.

The next morning, I called Aubrey German, a realtor I vaguely knew who had listed a house on Brown Street, directly across from Amory's school. I'd been driving by this house for years, and for the last six months I'd seen a "For Sale" sign in the front yard. Aubrey gave me the owner's address, and I sent her an impassioned email, offering the princely sum I'd been prepared to pay at the other house, including copies of all my character references, and throwing myself at her mercy. Would she consider renting the house to us? Just four days before our close of escrow, and also the first day of school, I heard back from Aubrey. I could come in and sign a year's lease. We had a new home.

It was about half the size of our house on Mee Lane, but it had three bedrooms, enough space for a desk in the master bedroom, and a small yard shaded by an enormous fig tree. I had already given away or sold nearly a quarter of our belongings. I had pared our collection of wine glasses down from sixty-four to just eight. And now we had landed in a sweet little house. And it was in town.

After the movers took the last of our furniture, the kids and I climbed into the car, and I idled on the road so they could get a final look at the only home they had ever really known. I glanced in the rearview mirror to watch their faces.

"Goodbye, Mee Lane house," Bronte said with a fake bravery in her voice.

"Goodbye, Mee Lane," Amory echoed. I pressed my foot to the

accelerator and sped down the road, not looking back. Goodbye, Mee Lane. And good riddance.

Brown Street was a dead-end street of ten small houses, a Hispanic Adventist Church, and, across from our house, a small apartment building. The population was a mix of white lower-middle-class couples and young Hispanic families, but the Mexican culture dominated the neighborhood. The views outside our windows had changed from vineyards and poplars and mountain vistas to the small yards of our neighbors, where *quinceañeras* and holiday parties were held. In the evenings after dinner, the street would fill with young children and their parents, all seemingly happy, every day. Now we heard the constant soundtrack of *norteño* music. The smell of *carnitas* cooking on a stove. Cries of *Mija, mija!* We had gone from rural isolation to being in the middle of a community, and I loved it.

For the first time in their lives, my children had a daily independence. On the first school day, Amory returned home from his elementary school across the street announcing that it was exactly ninety-eight steps from door to door. Bronte could hang out with her friends after middle school without calling to have me pick her up. And my reward to myself for surviving the previous two years was a bright blue Dutch-style bicycle, which I began to ride everywhere. I outfitted it with *panniers* and rode to the grocery store, to the movies, to the farmers' market. After all that miserable waiting, I finally had the life I'd dreamed about for so long.

Once I'd gotten well and truly settled, I began seeing Mike with some regularity. We rode our bikes around town, met for an early movie, got fish tacos at the takeout place, and sat outside under the big oak trees. He was casual and accessible—plans just sort of materialized without a lot of fuss. I began to think about having sex again—which shocked me, given my loss of appetite over the past few years. I imagined Mike's husky body and how it would look in my bed. But every date ended with the same quick bear hug. Not even the suggestion of a kiss. Had I been out of circulation for so long that I'd forgotten how all this worked?

One Monday, as I was sitting in the car waiting to pick Amory up from Little League, I got a text from Mike out of the blue. I'd thought it would be about our plans to drive into the city that weekend—because of my work on the brochure and website, I'd been invited to the opening night gala of the new Academy of Sciences in Golden Gate Park, and I'd asked him to be my date. But when I opened the text message, it read: *Do you like to write naked?*

Um, what? For a minute I thought perhaps I'd gotten a crank message from some stranger, but no, it was Mike's ID on my screen. It would be one thing if we'd already been intimate and he was taking it a little further. But he'd never even kissed me. It felt awkward, like a line had been crossed out of turn.

Not usually, I wrote back. *Why do you ask?* But he went silent.

A couple of days later, he struck again: *I want you to put your tongue in my ear.*

Excuse me? I responded. Again, no answer.

I couldn't figure it out. If he was so anxious to get physical, why didn't he make any moves in person when we were together? It finally dawned on me that Mike had probably been spending his time in online sex chat rooms. He was too intimidated to risk a face-to-face rejection, but he was more than comfortable having digital sex. By Friday, he'd tried it twice more. I picked up the phone and called him.

"What's going on?" I asked.

"What do you mean?" he asked, with a *who, me?* tone of innocence.

"Don't you find it a little strange that we haven't even kissed, and yet you're sending me sexually suggestive text messages?"

There was a short pause. Then he said, "I guess I should have explained that my sense of humor is kind of off-the-wall."

"You think it's funny? Because I find it very confusing."

"Ah, that's just me joking around."

"But there's such a disconnect between our face-to-face relation-ship and the one you seem to want to have through the phone."

Silence.

"It's making me uncomfortable, Mike."

"Yes, dear."

"Pardon me?"

"I said 'yes, dear.'"

"Can we have a real conversation about this?"

"No, dear."

"Are you patronizing me? Because that's what it feels like."

I finally hung up, feeling as if I'd just been trying to speak a new foreign language. Then I called a girlfriend and invited her to be my date for the Academy party.

Late Saturday morning, I got a call from Mike. "Just wondering what time you're picking me up," he said.

"Ah," I said. "After our conversation the other day, I figured our plans were off. I invited someone else."

"Oh. Uh, okay." He sounded wounded. "Well, what about a bike ride tomorrow, then?"

"Mike," I said. "I'm sorry, but I'm really getting the impression that we're on two different bike paths here. I tried to have a candid conversation with you about something that was making me uncom-fortable, and I felt like you just shut me down."

"Okay," he said. "See you later then." Apparently, candor was not something Mike enjoyed. Now I could look forward to random awkward encounters with him around town for the rest of my life. Awesome.

The first time Steve came to pick up the kids in our new house, I invited him in. He scanned the small living room—which was filled with about half the furniture that had fit in our previous living room and already looked like we'd been living there for years. It was so odd to see him there amid our familiar things, but in a different house. My house. He was wearing his new favorite outfit—a camo T-shirt under a pair of denim overalls—and he looked out of place. "This is really nice," he said. It was an accusation, not a compliment. "How can you afford it?"

I tried to read his subtext. Was he accusing me of somehow siphoning funds from our joint account, or of cheating on my financial statements the way he had? Or was he just surprised that I had landed on my feet?

"Well, that's my problem now," I said cheerfully. "I'll go get the kids."

Now, about a month later, he was standing there again as Bronte and Amory pulled their things together for another week with their dad.

"By the way, I've decided to give up the Pratt house when the lease expires next month," he said casually. Had he been there a year already? It didn't seem possible that we'd been separated that long. "It's just too expensive."

I couldn't imagine a better or more affordable place for him in St. Helena. And besides the four properties he would receive in the divorce, he would also receive the majority of our retirement savings. He was far from broke. But I refused to react.

"Oh, did you find a new place?" I asked.

"Yep." He grinned.

"Where is it?" I was almost afraid to ask. Now that Steve was unemployed, there was no limit to his imagination.

"I'm getting an RV. I'll park it at the Napa Fairgrounds during the week, and we can go places on the weekends."

"You're kidding me." My refusal to react was caving already.

"It'll be great! It'll be an adventure!" He was smiling, silently goading me. He'd been looking forward to this.

"Have you told the kids about it?" Back to poker face.

"Yeah, they're really excited. I'm taking them to see it today."

I looked at him blankly. This was the man with whom I had traveled first class, the one who preferred a town car instead of a cab at the airport. The one who liked to buy houses with land. Was he so changed in his tastes, or was he trying to dramatize how far he had fallen since I'd ended the marriage? *Look what I've become since you left me.* Had it been only the two of us, I would have watched with amusement. But he was taking our children along for the ride down this road of erratic choices—he knew that was the way to get to me. I stood on the porch and watched the three of them clamber into his truck and drive off.

For the first few weeks of RV life, the kids were stoic, but soon the complaints began. There was no privacy. They had to use the communal, cinder-block bathrooms at the fairground to take their showers. It took forty-five minutes to get to and from school each day. "Tell your dad" was all I could say. I was determined not to be the parent who bad-mouthed her ex to the kids, but I also didn't want them to think I approved of his decisions. How could I support them without putting them in the middle of a fight—one that Steve would certainly enjoy?

One day, as I was driving up Main Street past the post office, I spotted Steve's big black truck parked at the curb. As I drove by, I watched him sitting in the truck's cab, reading his mail. For one split instant, I saw him with a flash of empathy. It took me completely by surprise. In that moment, he was just a lonely man reading his mail, a man whose life had largely fallen apart. My heart opened, like those time-lapse films of flowers unfurling in the sunlight.

How had it come to this—me observing my husband like a near stranger? How was this sad, graying man in overalls possibly related to the confident, swashbuckling guy I had married? I drove a few blocks and had to pull over, because the tears were blinding me. I knew my feelings of compassion would quickly pass, that I'd be back to hating him again, and for good reason. But for a while I sat in my car and cried hard.

Not surprisingly, Steve's RV life didn't pan out. After a few weeks living in the fairground's parking lot, both kids were back with me fulltime until Steve got a real house. Now he'd found one—in Pope Valley, twelve miles from St. Helena on a twisty mountain road.

"You'll be spending half your day driving to and from town for drop-offs and pick-ups," I pointed out, trying to keep my voice out of the whiny registers.

"I don't mind," he said cheerfully. "It'll be worth it to be out in the country."

Within a week, he'd moved in and brought the goats and chickens back down from the farm. It was only a two-bedroom place, but "I'll just sleep on the sofa when the kids are here," he assured me. Months later I would learn that Amory slept out in the RV parked next to the house, with a space heater powered by a fifty-foot extension cord running from the kitchen.

Chapter 14

Broken Bones

Two days after the close of escrow, Mitzi called. We hadn't spoken much since that conversation about a weekend at the farm. And, though I knew she'd done her best, the final sale price was hardly worth celebrating.

"Congratulations!" she gushed, but then quickly got to the point. "When can I expect your half of the commission check?" I promised I'd put it in the mail that day, but she asked that I deliver it myself to her broker. We hardly spoke after that. And I knew that when the time came to buy something new, I'd be using a different agent.

One afternoon, Amory and I pulled into our driveway and watched a young father running behind his son's bike, holding on to the back fender as he taught him how to ride without training wheels. My mind raced back about eight years, the first day of summer day camp, when six-year-old Bronte was instructed to bring her bike for a trip to the park. As we were getting ready to leave the house, she worked herself into a tearful state, not wanting to bring her pink bike with its babyish training wheels. In just thirty minutes, I'd removed the wheels and run up and down Mee Lane pushing Bronte until she found her balance and her confidence. I watched her sail down the road under her own power: wobbling a bit, about to fall, then evening out. She was going to do it! As we triumphantly loaded the bike into the back of the SUV, I remember thinking how Steve was missing out on these moments, how great it would have been for him to be there. Wasn't this something dads were supposed to do?

Four years later, the scene repeated itself, when Amory decided one morning before school that he couldn't wait to take the training wheels off his bike. Once again, I ran up and down the road with him, and this time I cursed Steve for missing both chances to teach his children how to ride their two-wheelers.

Now, as we watched the young dad and his son, I asked Amory, "Do you remember that magical feeling when you first realized you were balancing on your own?" I could even remember it on my own bike, nearly fifty years before.

"I sure do," he said. "I remember looking back, and you were holding on to one side of my bike, and Daddy was holding on to the other side, and you were both pushing me down the driveway, saying 'Pedal faster!'" Steve had appeared in Amory's memory like a ghost limb. The father who wasn't there but should have been.

I was stunned. "Huh" was all I said. I wanted so much to set his memory straight. *Your dad wasn't even in the same zip code*, I wanted to say. What was the cause of Amory's false memory? Was it an innocent mistake, or was he retroactively inserting his dad into a memory where we both wanted him to be?

One Sunday, Steve brought the kids back to my house with the news that Amory had eaten some bad chicken at a restaurant the night before and had been up all night vomiting. I put my hand on my son's forehead. He was dirty and tired, but he didn't feel feverish. He gave me a wan smile. "Aw, honey," I said. "Let's see if we can find some 7-Up." Bronte, who had eaten the same chicken, seemed fine.

By the following morning, Amory had thrown up again three times, which was an achievement because all he'd had was 7-Up and a little chicken soup. I called the school and said he wouldn't be in that day. Then I told Steve I wanted to keep Amory with me fulltime until he improved, and Steve didn't resist.

"I'm thinking you have a stomach flu and not food poisoning," I told him. "And the good news about stomach flu is that it usually doesn't last more than a day or two." It had already been two days. I kept pumping him with fluids as he lay listlessly on the sofa and watched cartoons.

By Thursday, we were seeing the pediatrician, Ray Mendelson—the man who had been Amory's doctor since the day he'd been born eleven years before. He was practically an uncle. Watching him examine Amory and quietly ask him questions made my heart swell. Everything was going to be okay.

Then Ray turned to me and said, "I'm not a specialist, but I'm thinking this could be post-viral gastroparesis." He explained how sometimes, after a virus, patients suffer from symptoms that suggest an obstruction of the stomach, without any evidence of a mechanical blockage. It could be caused by hormones or diabetes or a reaction to certain medications. "In this case, I suspect Amory may have had some kind of acute viral infection in his stomach, which has temporarily caused this reaction," he explained.

"Okay," I said. "How do we cure it?"

"Unfortunately, there's really nothing we can do. But it usually resolves itself in three to six months."

"Six months!" Amory had already missed a week of school and Little League practice. He'd been a star player—he'd finally found a sport he enjoyed and excelled at.

"Just to rule out anything more serious, I'm happy to order some tests up at the hospital," Ray said.

I called Steve to let him know. "Keep me posted," he said. His tone said he was concerned about his son. But he didn't offer to help.

We spent the next week going back and forth to the hospital up the hill. A CAT scan, an EKG, a bariatric X-ray, a gastric-emptying study, some bloodwork. Amory was a trouper, and I tried not to let him see my fear. I willed myself not to think about the words "brain tumor" or "stomach cancer." At home, every hour or two, he'd go into the bathroom and close the door, and I'd hear him vomiting, bravely.

The tests showed nothing. Meanwhile, the vomiting continued. Five, six times a day, including through the night.

I called UC San Francisco Medical Center and booked an appointment with a pediatric gastroenterologist. I had heard of friends going to UCSF for cancer treatments or high-level cardiac issues. My kids had never seen more than the ER at St. Helena Hospital for an ear infection or infected splinter.

Dr. Hirschfeld was a worried-looking man with overgrown eyebrows—he looked like the kind of guy who taught at a research university, not one who chose to work with children. He reviewed the test results from St. Helena Hospital, instructed his physician's assistant, Shelly, to perform a few more physical exams on Amory, and left the room. Shelly was an angelic young blonde woman with enough bedside manner for both of them. She performed the exams on Amory, then left and returned with Dr. Hirschfeld. Amory had kept his Pittsburgh Steelers cap on and now sat on the table looking scrawny and apprehensive in his paper gown.

"The evidence all points to gastroparesis," Dr. Hirschfeld said. "And your pediatrician is right: There's no known remedy for it. But it should resolve within a few months." He recommended a diet of Gatorade, cooked vegetables, blended fruit, and Ensure nutrition shakes. Shelly gave me her business card, and as we left, I felt like the sky had brightened a tiny bit. We drove the two hours home, stopping once to order Amory a smoothie and again for him to vomit it back up.

Where was Steve that day? We kept in touch by phone, and of course he was worried. He loved his children—I never doubted that.

But he was also happy to let me spend my days ferrying Amory to doctors and labs while he worried from the comfort of his own home. And part of me was glad of it. I wanted to be the parent in the waiting room, the one in control of decisions and Amory's care. Fortunately, Steve didn't argue. We had agreed that Amory would stay with me until he was completely cured. I resented that I was holding the laboring oar alone during this ordeal, but I knew I was meant to do it.

Although I was no longer worried about Amory dying from some undiagnosed illness, the days and weeks dragged on with little improvement. During the day I worked in my home office while he lay on the couch in front of the TV. At night I'd play Mario Kart video games with him for an hour or two. It was a game I'd never imagined I'd ever want to play, but he looked forward to it all day, and soon I did too. How would I have managed to care for him if I'd had a real job in a real office? I wondered.

As we turned the corner into spring, Amory's symptoms began to subside. He was vomiting only four times a day, then three. He was keeping up with his homework, and we were talking about him returning to school. The Little League coach called to ask if he could please come back in time for the playoffs, and while Amory was eager to rejoin the team, what he really wanted was to go on the annual sixth grade school field trip for three days at the Oregon Shakespeare Festival. He was still vomiting several times a day, but Jacqueline, the school's director, assured me that Amory could share a room with one of the school dads, who would be there to help.

After seeing my youngest child as ill as he'd ever been, my reaction was to say no. But Amory pleaded—this was the first thing in six months that he'd gotten excited about. So I reluctantly agreed, and he promised to call on the teacher's cell phone every night. As I packed him into her Subaru early Wednesday morning, I imagined him sleeping in a strange Ashland bed and breakfast with the only bathroom down the hall. Amory had never even been to sleepaway camp. Worries and fears slithered around my heart like black snakes.

As promised, he called home every evening. Except for getting sick during a performance and having to vomit into his beloved Steelers cap, all had gone well. But three days later, as his class was preparing to leave Ashland for the trip home, Amory called again. "Mom, I hurt my arms," he said. He knew how to use the sad, vulnerable tone of voice to get my immediate sympathy and, after the past six months, I was already there.

"Sweetie, what happened?" *Arms? Both arms?*

"I was on the swings and I jumped and when I fell, I landed on my arms."

"In the sand?"

"There was a cement curb."

The snakes of worry and fear returned. *Just get him home,* I thought. "Aw, honey. Can you get some painkillers from Miss Jacqueline?"

"I already did. But my arms still hurt."

"Well, you'll be home later today. It won't be long." *Yes, it would. It was a seven-hour drive.*

"Okay." The pathos in his voice broke my heart all over again. I should never have let him go. I had wanted to let him do something fun, but now he was not only sick but injured. What kind of mother was I?

That evening, the Subaru pulled up in front of our house, and Amory climbed out. He looked at me with the eyes of a condemned man. For seven hours, he'd been seated in the middle of the car, surrounded by shrieking preteen girls. He held his arms gingerly in front of him while the school director and the chaperone dad got his duffel from the trunk and laid it on the sidewalk.

Jacqueline came up to us and tousled Amory's hair. "You've got quite the little actor here," she said. She gave me her version of the accident. "He's a bit sore, but he'll be fine," she said as she grasped his right wrist and gave it a little shake.

Amory stared at me with burning eyes. Clearly, he hurt a lot more than he was letting on. I said quick goodbyes and got Amory bundled up on the couch, his now familiar residence. "If you're not feeling a lot better in the morning, I'll take you up to the hospital for X-rays," I said. I expected him to put up resistance, but he just nodded and asked for some dinner.

"Well, you've got a two-fer," the radiologist said cheerfully the next morning.

"Two . . . ?"

"Broken arms," he said. "The left is a clean break at the wrist. And the right shows a fracture to the radius." He gave me the number of an orthopedic surgeon in Napa, and we shuffled back to the car. Amory's arms were swaddled with Ace bandages—he would need a full cast on his right one, a partial cast on the left. I tried to read his expression—was it fear or pride?

I drove home, shaking my head and muttering. My son would miss at least another week of school. I'd have to tell his Little League coach. I would also tell Steve, of course, and he would be sympathetic but of no actual help.

More than ever, life felt frail and arbitrary. *How can I be working so hard and still have things go so terribly wrong?* I thought. I knew it was irrational, but I was beginning to feel cursed. It was as if Amory—the younger, more sensitive child—was the lightning rod for all the bad energy that was swirling around my house, my marriage, my family. I lay in bed at night and asked God how many more shoes would be dropped. It felt as if my floor were littered with shoes already.

While Amory was out of school, Bronte had been taking driver training in the afternoons. Steve had taught both kids to drive his truck years before, out in the vineyards surrounding our house or around the property at the farm. But this was different—city streets and highways, other drivers, maybe even drunk drivers. I was watching my children slip away, and suddenly it was happening in double time.

Six weeks and several visits to the doctor after Amory's accident, we drove to the orthopedic surgeon in Napa for what we hoped would be the final visit. To Amory's delight and my relief, the doctor cut off both casts and gave Amory a couple of soft wrist supports to wear during sports. As we drove home in the car, I glanced over at my son in the passenger seat, gazing in appreciation at his own arms, now white and scrawny from their weeks in the casts.

"I'm a real boy!" he exclaimed, invoking Pinocchio. And I sent up yet another silent prayer to God, thanking him for giving me a child who could make me laugh under almost any circumstances.

Chapter 15
Kangaroo Court

After we'd been living on Brown Street for about seven months, I contemplated the next step. This house had been a port in the storm, but I couldn't continue paying the exorbitant rent. And now that I'd finally gotten the proceeds from the sale of our house on Mee Lane, I had enough capital to use as a down payment on my own house.

In our divorce settlement, I'd proposed to Steve that I get the full proceeds from our primary residence, while he would get the other four properties we owned. I loved this idea: In one act, I could divest myself of the real estate that meant nothing to me, while granting me the resources to start over with a home of my own. The lawyers had penciled it out, and my proposal came out almost exactly even for both parties. God bless California's community property laws.

Steve liked this idea too. He'd always said, "I've never regretted the properties I've bought, only the properties I've sold." And this arrangement allowed him to keep the farm in Nevada City, the loft in Oakland, and two rental properties in Modesto. He would come out of the divorce with his real estate empire still relatively intact, and I would have enough to scale down and achieve my independence. The only catch was that the loans on all four properties still carried both our names. Banks don't care about divorce—the only way to remove me from the title was for Steve to either sell or refinance the properties, so my lawyer had inserted a clause that he was required to do so by April of 2010. That gave him nearly a year.

As I looked at houses to buy, my choices gradually sank from charming, renovated vintage homes on the desirable west side of St. Helena—now selling for well over a million dollars—to cookie-cutter condos on the more working-class east side of town.

One Sunday I spotted an open house sign at a new five-home development. The house at the back caught my eye—its master bedroom windows looked out onto a tree-filled lot next door and to the eastern hills beyond. Three bedrooms, two and a half baths, and even a little loft office, so I wouldn't have to sleep and work in the same room. There was no family room or dining room—just a small living area—but a nice-sized kitchen. And no real yard for the dog, but she was an inside dog anyway. I wanted this house.

I hired a new real estate agent and began negotiations with the developer. We arrived at a mutually agreeable figure, the seller agreed to finance me, and now all I needed was for Steve and the lawyers to release the funds for a down payment.

I didn't tell Steve about my plans—I just couldn't trust him not to try and sabotage my next move. And for Steve, real estate held a symbolic power—he loved to acquire new territory. This would be the first house I'd bought on my own, and I could imagine Steve's displeasure at this demonstration of financial independence. But inside, I was launching fireworks, dancing polkas, decorating cakes.

One evening in March, I ventured out to meet my friend Sally for drinks. We sat at the bar and ordered mojitos and ceviche. It had been ages since I'd talked with her, and there was a lot of catching up to do.

Sally had a bawdy sense of humor and a raucous laugh. We enter-
tained each other with our pathetic history of dating in the "middle
ages." After a while, she paused, stirring her mojito with its plastic
straw. "So," she said, "I'm trying to decide whether I should tell you
something or not."

"Yes, you should," I said. Sally looked dubious. "Oh. Is it about my
estranged husband?" I asked.

"Bingo."

"Oh God. What's he done now?"

"Well . . . I guess you haven't heard about his motorcycle trip to
Reno."

"Uh, no?"

She paused and took a sip of her drink. "With Mitzi."

No words passed as I gazed out into some middle distance trying
to process this news. I pictured Mitzi dressed in black leather and
perched behind Steve on his Harley, her arms wrapped around his
waist. I imagined her perfectly styled blonde bob, what it must have
looked like when she removed the helmet after six hours of hard road.
Her perky enthusiasm for a sport I'd always hated.

I remembered back in the fall when she'd asked my permission
to go up to the farm and I'd said no. The time I'd suggested to Steve,
months earlier, that perhaps we needed to change agents after two
years without a sale and he'd refused. The day we closed escrow and
Mitzi had phoned to remind me to get over to the title company
ASAP to sign the final papers so she could claim her commission.
That was the last call I'd had from her. Suddenly it made perfect sense
that they'd been seeing each other behind my back. Only I had been
too obtuse to see it.

My first reaction was to blame Mitzi. Steve had already proven
himself to be without a strand of moral fiber and willing to do anything to hurt me. But Mitzi? My old friend, whom I'd convinced Steve
to hire as our realtor? The one who'd said, "Of course, the friendship

comes first"? I couldn't believe she was capable of this kind of conflict of interest, this personal betrayal. And then I could, and I saw once again how naïve I'd been.

I had literally lost my breath. When I found it again, I asked, "Do the kids know?" Sally lived down the street from the Meuhlings and often drove Mitzi's daughter, Brooke, to school with her own son, Jack. Sally always knew everything.

"Amory doesn't know. But apparently, since Brooke knows, Steve and Mitzi told Bronte so she wouldn't hear about it at school."

I stared at the raw fish on my plate and listened to the cracking sound I was sure my heart was making. They'd put Bronte in the position of keeping this secret from me for how long now? I did the math: seven months. Most of her freshman year. For the rest of the night, I was numb.

The next morning, I called Mitzi's office and asked to speak with her broker. I identified myself and said I had a problem I needed to discuss. "Of course," she said in a sparkly voice. "What can I do to help?"

When I gave her the short version—how her agent, my friend, had started an affair with my estranged husband while she was representing both of us—she said, "I'm speechless. I don't know what to say. What can I do for you?"

"I'm not sure yet," I said. "But I thought you should know right away."

A few days later, when the shock had eased, I wrote a letter to the broker explaining that I'd figured out what I wanted: to be reimbursed my half of the commission. If I could recover the $19,300 I had just paid to Mitzi, I would consider the case closed. I followed up with a phone call.

"I've talked with our regional broker in Napa," she said, "and unfortunately, there is no way we can reimburse you for your portion of the commission." Now her voice was cool and businesslike.

"We've also talked to Mitzi, and she has a very different version of what happened."

"Oh, really?" I said. "What's her version?"

"She says that you knew about their relationship all along and had given it your blessing." In my mind, bonfires were burning. Orange flames, flying ashes. The sky clotted with black smoke. Burn it all down. The smell of burning blonde hair.

By the time we met for our weekly appointment with the therapist, I was still on a simmering boil. But the truth was that, as much as I naïvely kept hoping Steve would behave like a rational adult, his childishness never surprised me. By now it was clear that he would do anything to hurt me, to exact revenge on me for ending our marriage, and he outdid himself with each new maneuver. When I confronted him on Patricia's couch, asking how he could possibly think that getting involved with Mitzi was okay while she was representing us both, he smiled and said, "It's none of your business, Kirsten, who I go out with. You just can't stand that this is out of your control."

"And your daughter?" I seethed. "You see nothing wrong with forcing her to keep this secret from me all this time?"

"Bronte's fine with it." Steve shrugged. "She and Brooke are friends anyway."

The next week, after the shouting had died down, I worked up the nerve to talk to Bronte. She'd been angry, standoffish, and mostly silent since we'd moved from Mee Lane to Brown Street. I wasn't sure if it was just typical teenage hormones or if she blamed me for the separation and divorce. Or both. Now I approached her tentatively, not wanting to scare her off from what was going to be a tricky conversation. The media psychologists all advised having such conversations in the car, both facing forward, to avoid unnecessary hostility or conflict.

We were driving back from the barn where she kept her horse. She was always happier and more relaxed after riding.

"Bronte," I began, searching for a subtle entry point. "I've just learned about what's been going on between your dad and Mitzi."

No sound from the passenger seat.

"I didn't know about it," I said.

Nothing. I snuck a peek and saw her staring out the side window, her head turned as far from my voice as possible.

"And I guess they told you about it so you wouldn't hear it from Brooke."

"Yeah. So?" A crack in the wall. Pennies from heaven.

"So, I feel terrible that you were put in that position. Of having to keep that secret from me."

"You know what? I really don't care." She was slouched down in her seat, still staring out the window.

"It didn't make you feel uncomfortable?"

"No."

We were about to turn onto the highway now. I had fifteen minutes left.

"Bronte, they shouldn't have done that. They had no right to put you . . ."

"I don't care! I DON'T CARE! Can we just stop?"

"Honey, I just want to . . ."

"STOP! I don't want to have this conversation!"

Silence. "Can you . . ."

"NO!"

We drove the rest of the way in silence.

So that went well, I thought as we pulled into the garage.

After getting nowhere with Mitzi's brokerage, I'd filed a disciplinary complaint against her with the North Bay Association of Realtors. Hell hath no fury like a woman scorned—I was determined to chasten Mitzi publicly (and through her, Steve). Let me be clear: By calling attention to our sordid triangle, I knew I was opening the door to possible further humiliation. But I refused to just roll over and ignore what they had done. It was beyond bad behavior, in my mind. It was unethical. I wasn't going to let them get away with it.

Although the association couldn't award any financial damages, it would at least give me the chance to call Mitzi out publicly for her misconduct. She and I would be summoned to appear before a NorBAR "Professional Standards Hearing Panel" in May concerning Articles 1 and 2 of the Code of Ethics of the National Association of Realtors. Included in my two-page complaint was a timeline of our home's sale and a summary of what I knew about Mitzi and Steve's relationship.

In April, I learned that Mitzi Meuhling and Steve Beckwith had been having an affair for what I believe was about six months, I wrote. *This means that for about four months of the time she was under contract to us, Mitzi was sleeping with my estranged husband.*

I went on to describe how, as a close friend, I had shared many confidences with Mitzi about my relationship with Steve, as well as financial details of our divorce settlement and how it would be affected by the sale of our home. I explained how Mitzi had excluded me from conversations with Steve about the house, saying she knew I was under pressure with work and hadn't wanted to stress me out. I detailed the many times we socialized together—when I took Mitzi's family out to dinner and even gave her extra food from my pantry when we moved—ignorant of the fact that she and Steve were sleeping together. And I ended with the devastating news that Bronte had been told of the relationship and had been expected to withhold it from me.

I was continuing in the assumption that we were merely friends and realtor/client, while my daughter knew otherwise, I wrote. *I find this extremely upsetting, and my daughter has undergone therapy about Steve and Mitzi's relationship.*

Now, on a Thursday morning in May, I was driving to an office in

Santa Rosa for the formal hearing. There would be three appointed panel members—other realtors plus an attorney—who would hear our case. I walked into a large conference room where long tables had been arranged in a U shape with chairs around the perimeter. At the bottom of the U, the three panel members sat with their notepads and coffee. I was offered a seat on one of the side tables and looked across to the other side, where Mitzi would soon be seated.

I opened my folder and reviewed the script and timeline I'd brought, summing up the particulars of Mitzi's misdeeds. My heart was fluttering around in my rib cage, trying to escape, but I kept breathing deeply and reminding myself that I couldn't be more prepared. What I didn't know was what Mitzi could possibly say to exonerate herself. It seemed like such a black-and-white case to me—how could it be anything but unethical for her to have slept with a client while representing both him and his estranged wife? Once again, my blind spot was massive. A rearview mirror couldn't have helped me.

I heard the outer door open, a flurry of voices, and then Mitzi entered the room. She was wearing a fitted black-and-white ging-ham-checked blouse, snug black slacks, and white patent leather mules. When I'd gotten dressed that morning in my linen Eileen Fisher smock, leggings, and ballet flats, I'd thought I looked good. But now, amid all the shiny real estate people, I wondered: Would the Professional Standards Hearing Panel view me as the artsy but frumpy ex-wife, bitter and rejected?

I thought back to a conversation with my friend, Denise, a few months before. "Well, she *is* fairly attractive," I'd said about Mitzi, trying to sound reasonable.

"Attractive? Mitzi?" Denise wrinkled her nose and cocked her head, as if trying this description on for size. "Okay, maybe a little. In a kind of *real estate* way."

Now I was surrounded by that culture, where all the women wore form-fitting, jewel-toned clothes and big gold accessories. I was definitely not among my people.

I watched Mitzi beam her real estate smile at the panel and take a seat. Two other women followed: the broker and the managing broker, both of whom I had corresponded with before filing my complaint. It hadn't occurred to me that Mitzi would bring reinforcements. I'd thought that we would each read our prepared statements and be done.

The door opened again, and in walked Steve, smiling broadly, who then took a seat in the line of people facing me. He was wearing khaki slacks, a cashmere sweater, and a nice sport jacket—attractive attire I hadn't seen on him in years. Where were the overalls now, I wondered. Then it dawned on me: My husband—the experienced trial lawyer—was appearing on Mitzi's behalf. Apparently I had skimmed over the part in the hearing documents that explained we could bring witnesses. And now my own husband was about to testify against me—he had no doubt also counseled Mitzi on what to say. Here we were, at yet another new low in the saga of our ruined marriage. For all his betrayals, I hadn't imagined that even he would be capable of this. He looked me in the eye and gave me a smile I couldn't exactly interpret. Was it *Fancy meeting you here*? Or *Just doing what I've got to do*? Or *I'm sorry*?

But another thought quickly replaced that despair. I suddenly understood that I was about to be publicly humiliated in a big way. There was Mitzi, in her perky gingham Talbot's togs, with three witnesses and surrounded by a jury of her peers. And here was I, sitting alone at my long stretch of a table, feeling small and outnumbered. There was no way this would end well for me.

The head of the panel called the hearing to order and explained the guidelines. I would read my statement; Mitzi would read hers. Then each of the witnesses would make a statement. Each side would be permitted to cross-examine the witnesses. *Yes, cross-examine! We were actually in a trial!* Finally, the panel would be allowed to ask any final questions that might remain.

I cleared my throat and read my five-page statement. I cited how Mitzi had continued to see me both socially and as my agent, at one point telling me that she was seeing a man but refusing to tell me his name because "this is a small town." My delivery was shaky and emotional, but I held it together until I got to the part about Bronte keeping this news a secret from me. Now my voice broke, and I lost my composure for a few long seconds. Then I took a breath and continued reading. I occasionally looked up to see Steve carefully taking notes on a yellow legal pad, the way he would in court.

Now it was Mitzi's turn. She put on her sparkly half-glasses and began in her little breathy voice. "Kirsten claims that she learned about my relationship with Steve in March of 2008. This is not true. I called her in October 2007 before I ever accepted an invitation to coffee with Steve and gave her a heads-up that there might be a relationship on some level. She did not object."

At this, my mouth fell open. Mitzi looked back and mimicked my expression, the way little girls do in elementary school. Steve slid Mitzi a note he'd hastily written. She read it, nodded, and continued.

"Whenever a decision needed to be made, we went through a silly dance. I called Kirsten, she would call Steve, and Steve would call me. After a while I told her, 'I'm calling Steve first because you always go with what he says anyway.' She thanked me for not burdening her with all the little decisions."

She continued in this vein, taking barely recognizable facts and repurposing them to suit her fairy tale.

"I am sorry to trouble NorBAR with this unfair accusation," she concluded. "For a member of this association to discharge her duties and then be threatened with disciplinary action, personal and professional humiliation, and possible loss of pay is simply wrong." Mitzi took off her readers and turned to the panel, giving them her most charming, toothy smile. I imagined that scene in a horror movie where the pretty friend takes off a mask to reveal the disfigured villain underneath.

Mitzi's brokers each made a brief statement, attesting that Mitzi had assured them the relationship had been conducted with my full approval. Then Steve read his prepared statement, which claimed that Mitzi had informed me of their romance and I had been fine with it—until after I had paid her my half of the commission. Clearly, this was a sad combination of jealousy and buyer's remorse, he explained, in that the compensation I paid to Mitzi had aggravated my deep-seated resentment about their union.

He was basking in the attention, I thought. He hadn't appeared in a courtroom in years, and here he was, showing off his legal acumen. Plus, he was the common denominator in a love triangle. Two women fighting over him! His immense satisfaction was writ large on his no longer handsome face.

Then it was my turn for questioning. I might end up looking completely foolish, but I would not go down without a fight. I took a deep breath, called upon the spirits of Clarence Darrow and Perry Mason, and began asking questions.

"So, Mitzi, you say that you told me about your relationship with Steve back in October and that I gave you my consent. But I have no recollection of that conversation at all. Can you tell me what we said?"

"Well, I remember I was in the car, driving down on the Carneros Highway," she said, squinting at the ceiling as if to recall it exactly. "I told you that Steve had invited me out for coffee and a Danish." She smiled at the panel. "I thought that was so cute. 'Coffee and a Danish!'" Nobody smiled back.

For a moment I was taken aback. Her memory seemed so specific and fresh, I wondered whether I had, in fact, actually forgotten that this conversation had taken place. But no. You don't forget a thing like that. I imagined Steve coaching her on the details.

"And what did I say?"

"You said you understood and were fine with it. You gave me your blessing. After all, you didn't want him, so why not?" She giggled.

"I said that? I gave you 'my blessing'?"

"Well, not those words exactly."

"Mm-hmmm. And that was it? Because I don't remember ever having that conversation."

"Well, as I recall, you had a lot on your mind back then."

"Uh-huh. So, if I was fine with this relationship, why then did neither of you ever mention it to me again, even when we went out to dinner together? Why no acknowledgment of it in my presence? And why, when you told me you were seeing a man and I asked his name, would you not tell me?"

"Um, I don't really remember that."

"I guess my bottom-line question is—if your version is true and I had no objection to your relationship—why would I be sitting here now, filing this complaint?"

It went on like that for a while. I was getting the hang of this cross-examination thing: You phrased your questions so that, regardless of the answer, you were giving the jury your side of the story.

Then I turned to Steve. "So you decided to get involved with Mitzi while she was still representing both of us. If you had waited a few months, you could have done the same thing and it would have angered me, but it wouldn't have been professionally unethical. Why did you, as a member of the California Bar Association, feel that this was an acceptable thing to do?"

"I didn't see the point of waiting," he said. "What difference did it make?"

"Why didn't you at least tell me about the affair? In all the times we met and talked over that period of six months, you didn't mention it to me once. When I finally confronted you about it at the therapist's, you said it was none of my business. And yet now you insist that I knew about it all along."

"Kirsten, you know you've been having memory problems for the past few years."

I thought of the movie *Gaslight*.

"You're right, Steve, I do forget things. Like where I put my keys and my glasses. But I don't forget things like being told my husband is having an affair with my friend and real estate agent." I stopped and enjoyed the moment of silence that followed. Neither Steve nor Mitzi looked at me, and I thought I heard a snicker from the direction of the panel.

When it came time for Mitzi to ask questions of me, she had none. But one of the panel members had a question for Steve: "Why did you think it would be a good idea to get romantically involved with Mitzi?"

"Well"—he shrugged and gave the man a rakish grin—"you know, I was single . . . she was single. . . ."

How had this man ever succeeded as a litigator?

Finally, it was over. Or almost over. Mitzi asked if she could say one more thing. Then she leaned forward and gave me a soulful look. "I just want to say that I'm sorry for the way this happened, Kirsten. I'm sorry. I'm truly sorry. I just want to put this all behind us."

I have always been a sucker for a sincere *mea culpa*. The entire room turned to look at me, waiting for my reaction. I sighed.

"It would be easier to accept your apology, Mitzi," I finally said, "if you hadn't just sat here and lied to me for two hours in front of all these people."

Mitzi blanched and looked down. Chairs shuffled, throats cleared, and we were out in the parking lot finding our cars.

Driving home, I was speeding with adrenaline and relief. I was fist-punching the air. I still had only a fifty-fifty chance that the NorBAR board would find in my favor—I had no idea how they'd interpreted the two very different versions of events. We would learn the official outcome in three weeks. But in this moment, it didn't really matter. Movie finale music played in my head; credits rolled on the screen.

For today, I drove under the triumphal arch.

Chapter 16
The Nuremberg Defense

Four weeks after the hearing, I pulled from my mailbox a thick envelope with the familiar green NorBAR logo. I set it on the counter and scrutinized it, unopened. It felt so big and important, but what difference did it make, really? I would receive no financial compensation. Any victory would be symbolic at best. Still, the image of Mitzi sitting with her pack of witnesses, Steve among them, was burned onto my retinas. If she was acquitted of wrongdoing, it would be a victory for them, a public humiliation for me. I imagined Mitzi at her house, regarding an identical envelope with the same stakes inside.

I summoned my nerve and sliced the edge of the envelope. A cover letter that introduced *the Findings of Fact (Form D-11)*. I turned the page. Attached was a list of ten recommendations and boxes to be checked from *(1) No discipline recommended* to *(10) Expulsion*. The box that was checked was number three: *Reprimand—Place a Letter of Reprimand in member's file for 36 months*. They had determined that Mitzi had done a good job in the marketing and sale of the property. But they found fault with regard to Article 1: *The Realtor is obligated to treat all parties honestly.*

Although it could be argued in favor of respondent Meuhling that she merely acted irresponsibly and perhaps displayed bad judgment, they wrote, *the requirement for honesty goes beyond that and includes the need to show fairness and sincerity. The hearing panel finds that respondent Meuhling did not meet that standard.*

They hadn't bought Mitzi's story that she had told me about her romance with Steve. It wasn't a Scopes Trial victory, but it was something. I had put a reprimand in Mitzi's file for three years. Would it affect her business or her earning ability? Probably not. But it wasn't abject humiliation for me either. Now I could begin the process of letting the whole Steve and Mitzi thing go.

Haha! Yeah, right.

As I remembered the sight of Steve whispering in Mitzi's ear, slipping her notes, the conflagration of our marriage burned bright before me. Charred carcasses of automobiles. The smell of burning rubber, skin, clothing. There would be no survivors. I hated them both.

"Well, she didn't want him, so why shouldn't I have him?" That's what Mitzi had said, with her usual giggle. Why then, did it bother me so much to even think of them together? It was the same feeling I'd had when he dated Eileen, from chorus. It wasn't the idea of him seeing other women—they were welcome to him. But to be sleeping with someone I knew, and knew well—it felt like an unforgiveable breach of privacy. I would always be a shadow in that relationship. I'd always be the angry ex-wife. It wasn't just Steve's life that was being shared; it was my former life, too.

And there was this: Steve had once been a handsome, successful catch. I'd been proud to be married to him. Now he embarrassed me, with his redneck logic and his ridiculous outfits. It was humiliating to think that others would see him close up and think that I had chosen that. Had he been the same man I'd loved for so many years, there would have been regret and nostalgia, maybe even jealousy. But that man was no longer around.

Now that Steve and Mitzi seemed to be staying together for the long term, there was also the unthinkable idea that such a duplicitous person might actually become my children's stepmother. There was just no way to be happy about that.

Spring. A million different shades of green in the trees and vineyards. Yellow mornings that bled into hot afternoons. Bronte completed the tenth grade, and Amory graduated from his Montessori elementary school, headed for the gauntlet of middle school. After his graduation ceremony, I stood in the parking lot talking with Steve about the kids' plans for summer.

It was the first time we'd seen each other since the NorBAR hearing. We'd finally given up on the idea that therapy could help us keep things civil—who were we kidding? After his dressing up for the hearing, Steve was back to wearing overalls and cowboy boots. Out of nowhere he asked, "So when were you going to tell me you bought a house?"

He was trying to seem casual about it, but I knew that buying property was Steve's favorite thing in the world. He'd known of my intention to eventually buy a house in town, but I guess he was surprised to learn that I could actually do it without him. Of course Mitzi had told him. She must have seen my escrow posted in the local listings.

"I probably would have told you after close of escrow, when I was about to move in." I held his gaze—I was nearly free of him now. I could feel the late spring sun on my neck. Everything was still. I tried not to squirm or show my eagerness to run away.

"I guess my real question is why you've gone to such trouble to hide it from me," he said. "And where did you get the money to buy a house, anyway? You must have had a secret bank account I didn't know about." He looked back at me eye to eye, his boots planted firmly on the asphalt. He always loved to pull these surprise attacks, to see me squirm.

I stared back at him, slack-jawed. "We just sold a house, remember? I got the proceeds, remember? And you got the four other properties? It's always been my plan to buy something else once we sold Mee Lane. You knew that."

"Oh, I see." He recovered quickly. "You should really think twice, though, before you spend all that money in one place." Now his tone was paternal, the loving father giving helpful advice.

"I think I can handle it, thanks."

"So, why didn't you tell me?" Here we were, back at square one.

I took a breath. "I didn't tell you, Steve, because I thought it might upset you. I thought you might try to do something to screw it up for me."

Steve kicked at a rock on the pavement, sending it onto the grass. "Now, why would I do that?" He was suddenly kind, solicitous. "Kirsten, you're the mother of my children. I would *never* do anything to hurt you. Surely you know that, at least."

I laughed. "Oh, really?"

"What have I ever done to hurt you?"

"Hmmmm. Let's see. You slept with my friend behind my back? You told Bronte to keep it a secret from me? You appeared at the NorBAR hearing and testified against me? Do you need any other examples?"

Steve shook his head. "Kirsten. I only did that because they called me up and asked me to. I was only responding to their request. Besides"—he suddenly grinned—"you did a great job!"

"I'm pretty sure that's called the Nuremberg Defense," I said. "I guess twenty-two years of marriage meant less to you than pleasing Mitzi's real estate team."

"Now you're overreacting," Steve said.

"Whatever." I turned and walked back across the street, closing my front door.

—

Two weeks later, another moving van pulled up to our house and carried our things half a block to our new home on Allison Avenue. The same pleasant neighborhood, with schools and stores and friends just minutes away. Everything was bikeable. High ceilings and quiet neighbors. Finally, we had a place to call home for good.

Within a week, I was back at my desk writing. But I suddenly noticed that, between the house negotiations and escrow and the move, I hadn't been working much in the past few months. Now that the dust had literally settled, I realized I hadn't been billing much at all.

I'd already started shopping at Safeway instead of the smaller, more expensive Sunshine Foods. Our weekend dinners out were a thing of the past. Instead of browsing the bestsellers at the independent bookstore, I was now a regular library patron. And I'd begun running all my local errands on my blue bicycle, leaving the big SUV in the garage.

Did I miss my old, bigger life? Sometimes. But I reminded myself of the trade-off it required—dealing with Steve's growing appetites and addictions, living beyond our means, being trapped in a country house far from town—and I knew I was in a better place. I was pretty sure I was the subject of local gossip, other wives clucking about how far I'd fallen since the days when Steve and I had been one of the upwardly mobile couples on the scene. All I could do was hold my head up and hope that integrity and grace counted for something. They were all I had left. I thought back to the person I'd been when Steve Beckwith had first met me: an independent woman. A freelancer struggling to live month to month. A woman unsure of her future. After all the adventures of the past twenty years, here I was again. Only with two kids and a mortgage.

Chapter 17
A Diploma of Virtue

I met Gregory in my Tuesday evening yoga class—he placed his mat next to mine, and we chatted easily after class. I was immediately struck with his patrician good looks—wavy silver hair, tortoiseshell glasses, chiseled features, and piercing brown eyes. When he tossed around a few literary references and mentioned that he was working on a book, I was pretty much reeled in. So when he asked me out for coffee the following day, I said yes.

Gregory was an alumnus of the Graduate Theological Union in Berkeley and Harvard's John F. Kennedy School of Government, and he made his living as a body trainer and meditation teacher. Sixty-two years old, divorced once, no kids. Matters of the spirit were more important to him than financial success, he explained. His dream job? To be the Dalai Lama, haha. Over coffee he spoke softly and thoughtfully and had a sharp and logical mind. He also casually dropped the fact that he made only $25,000 a year. In my current state of recovery from living way beyond our means, I justified this as humble and sensible.

At the end of our first date, Gregory invited me to join him and some friends for dinner at his home later that week. At six o'clock,

I showed up with the peach-and-berry crisp I'd spent all afternoon making and found a note taped to the front door: *Last-minute meditation lesson, back at 7.*

I left the crisp sitting on the balcony railing and went home for an hour. When I returned, the door was open, and Gregory and his several friends were pouring cabernet and already enjoying my crisp. I took a big gulp of the cabernet.

Despite my instincts telling me that this was in no way a fit, we had a third date and easily fell into bed. It was a lovely little romp, but afterward, as we lay tangled in my duvet, I felt an overwhelming need to get this near stranger out of my house. Making love was one thing—spending the night together was the true intimacy.

I continued to see Gregory for a few weeks. I told myself that I was attracted to his thoughtful, articulate manner, but who was I kidding? I'd picked him because he was as different from Steve as a man could be. Meanwhile, I'd finally noticed that he lived an extremely self-focused life. He was paid for his meditation and body work classes in cash only—why pay taxes? His wine collection was the result of many generous friends. His car was loaned to him by another friend. He lived elegantly upon the kindness of strangers. Meanwhile, he was convinced that his collection of verbose essays would one day soar to the top of *The New York Times'* best-seller list.

One day the phone calls and emails just stopped, each of us too ambivalent to continue. *No dating men from St. Helena* became my new rule. When I bumped into Gregory at the Roastery or the Model Bakery, I shuddered. I couldn't imagine what I'd seen in him. Now all I saw was an effete, aging fool.

Later that month, I opened my mail to find a divorce decree, with my name, Steve's name, our children's names, and many checked boxes, signed and endorsed by the Clerk of the Napa Superior Court. I stood in the dining room, still holding the serrated knife that had liberated this simple document. My mind flickered with images from the past twenty-two years, all the family videos and meaningful moments that were now cast into a kind of sad, sepia-toned montage. It was done. I was free. It felt like a graduation, I thought, and remembered the Edith Wharton quote: *A divorce is in itself a diploma of virtue.*

And yet, there would be more struggle, I knew. Until the children were both on their own and out from under our mutual care, Steve would remain a determined adversary. I had taken something away from him, and he would make me pay for it.

I wasn't sure about James Kiehl when I first saw his profile on Match. His primary photo seemed to date from the seventies, with aviator-style glasses and a helmet of hair. But the other photos weren't so bad, and he seemed like he might even be a good guy. He lived in Napa, his politics were liberal, and he talked a lot about philanthropy. When he "Liked" my photo, I "Liked" him back and thought, what the hell. We exchanged emails to arrange a rendezvous.

"Coffee or a glass of wine," I said, sticking to my rule, and suggested a place in the midpoint of Yountville. But he said he was willing to come to St. Helena and suggested drinks at a nice restaurant just two blocks from my house. I couldn't argue with the convenience.

"Come hungry," he said.

When I arrived on my bike, I found Jim waiting in the pretty, tree-filled courtyard. He looked better than his photo—he'd updated his glasses and wore all black, including a beautiful cashmere jacket. I smiled and introduced myself. He grinned. "I have so many stories to tell you," he said, taking my arm. "So many stories."

The host led us not to the bar but to a reserved table by the window, where a bouquet of a dozen roses awaited us. Confused, I looked up at him. "I went ahead and made us a reservation for dinner," he said, still grinning. He was so pleased with himself—such a debonair ladies' man!—but once again I felt like I was a player in somebody else's script. The gesture was flattering, sure, but the roses weren't about me. They were about Jim impressing me. He'd completely ignored my request to keep it simple. His first moves were exactly like Steve Beckwith's.

Jim ordered us an appetizer and sat back in his chair. I began with a simple question—"So you've recently moved to Napa?"—and the stories began. And then they went on and on. Twenty minutes later dinner arrived, and Jim kept talking. His promise had not been an empty one: He had so many stories.

The next day, he emailed to ask me out again—this time for dinner and dancing in Napa. I decided to give him another shot. Maybe this time he'd relax enough to have a two-way conversation.

Jim had suggested that we meet at his house and then drive together to the restaurant. At the appointed hour, I pulled up to the curb. His house was a large, two-story faux-Mediterranean affair in a neighborhood of similarly faux houses. As I approached the porch, I was greeted by a collection of carved wooden bears and folksy signs welcoming me to "Jim's Place." This is perhaps the most tragic fall-out of most divorces, I thought: financially successful men without proper supervision in the decorating realm. We drove across town to the restaurant, where a seventies-era trio of cool, middle-aged musicians was playing "Just the Two of Us." We quickly ordered a first course, and the stories began again.

By the time we were halfway through our meal, something snapped in my brain. I looked at Jim and saw his mouth moving, but I'd reached my limit with his words. I'd heard about his entire academic and professional career, learned the stories of both his ex-wives, knew the names and had seen photos of his three children and two grandchildren. Meanwhile, he hadn't asked a single question about me. I thought of all the women in this valley who would be more than happy to sign up for a lifetime with this man. Why couldn't I be one of them?

The waiter brought the dessert menus. I fumbled something about having to work in the morning. The next morning was Saturday—it was a pathetically obvious ruse, but it was all I had.

"Are you sure?" Jim asked, wounded, confused.

"So sure," I said, and mumbled an apology. We walked quickly to the car, and I listened to another chapter of his life story on the way home. When he pulled into his driveway and walked around to help me out of the car, I sprang out, gave him a quick hug on the sidewalk, and thanked him for a pleasant evening. As my tires screeched out of the cul-de-sac, I caught sight of him in my rearview mirror, standing at the curb looking dumbfounded.

Chapter 18
All the Bells and Whistles

In late July, I invited Hope and Ruby up from the city—two old friends who had known me since the eighties when we'd worked together in advertising. The kids were with Steve that weekend, and we were celebrating my divorce by watching Jane Austen movies and eating one lavish meal after another. Now we were gathered around a Scrabble board, hooting with laughter about old times. When the phone rang showing Steve's caller ID, I hesitated, but I knew he wouldn't be calling unless it was about one of the kids.

"I think I may have mentioned that I've been helping Bronte look at cars," Steve said, without introduction. Our divorce settlement had stated that we would split the costs of a car for each child as it became necessary. There was nothing about timing or a specific financial figure. Now, one week after Bronte had turned sixteen, Steve was dying to buy her a used car. He welcomed any excuse to spend money.

"Well, we're sitting in the office of Jimmy Vasser Chevrolet," he continued. "Bronte's found a nice truck that she's fallen in love with. I just need your agreement that we can buy it for her."

"You know I've got guests staying for the weekend," I said, hearing my voice veer into a whine. "I'm not prepared to agree about a major purchase on the spur of the moment. We haven't even discussed how much we're going to spend." I looked longingly at the Scrabble board, the tea and macarons that awaited me on the table. Steve had instinctively known I wouldn't want to talk about money this weekend.

"If it were left up to you, this would never happen," he said. "Somebody had to help her buy her first car."

"She turned sixteen last week! What's the rush?"

"She's turned sixteen, and we promised we'd buy her a car. Of course she's anxious to find one. Kirsten, this is a really great deal. It's a 2008 Chevy Silverado truck, a Joe Gibbs package. It's got all the bells and whistles. It's perfect."

"How much?"

"Sixteen thousand five hundred."

I swallowed hard. The truth was, with so little work and a new house, the idea of buying a car at all made me queasy.

"There's no way I can afford that, Steve. We haven't even discussed price yet, and you arbitrarily think I can fork out eight thousand dollars for a car on the spot?"

I looked up at Hope's and Ruby's faces. They were staring at me with grim expressions of disbelief.

"This is so typical of you," Steve said. "You foolishly spent all your money on a house, and now you can't even afford to buy your daughter a truck." He had his lawyer voice on.

"Yeah, I guess I must have my priorities pretty confused. I put housing ahead of wheels for my teenaged daughter. I'm *not* going to be pressured into making an impulse purchase just because you've promised her something prematurely."

My heart raced. When would I learn to anticipate this stuff?

"She's sitting here with her heart set on this truck," Steve said. "I'll just tell her that you refuse to buy it for her. You continue to think of no one but yourself."

The manipulation. Would it never end?

"I need to get back to my guests now, Steve. Call me later in the week. But I'm not going to agree to this on the spot." I hung up the phone, shaking with anger.

On Monday, when he knew my guests had left, Steve started on round two.

He agreed to finance the truck himself, pay for all the auto insurance for the first year, and not require a payment from me for six months. He was tireless when it came to something he wanted to buy. I just didn't have the strength or the energy to match it—and deal with Bronte's anger to boot. She already seemed to hate me as it was. Once again, I capitulated.

As I watched my savings account dwindle—the remainder of my money from the sale of our house—I began to see a hairball in my career plan. All the other freelance writers I knew were either single without children or married with a second source of income. I didn't know of another single freelancer who was supporting two children on one feast-or-famine income. And now I understood why.

I began surveying online job boards and registered with a few creative agencies in San Francisco. Then, through the magic of networking, I found a six-month contract position at the Haas School of Business at UC Berkeley—taking over for a marketing communications manager who was going on maternity leave. I couldn't believe my good luck. Berkeley was my old stomping ground—from my undergraduate years in the seventies and working there in the early nineties to my more recent freelance work.

And so began my road warrior period, commuting to the Bay Area five days a week. I left the house at seven in the morning, drove to El Cerrito, hopped on a BART train, and hopped off three stops later in downtown Berkeley. Then I reversed the process each evening.

If you overlooked the thirteen-hour day, I loved being in Berkeley again. I was surrounded by smart, driven people who believed in what they were doing. I spent my days writing marketing copy, supervising photo shoots, attending meetings. And did I mention the food? The streets of Berkeley were fragrant with fish oil and sweet pork and cilantro—smells I'd missed in the Napa Valley. At the end of the day, I would walk the mile downhill through campus, recalling my undergraduate years and remembering the lens of hope and possibility through which I had seen the world back then. I could usually spot the afternoon fog sneaking under the Golden Gate Bridge in the distance and feel a whisper of optimism again.

On the weeks when I had the kids, the house vibrated with adolescent anger—specifically, Bronte's. Ever since she turned twelve, I'd been enduring the eye-rolling, the exasperated "what-*evers*," and that little gagging sound from the back of the throat that teenage girls make when they scoff at you. But this was different—more poisonous, more personal. Bronte was my first teenager, so I didn't know if it was simply normal behavior or if the divorce and all the moving around had triggered a deep-seated hatred for me. Our conversations usually followed a similar pattern:

"Can we talk about this? You seem really upset."

"Mom." She wouldn't even look up from her phone.

"Just talk to me for a minute, please?"

"Mom!" Usually punctuated by the slamming of a door.

One early morning I was eating oatmeal at the kitchen counter before driving to the BART train. I heard the front door click open, and in walked my daughter. She scurried up the stairs, and I followed her.

"And where have you been, may I ask?"

"I just went out to my truck to get some homework."

"No, you didn't. It's five thirty in the morning. You're never up at this hour."

"YES, I DID! HOW DO YOU EVEN KNOW?"

"Keep your voice down, Amory's asleep. And plan on continuing this conversation with me tonight. I have to get to work."

And that's how I learned that my sixteen-year-old daughter had been spending every night with her boyfriend, Sam, sneaking out after I was asleep and sneaking back in before I awoke at five. That morning her alarm clock had failed.

The next night, I sat across from Bronte and Sam at our dining room table. Rather than face my wrath alone, she'd decided to bring Sam, who had arrived bearing a Safeway bouquet. I thanked him and laid the flowers on the counter.

Sam was twenty, with a job at his dad's hardware store and a second job as a volunteer fireman. Bronte had been staying at his apartment but had also been spending a lot of time with his family. With them, of course, she was a perfect daughter. She wanted to spend summer vacation with them.

Once again I felt my heart pinch. Would I never get to be the fun mom, the respected mom, the beloved mom? I already knew the answer.

Sam seemed like a sweet young man. But he was twenty. And Bronte was sixteen. And they were having sex every night.

"Sam," I began, "are you familiar with the term 'statutory rape'?"

Sam flushed and looked down. "Yes, ma'am."

"I don't mean to imply that you've raped my daughter. It's just the term they use to describe sexual activity when one of the partners is below the legal age of consent."

Bronte made the scoffing noise. "Mom. I don't *believe* you!"

"I guess I can't be too surprised that you're having sex. But I *am* shocked that you've been practically living together behind my back. Bronte's only a sophomore in high school, Sam. As you know."

Sam was suddenly crying, but my eyes were on Bronte, who was sitting with her arms crossed, scowling, sending death rays of hate directly into my eyes.

"You're just too young to be living this double life," I said to her. "Look. I know I can't prevent you from seeing each other. But I think you should consider taking a break and letting things cool off for a while. And you certainly can't continue to stay over at Sam's at night. You have another two years of being part of this family, and I want you here."

Sam was wiping his eyes and nodding. "Yes, ma'am."

But Bronte was venomous. "You can't make us stop seeing each other! I refuse to play by your ridiculous rules." She stood up and marched out the door, Sam following sheepishly behind.

It suddenly hit me that Bronte was modeling her behavior after her dad: angry and my-way-or-the-highway. And Sam was me—trying to smooth things over. Our relationship was repeating itself in miniature, right before my eyes.

Summer 2009 passed by in a blur. I was gone thirteen hours a day during the week, so the kids were, by necessity, on their own when they stayed with me. I tried hard to make our home as loving and light and fun as it always was, but I wasn't fooling anyone. And sometimes I was just too tired to care.

Then, in September, something remarkable happened. Mitzi moved, with her two kids, down south to Costa Mesa to her mother's house. Was the reprimand I'd had placed in her file just enough to make her pack her greasy carpetbag and retreat from St. Helena? Or did it have nothing to do with me at all? Whatever the reason, her departure felt like a blessing.

Bronte was now in eleventh grade and Amory in eighth. Once Bronte got her truck, Steve was off the hook for driving her to and from school, her horseback riding lessons, and her evening meetings for Future Farmers of America. Now she was regularly driving back to Steve's house after dark on a twisty twelve miles up the mountain toward Pope Valley, a road that was notorious for its sharp curves and lack of railings.

"She's a solid driver," Steve said. "She'll be fine. Stop worrying so much."

Once again, I was the bad cop.

Chapter 19
How the Light Gets In

December arrived, as usual, too quickly. Christmas would follow our new holiday protocol: Steve would get the kids for Christmas Eve, then bring them back to my house that night. He never did bother to buy a tree, not one time, so the kids always wanted to wake up at my place, where there was a semblance of the old family traditions. Steve would come by around nine or ten, we'd open gifts together, and I'd make some fancy breakfast like eggnog French toast or scrambled eggs with smoked salmon. We'd been doing it for three years now, and Steve and I had gotten pretty good at feigning holiday cheer. I'm sure we were each counting the years until both kids were adults and we didn't have to perform this charade anymore.

This Christmas was no different. We'd talked beforehand about what the kids wanted and what we would each be getting them. Budgets were still fairly tight for both of us, so it was agreed that we'd play it simple this year, again. Steve was planning to give "just a few small things," in his words.

He arrived that morning, and we sat in our usual tiny circle, with Steve passing out the gifts arrayed under the tree. A sweater for Bronte. A carry-on bag for Amory. Some horse tack for Bronte.

Several video games for Amory. When the boxes had all been opened and we sat in a disarray of wrapping paper, Steve reached behind the tree, where two white envelopes lay hidden. He gave one to each of the kids with a little bow and a smile, like he was on stage playing Bob Frigging Cratchit. And I knew I was about to be ambushed.

Bronte and Amory tore open the envelopes, and their faces brightened. "Club Med! When are we going?" Bronte squealed.

"Ixtapa? Wow, thanks, Daddy!" Amory was beaming now too. Steve giddily explained how they'd be going in July, and Mitzi and her kids would be coming along, to make it even more fun.

"Well, isn't that exciting?" I said, miming joy and surprise.

Later, as Steve gathered his things to go, I stood waiting to see him out. "Funny you didn't mention Club Med when we were discussing our gifts," I said.

"I wanted to keep it a surprise, is all," he said in his *aw shucks, ma'am* tone.

"And did you enjoy that?"

"The kids seemed really happy about it. You're not going to begrudge them that, are you?"

"Wouldn't dream of it," I said. I stood in the doorway, listening to a single mockingbird whistling into the chilly air from the branches of a neighboring tree as I watched his black truck drive away—once again wishing it were the last time I'd ever see his taillights. Not for the first time, I imagined him dead.

New Year's Day. I liked nothing better than to start the new year with a flurry of activity. I was rarely happier than when I was productive, checking items off my long to-do lists, which I kept every day, even on weekends. Today it was eight in the morning, and I was in the front yard pruning the crepe myrtle tree. Dolce, our yellow lab, had taken advantage of the open front door and come out to sniff the smells of new beginnings and to sit contentedly nearby.

The first day of the year always made me see omens, even more than usual. Between the drought and the cold snap, the myrtle tree looked dead—its parched branches covered in dried seed pods. Now I thought of the clearing away of the dead brush as a meaningful ritual, making room for new growth. As they fell to the ground, the dried pods rattled like tiny brass bells. *Ring the bells that still can ring*, wrote Leonard Cohen in "Anthem." It was one of my favorite lyrics. *Forget your perfect offering. There is a crack in everything—that's how the light gets in.* I was feeling clean. That dead myrtle had annoyed me every time I passed it. Now it would remind me of new beginnings.

Later that month, Steve called to tell me he'd decided to move full-time to Costa Mesa. He'd been doing some contract work for a law firm in nearby Irvine that was becoming fairly regular. Apparently, his interest in sharing equal custody of our children had waned.

"Of course, I'll need to pay you some support if you have them fulltime," he said. If only he'd been so accommodating a year or two before. I told him I found it paradoxical that he'd made this choice now, when I actually needed his help raising the kids while I was spending thirteen hours a day at work and on the road.

"Again, this is not about you," Steve said. "This is the first good work I've had in a while."

He was right about that, of course. But he'd also found work right in the very town where Mitzi now lived. What a small world!

Steve called again in February to tell me he wanted to take the kids to the mountains for a few days during spring break. They'd stay in Reno at Circus Circus, play video games and laser tag, and visit Steve's favorite destination, the massive Cabela's retail store. I'd already made plans to take Amory skiing later that week, so we coordinated a rendezvous in downtown Truckee where I would take Amory. Steve would return home with Bronte.

About a week before they were scheduled to leave, Amory let it slip that Mitzi and her two kids would also be going on the Reno trip.

"Wow," I said. "That's a lot of people in Daddy's truck. Or are they driving separately from Costa Mesa?"

"Mitzi and Easton are coming with us, but Bronte and Brooke are driving in her truck," he said, before he realized he'd revealed too much. I was on the phone before he could try to take it back.

"She's not even seventeen! She hasn't had 'her year' yet!" I wailed.

"She's a great driver," Steve countered.

"They have this law for a reason, Steve. Teens talk and text, and their accident rates go way up." I held the phone with one hand and madly scrubbed kitchen grout with another. "Plus Bronte's never even driven in the snow. And there's a huge storm headed in next week!"

"That's why we're leaving early," he said, calm and smug.

"*Why* would you deliberately put your own child in harm's way?" I was near tears.

"You need to mind your own business, Kirsten. Again. You just can't stand the idea of us going away with the Muehlings."

I tried reasoning with Bronte, but she insisted that it was between me and her father. I wondered if I could alert the Highway Patrol to pull them over on Highway 80. I harangued Steve by phone every other day. Finally, just before they were set to leave, he called.

"Mitzi's going to ride with the girls," he said. "Are you happy now?" I was. Not that there was much that Mitzi could do if Bronte went into a spin on an icy mountain pass. But at least there would be a legal adult present.

A few weeks later, when we met in a Truckee parking lot at the appointed day and hour, I watched Amory climb out of Steve's car and Mitzi get out of Bronte's truck to stretch her legs. Years later, when she wasn't so angry at me, Bronte revealed that Mitzi had actually ridden in Steve's truck after all. They'd merely stopped a few miles up the road for her to get into Bronte's truck to keep up the appearance of Steve's lie. How they must have laughed over that one.

Shortly after the Reno trip, Steve emailed that he and Mitzi were engaged, that he'd just told the kids, that they seemed fine with it, and that there probably wouldn't be a wedding for more than a year.

I had expected this news eventually, but even I was surprised at how quickly he had rushed to put a ring on her finger. And I could only guess at the pleasure with which Steve had written to tell me about it. *I win!* his subtext seemed to say. *I found happiness before you did!* That may have stung, but what really hurt was that the kids "seemed fine with it." And the notion that Mitzi would have anything to do with raising my children made me physically ill.

It came as no surprise when Steve called a few days later to chat. No doubt he wanted to enjoy whatever effect his message had had on me. "You got my email?" he began.

"I did," I finally said. Long pause. "I guess congratulations are in order. I think you'll be perfect together. In fact, you deserve each other."

Steve chuckled. "You mean the dark knight and his evil princess?"

"Your words, not mine."

He went on to explain that although they hadn't set a date, they planned to move back to St. Helena within a few months and buy a five-bedroom house so that all the kids could have their own rooms. I thought about the prospect of living in the same town with the new Mrs. Beckwith. Back when we were friends, people had often confused us or thought we were related. Now we would also share the same man's last name. The next day, I contacted the Napa Superior Court to begin the process of returning to my maiden name of Mickelwait.

June, again. It was hard to believe that it had been a whole year since our divorce had become final. Steve and I were still so entrenched—family-wise, financially, emotionally. Would this anxiety and anger never run its course?

"I honestly don't think we'll be done with this until one of us dies," I complained to my friend and neighbor, Jane.

"It'll be better once the kids are on their own," she said. "You just have to get through college and two weddings." Those years stretched out before me like a jail sentence.

Besides being the first anniversary of our divorce, this month was significant for another reason. According to our marital settlement agreement, Steve had been given one year to get my name off the four loans we shared. That year was up. I sent him an email reminding him of this and then hunkered down and waited for either shrapnel or bullshit to fly.

Two days later Steve emailed to explain that because his recent employment record had been so spotty, he couldn't expect any bank to refinance the loans. He asked for my patience as he worked to "rebuild his resources." And so began the postdivorce conflict phase, in which I tried to enforce the terms to which Steve had agreed in our settlement. He couldn't refinance the properties and refused to sell them. I could go ahead and sue him, he said, but we both knew I had neither the time nor the money. So I was resigned to wait until he could refinance, which he assured me would be within the year.

Aside from the loans—which worried me only occasionally—everything seemed stable for a while. We had a real house to live in. I had a real job. Amory was playing basketball and shooting up like a cornstalk on steroids. Bronte was pretty much gone—now that she had her own truck, she came and went as she pleased. She'd achieved an unprecedented trifecta for St. Helena's FFA, serving simultaneous terms as chapter president, sectional president, and regional vice president. She continued to ride her horse almost daily and raised sheep for auction. The wheels may have been coming off in her family life, but she would probably do well on her own out in the real world.

With Steve spending most of his time in Southern California—occasionally coming home for a few days to see the kids—I finally had a little breathing room.

Chapter 20
Fugue State

At Berkeley Haas, my contract position was due to expire. Within a few weeks of mounting another job search, I was hired to be the communications director for the Riordan Family Foundation in San Francisco.

I was already familiar with the Riordan Foundation. Its eighty-year-old chairman, Tom Riordan, was notorious for being difficult and narcissistic. And although the foundation was publicly known for supporting programs to help the poor, rehabilitate the homeless and drug addicted, and endow local arts and culture, it was whispered in nonprofit circles that Riordan really used it as a checkbook for his own conservative political causes. He was regularly pictured in the social columns with a series of ever younger wives.

I would be reporting to the program director but would have enormous autonomy, creating my own communications plan, advertising campaign, publications, and social media strategy. And although I faced an even longer commute, the job paid more. Even working full-time and freelancing on weekends, I was still struggling financially.

Around the same time, a man on Match caught my attention. Altamoda211's profile said his profession was "service industry/

entrepreneur" (a waiter, I thought). He was a New York native but lived in San Francisco and loved the outdoors. Didn't read a lot, but favored Jane Austen movies. Enjoyed nightclubs, dancing, and museums and spoke Spanish. Played the guitar and the saxophone. Loved Pablo Neruda. But it wasn't the words so much as the photos that caught my eye. Here was a man who knew how to dress and pose rakishly for the camera. Here he was, standing in front of the Museum of Modern Art. Here he was, sitting on his Vespa, a well-tailored leg extended for balance. Combine that with the Jane Austen and Neruda, and we might just have something.

In a rare moment of perfect timing, Steve had just the week before emailed to say he'd be moving back to Pope Valley fulltime, with occasional trips to Irvine as needed for work. I'd heard through the grapevine that he and Mitzi were still engaged, but things had cooled down a bit. So we were back to fifty-fifty custody at a moment when I was starting an ambitious new work routine *and* had met an interesting man.

It was around this time that the kids would return home from a weekend with Steve and casually comment about his health. "Daddy just stayed in bed, he wasn't feeling well," they said. Or "Daddy didn't go, he just wanted to stay home." From his chronic back problems to his gastric bypass surgery, Steve always seemed to have some physical ailment. And he never took care of himself. I suspected he was eating too much of all the wrong foods, wreaking havoc with his altered digestive system. Now when he came to pick up or drop off the children, I was startled to see how much he'd aged, looking much older than his sixty years. Well, it wasn't my problem anymore. My only concern was how it would affect Bronte and Amory.

In the previous two weeks, I'd emailed and spoken on the phone a few times with the man from Match. Eddie Cabrera was sixty with a voice that was both high and husky. His squeaky laugh was unbearably attractive. He called precisely when he said he would, and our conversations moved from subject to subject easily. I sensed that our lifestyles were different and that this would probably not be a relationship with long-term potential. But I felt an attraction to Eddie that I hadn't felt in a long time. I sensed we could have some fun together, for however long it lasted. We agreed to meet on Friday after work, which happened to be my last day at Haas.

By the time I left my office in Berkeley to take BART into the city, I was weighted down with two large shopping bags—the contents of my desk plus an orchid plant and a bottle of wine I'd received as going-away gifts—as well as my purse and briefcase. I lumbered off of BART at the Embarcadero station and shuffled the long block to our designated meeting place—the outdoor terrace of a restaurant at the Ferry Building. Arriving about fifteen minutes early, I found a table near the water, stashed my bags under my chair, ordered a glass of sauvignon blanc, and opened my book.

Within minutes I heard a familiar, husky voice. "Already started without me, I see." I looked up to see the man from the photos, only better looking, with wireless glasses and an impish grin. He had a newspaper folded under one arm, and I loved that we'd both arrived early prepared with something to read.

A waitress arrived, and we ordered a couple of appetizers and a nonalcoholic beer for Eddie, who didn't drink. There was that inevitable brief interlude of awkwardness and requisite small talk, but we soon settled into a real conversation. Eddie seemed shy but quick to laugh. He had short-cropped, salt-and-pepper hair that revealed a beautifully square head, like the bust of a Roman emperor. And although he was no intellectual, he had a quiet street smartness about him that was very appealing.

"So how'd the last day on the job go?" he asked.

"Kind of sad," I said. "But I'm excited to start a new chapter on Monday."

"The Riordan Foundation. That guy Tom Riordan sure is in the social pages a lot with his teenage bride."

I laughed. "Yeah. Not sure what I'm stepping into."

"Well, hopefully you'll be able to scrape it off your shoe soon enough." This guy was no fool.

"The program director said the staff gets invited to absolutely everything—openings, exhibits, fundraisers, all those things. Should be fun," I said. Eddie was so easy to look at. I felt him sizing me up too.

"Well, maybe I can be your plus-one sometime."

"Maybe you can."

Eddie had the most intriguing eyes I'd ever seen: dark brown, almost black irises circled by a chalky ring of white. Something to do with his cholesterol, he later told me. For now, I couldn't stop looking into them. He was born and raised in Spanish Harlem, he said, which explained the broad New York accent. Although he'd moved to San Francisco more than forty years before, he firmly held on to his inner-city roots. He was Puerto Rican—New Yo'Rican, he proudly called it—and I pictured him in *West Side Story*, dancing with a gang of handsome thugs.

"So, what exactly do you do in the service industry?" I finally asked.

He paused, then said, "I drive a cab." I tried to muffle any outward expression of my disappointment, but he was prepared for the look on my face. "I have my own medallion," he said. These were issued by lottery for a huge sum, and once you had one, you could earn good money each month letting another driver use your cab in the hours you weren't driving. It meant that, after he retired, he'd have guaranteed income.

Okay, I thought. Not what I'd expected. But here was a guy with a modest but sound financial plan, unlike my ex-husband. He lived lower to the ground, had a smaller economic footprint. That was appealing.

The sinking September sun cast yellow highlights on the water, and the East Bay hills took on a rosy glow. "Let's go for a walk," Eddie said suddenly and signaled for the check.

When he stood up, I got the full-body view. Not tall, but with beautiful posture, as if he were aware of female eyes assessing him. He wore a black knit jacket with interesting details on the pockets and lapels, a black polo shirt with the collar turned up, nicely tailored jeans, and a hipster version of wingtip shoes. I took it all in as if I were looking at pastries in the glass display of a bakery. We walked through the Ferry Building to Market Street, which was still bustling with office workers headed for buses, trains, and ferries. "Take my arm," Eddie whispered. I did, and felt the texture of the knit around his bicep.

As we walked along the Embarcadero and curved back onto Market Street, my head swam. The beautiful city. The delicate light. The dinnertime smells coming from the open doors of restaurants. And a handsome, smart, elegant man on my arm. A man who drove a cab. But whatever. It felt great.

I suddenly found his lips on mine in the gentlest, most sensual kiss I'd ever received. My legs buckled a bit.

Eddie finally pulled back. "I just had to go for it." He grinned.

When I'd finally caught my breath, I said, "Can we do that again?" And we did. Part of me left my body and watched us from a few feet away, imagining what the passersby must be thinking about these two people over fifty making out in the middle of a public street, and I said so aloud.

"Screw 'em," Eddie said. "I'm a man who's just met a fascinating, beautiful woman, and I just did what had to be done."

He turned and led me to the stairs that descended to the Embarcadero BART train, and kissed me again. "Call me," he said. "Sooner rather than later."

I stumbled down the stairs and waited for the train. When it arrived, I hauled my bags on board and sank into a seat near the door. For the forty-five-minute ride back to El Cerrito, then the hour-long drive to St. Helena, I was in a fugue state. I parked in the garage, fed the dog, and fell into an armchair in the living room. When was the last time I'd felt like this? Had I *ever* felt like this? It seemed ridiculous. I was fifty-five years old but feeling like I was back at summer camp in 1967 after slow dancing with my first crush to "Cherish" by the Association.

I couldn't wait to see what would come next.

On Monday morning, I took my first commute by ferry to the city. I started a new job. And apparently I had a new boyfriend. How could my life have changed so much in just three days? It felt as if I'd been dropped into a movie about someone else's life.

The Riordan Foundation office was in a high-rise on New Montgomery Street. By the time I arrived at the bank of elevators in my building, I'd walked almost a mile from the Ferry Building. I set to work familiarizing myself with files, contacts, the forty-year history of the Riordan Foundation's philanthropy, and the basic Catholic principles on which its programming was based—helping the poor and making high-quality education accessible to everyone.

Within my first week on the job, however, I could begin to see the chinks in the armor of the foundation's culture. And it soon became apparent that Tom Riordan did indeed run the place as his personal checkbook—supporting conservative causes, political candidates, and even mistresses in addition to the funding priorities described in the foundation's charter.

My boss, Monica, had worked at Riordan for nearly ten years. She'd fought the good fight, picking her battles and standing up to Tom when it mattered. But within my first month I could see her resolve weakening. Observing the shrugs, the heavy sighs, and the dramatic rolling of eyes, I was pretty sure she was planning her exit strategy. Before that happened, I needed to prove my value, to ensure my own longevity.

That first week, Eddie and I met three times for drinks after work. It was finally Steve's turn to have the kids, so I would board the last ferry at seven fifteen, which meant pulling into my driveway at about nine thirty. A quick bite, feed the dog, read for five minutes, and fall asleep, only to awaken at five o'clock the next morning and do it again. But it was worth it. After work, Eddie would be waiting for me on his Vespa at the curb in front of my building and whisk me to North Beach, to the waterfront, or to a rooftop wine bar, and the romance bloomed quickly. I'd return home in the same gauzy dream state as I had on our first date. I was so ready for something different from my life of the past few years—for something *fun*. This certainly fit the bill.

During the day, I tried to concentrate on the new job. I knew I had to make a solid first impression with this crowd and prove my value quickly. The position came with a lot of power and self-direction, not to mention a communications budget of nearly $200,000. Within the first year I would create and execute a full communications strategy, from web to print advertising. The dysfunctional office culture often meant unpleasant surprises—in staff meetings, in communiqués from Tom Riordan, in quixotic demands by the CEO—but still I awoke every morning eager to get to work. I felt as if my years of experience were finally being utilized, and I'd been given the opportunity to make a tangible difference in the way that Riordan was publicly perceived. So far, the good points outweighed the bad.

Soon, the physical chemistry between Eddie and me had gone about as far as it could go in a public place. He'd shown himself to be a man of his word, calling and showing up as promised. He felt familiar and yet exotic, and I liked that he was leaving the next step up to me.

For our fifth date, I invited him up to St. Helena for dinner. We both knew what that meant.

On Saturday night, Eddie arrived at my doorstep promptly at five, holding a grocery bag and a bouquet of big sunflowers. He walked in the door, and I nuzzled my nose into his collar, inhaling his signature vetiver scent. My palm on the back of his closely cropped head. His hands sliding down to the back pockets of my jeans and gently grabbing the flesh underneath the denim. My arms wrapped around his shoulders, pressing my breasts against his chest. Little moans of stifled pleasure. Delayed gratification. The pot that had been simmering on a low flame these past few weeks was suddenly bubbling over.

My plan had been to serve an early dinner to leave plenty of time for what would invariably follow. But we didn't even make it that far. This time there were no bystanders or onlookers as there had been on every single date in the city. It was just us and the dog, who lay sleeping, oblivious, in the corner.

Somehow we maneuvered the carpeted stairs, the hallway, the short distance to my king-sized bed. Whispers of desire and delight.

"I've been wanting this for three weeks, *mi amor*."

"Me too."

"I haven't stopped thinking about you."

"Me neither."

"You're so beautiful."

"So are you."

He laughed and sat back to look at me. "You're definitely letting me take the lead on the love talk, aren't you?"

I said nothing but pulled him down onto the bed.

Fingers and buttons and elastic and hooks and suddenly nothing but skin against my soft linen sheets. I'd been wanting Eddie for more than three weeks too, but *this*—I had been wanting *this* for years. To feel this intensity of desire, to finally say *yes* to someone and truly mean it. To give myself fully, body and soul. It just felt so good to let my heart open wide, like one of those sunflowers facing the light.

There was also Eddie's foreignness—his broad New York accent, his caramel-colored skin, his European flair for fashion. Being with him took me backward, past single parenthood, past motherhood, past marriage and mortgages and putting everyone else's needs ahead of my own. It took me back to my twenties and to Rome, to a life amid Baroque palaces where I lived day-to-day and followed my curiosity and my heart and wrote passionate, profound thoughts in my journal. I hadn't been looking for it, hadn't dared hope for it, but here it was, right in my own bed.

Eddie was a master at lovemaking. We romped and laughed and lay quietly talking and then made love some more. And then suddenly Eddie sat up and said, "I'm starving. When do we eat?" Outside my windows the light was now a bluish bruise, and I checked the clock beside my bed. Seven fifteen. We'd been in bed for two hours.

We went on a search-and-recovery mission for our clothes—tangled in sheets and tossed over furniture, like my bedroom had been the scene of a home invasion—and wandered downstairs in the darkening light. Once in the kitchen, I started pulling out ingredients—spaghetti and fresh clams, parsley and garlic.

A few days earlier, I'd asked Eddie what he'd like for dinner. Any food allergies? Any dislikes? "What about spaghetti with clam sauce?" I'd asked. It was a dish I made confidently—it wouldn't be the first time I'd made it for a new man.

"If you want spaghetti with clam sauce, I'll have to make it for you," Eddie had joked. "Nobody makes it better than me."

"Oh really?" In the end, he capitulated.

Now, as I sautéed the garlic and boiled the water for pasta, I asked, "So what's in the bag?"

"Oh, just some reinforcements. Just in case."

I put down my spatula, walked over to the grocery bag, and looked inside. I pulled out a can of Progresso clam sauce, a box of pasta, a few other items.

"You brought your own ingredients?" I was confused.

"Yeah, just as a backup." He grinned sheepishly.

"You didn't trust that I could make this meal?"

"Well, I wasn't sure." More grinning.

"No. Seriously?" I stepped back and tried to straighten my thoughts. "The first time I cook for you, and you bring your own backup meal? What is this, a competition?" I said it with a smile, but inside I was offended.

"*Mi amor*, it smells delicious. Keep going." Kissing ensued.

The past two hours had been so magical, I didn't want to ruin it now. I turned the other cheek and resumed cooking. In twenty minutes, we sat down to a platter of spaghetti, fresh clams, and freshly grated Parmesan, with a Caesar salad on the side.

When we were finished, Eddie pushed himself back from the table and wiped his mouth with his napkin. "That was amazing," he said. Then, "I'm already thinking of how to improve it."

"You bastard," I said. But I already knew: This was old-school machismo at work. I would deal with it with a sense of humor, or this relationship would perish. I could do that.

After cleaning up the kitchen, we ended up kissing again, then found our way up the stairs as before and back into my bed. We spent a mostly sleepless night replaying our earlier moves, plus a few more. The next morning I awoke with a sleep-deprived love hangover that was a lot harsher at fifty-five than any I had remembered from twenty-five or even thirty-five.

Chapter 21
Pyramid Scheme

Life at the Riordan Foundation continued to amaze me. All my previous jobs had been for nonprofit clients at the other end of the fundraising spectrum—where you groveled for every penny and spent it as if it would be your last. To have the budget to place ads, to hire designers and photographers, and to take editors or grantees out to lunch—I felt as if I had just married very well.

But, like marrying a wealthy old man for his money, it slowly became apparent that this marriage came with a steep price. Dealing with prickly personalities and daily dramas meant that every day I stepped off the elevator gingerly, wondering what new tragicomedy awaited me behind the locked black security door with the brass plaque that read *Riordan Foundation*.

It had been a year since my showdown with Bronte and Sam. At home, Bronte continued to be emotionally absent, hostile, incommunicative. But I couldn't despair entirely, because elsewhere she was thriving. Her grades were average (below average in French and English), but in Agricultural Science she was a rock star. Her science fair project—measuring Omega 3 levels in eggs from chickens fed flaxseed, proven to reduce LDL cholesterol in humans—won first place at the FFA regionals, as well as the state finals. She went on to win fourth place in the biochemistry division at the nationals in Indianapolis. She got elected vice president of the FFA that fall and was a leader at the FFA pumpkin patch, where they raised more than $10,000 selling the squash they'd grown.

I knew she'd be fine in the long term. But she acted as if I had no place in her life, and that broke my heart.

Eddie and I began to fall into a comfortable routine. On the weeks when I had the kids, we'd often meet for lunch or coffee during the workday. The weeks when they were with Steve, I'd drive down to the city on Thursday morning and park my car in Eddie's neighborhood in lower Pacific Heights, near the Muni bus barn. Then he'd drive me on his Vespa to the Riordan Foundation—my arms around his waist and my nose at the nape of his sweet-smelling neck—and pick me up that evening for the weekend. "Sexiest commute ever!" I told my friends. I loved my new double life, split between country calm and urban hustle. It pleased me to think that my friends and colleagues in each world wouldn't recognize the woman I was in the other.

And Eddie's life was indeed foreign to the world I'd lived in since my thirties. The first time he invited me to his place, I tried to prepare myself for an apartment that had long been the domain of a single male. His building was a pale green, 1920s vintage apartment complex that looked as if it hadn't been painted in decades. As I walked up the carpeted stairs—no elevator—to the fourth floor, I could feel the rotting wood depress under the carpet, and generations of cooking smells seemed to emanate from the walls.

When he opened the door, I walked into a tiny vestibule leading to four small rooms. A workout bench with barbells stood in one corner of the bedroom. The kitchen and bathroom had clearly not been renovated since the year of construction—deteriorating tiles exposing moldy lath and plaster, peeling linoleum on the floors. But the place was otherwise clean, and the walls had recently been painted a stylish taupe gray. There was an elegant microfiber couch and massive flat-screen TV in the living room.

"Welcome to my humble abode," he said, grinning sheepishly. Within ten minutes, we'd fallen into his platform bed, and didn't leave for five hours.

When we finally emerged, ravenously hungry, I strolled around the apartment while Eddie scrambled some eggs with cheese and spinach. On the gray walls were a few well-chosen framed black-and-white photos: his mother, in Puerto Rico in the forties; John Lennon, in his "Imagine" period; and the classic shot, *A Great Day in Harlem, Jazz Greats.* Eddie stood behind me and rubbed my shoulders, pointing out Art Blakey, Thelonius Monk, Sonny Rollins. Dizzy Gillespie was sticking out his tongue.

"Who's she?" I pointed to the one white woman in the group, dressed in a sexy halter dress.

"Ah, that's Marian McPartland."

My own mother had loved listening to McPartland's show, *Piano Jazz*, on NPR when she made dinner in the evenings, and something about this exchange made my heart open just a little more. Eddie was a cultural oxymoron.

After decades of Steve's overspending, I also found it appealing that Eddie lived within his means. One Saturday we were walking down California Street near Laurel Village and passed a row of condos—attractive faux-Victorian townhouses in pastel colors. "Those units sold two years ago for about two hundred and fifty thousand each," Eddie said offhandedly. He made it his business to know everything about his neighborhood.

"Wow," I said. "Too bad you didn't jump on it. That's a great price." Only in San Francisco would a condo selling for a quarter of a million dollars be considered a bargain.

"Kirsten," Eddie said, "not everyone needs to own a house."

I was gobsmacked. He was right. It said so much about me that I assumed that home ownership was essential to adulthood. Eddie was perfectly happy in his run-down, walk-up grad pad for $925 a month. Filled with thousands of dollars of expensive men's clothes. He knew his priorities.

Amory was surviving seventh grade at Robert Louis Stevenson Middle School. Not yet thirteen, he was already six feet tall and easily made the basketball team. He got invited to serve as a Safe School Ambassador, and the one class in which he excelled was history (thank you, *Total War* computer games). But he needed more direction and supervision than Bronte—he was an adolescent boy, after all—and I wasn't home as much as I needed to be. I had to trust him to get himself to and from school on his bike, to come home directly after basketball practice, to do his own homework. So much was falling between the cracks—the regular phone calls to check on him from work, from the ferry, from the car just weren't enough. More than once, Steve and I got called in for a conference with the teachers and counselor to discuss Amory's academic performance. How was I supposed to keep all these frigging balls in the air?

Every weekday morning I would leave the ferryboat and walk to Market Street.

Often there would be a text from Eddie as my ferry was rolling into its berth in the morning. *I'm near the Embarcadero, pick you up in five, mi amor.* And there he'd be waiting, my own private taxi, to drive me the mile to my corner of Market and New Montgomery Streets.

"Let me look at you, babe—I love the color of that pashmina with your eyes." (How many heterosexual men even knew what a pashmina was?) Then he'd give me a hard kiss and I'd promise to call on my way home.

I found Eddie's sense of style—his bravado and his swagger—impossibly attractive. Over the course of our romance, he bought me many gifts, usually clothing. And as much as I delighted in the things themselves, the real gift was his unerring taste. Men had bought me presents before, and I almost always cringed when opening them. I dreaded unwrapping the spangled sweater, the overly detailed leather jacket, the fussy jewelry.

With Eddie, though, I would actually love it. A thick boiled wool scarf in gray and acid green. A tiny black silk vest with covered buttons and hidden pockets. A pair of metallic Converse sneakers. One time he bought me a pair of skinny jeans that fit perfectly, when I hadn't even been at the store with him. It made me feel seen, and understood, and adored.

And I would admire him in turn. With his obsidian eyes and barrel-chested masculinity, Eddie was a Pablo Picasso doppelgänger, only with a cap of short silver hair. The intensity, the testosterone, the hands-on-hips Superman stance—they shared a romantic, Hispanic archetype. It had been so long since I'd felt this kind of chemistry.

Without the sugar rush of this new romance, I wondered if I'd be able to survive everything else that was going on in my life.

October brought its usual pleasures of burgundy-colored leaves and sad autumn smells. Steve was back sharing custody, thank God. In particular, Bronte seemed to flourish in his rural outpost—she preferred the open country, and many of her FFA friends also lived in Pope Valley. Steve and Amory built a chicken coop, which was now home to seventy-one laying chickens, and Bronte started a thriving egg business. She made deliveries all over St. Helena, keeping a detailed database of how many dozen went to each address.

When the kids stayed with me, though, the animosity between

Bronte and me seemed to grow daily. Was this just normal moth-er-daughter tension, or did she blame me for everything that had gone wrong over the past few years? I began to dread every encounter with the stranger who was inhabiting my daughter's seventeen-year-old body.

One Sunday after Eddie had stayed over on the weekend while the kids were at Steve's, I noticed he'd left a pair of running shoes next to the bed. My first instinct was to put them in the closet—hiding them, keeping my new life a secret. But then I thought: Why? Why should I hide the fact that I had a social life too, just like Steve did? It had been three years since we'd separated. I was allowed to move on. I took the shoes out and left them near my bedroom door. A subtle gesture that would let them figure it out on their own. In that moment I didn't see it for what it was: classic avoidance.

Yeah, Mom. Bad call.

A day or two later, Bronte and I clashed over some trifling thing. She had eaten an entire container of ice cream in one sitting, or some other minor infraction. When I confronted her, the argument esca-lated like a flame to lighter fluid.

"And that wasn't a friend you had over last weekend!" she sud-denly fired back, catching me completely off guard.

"What? What are you talking about?"

"You said you were having a friend stay over while we were at Daddy's. But that wasn't a 'friend,'" she said, furiously making claw-like air quotes. "It was a *man*!"

Bronte's eyes bored into mine. When was the last time she'd even looked at me? She wore the flannel pajamas I'd given her last Christmas, and her hair was tied in a sloppy knot on the top of her head. She was a beautiful girl, even when she was furious at me, which was always. But now more than ever.

"Oh, I get it," I said. "I guess I should have told you directly." A point that was now abundantly obvious to me. "Okay, yes, I'm seeing someone new. But only when you're at your dad's. I wasn't going to introduce you to him anytime soon."

"How could you *do* that? While Amory and I are still at home? Why couldn't you just wait until I'm away at college?"

"Bronte, your dad is engaged. You have a boyfriend. Even Amory has a girlfriend. Why on earth would you think I'm not allowed to date too?"

"Because you're our *mom!*" She was crying now. "And he's a *stranger!*"

"Wait a minute," I said. I walked around the kitchen counter to get closer, but Bronte backed away. "Your dad is engaged to my former close friend, and you think this is *worse?*"

"Yes!" she wailed. "Mitzi's a friend, I know her! I don't want to meet some strange man you picked up somewhere."

"Bronte, that's just not fair."

"I don't *care* if it's fair! It's how I feel." She stared at me with angry, reddened eyes. "All you had to do was wait one more year, until I went away. Just one year! You're so selfish. All you do is think of yourself!" And she stomped upstairs, slamming the door to her room. Steve's own words, now repeated by our daughter, echoed in my head.

The next day I returned home from work and poked my head into Bronte's room. The entire room had been stripped—the bed was still there, but the bedding, the desk, the chair, the bookshelves, and everything else was gone. I felt the adrenaline wash over me like a cold shower. She'd needed a second person to help her move the bigger items. Probably Sam. The bare white walls and stained gray carpet suddenly seemed like a projection of my own cold heart. I could feel the many cantilevers of my double life falling down around me. Had she decamped to Steve's? Or moved in with Sam?

"No, she's with me." I could hear the satisfaction in Steve's voice. He'd clearly been expecting my call.

Stunned silence on my end.

"I knew you two weren't getting along, so I told her she could stay with me fulltime for a while."

"Oh, you did? When I wanted to cancel our country club membership, you yelled at me for trying to change the terms of our settlement, but you singlehandedly decide to alter our custody agreement?" I was pacing again. I was holding the phone like a grenade to my ear. I was yelling. "Our entire divorce is built around our shared custody! You can't just switch it up because Bronte and I aren't getting along!"

"Well, she was pretty upset at you." *Me, the bad mother.*

"She's been upset at me for three years, Steve. You can't take these matters into your own hands without any mutual discussion. Give me a fucking break!"

A pause. "Yeah, I guess I should've called you first."

"You think?"

"She says she doesn't want to move back until you stop seeing this new guy," he said softly. He must have been proud of his daughter—she'd learned her manipulation techniques from him.

Of course I dragged Bronte to the therapist with me—not Patricia, who had moderated my separation from Steve, but a new woman, Barbara, who was the psychological counselor at the high school. What was I expecting? That Bronte would suddenly break the brittle shell of her teenaged fury and fall into my arms with words of forgiveness? The session was just a more public performance of our domestic drama, with Bronte railing against me for my selfish act of dating someone other than her father.

No matter what I said, no matter how well crafted my logic, she always returned to the same refrain: *I don't care if it's fair. It's how I feel.* Her feelings trumped everything else. Just like her dad's.

When our fifty minutes were up, Barbara asked Bronte to leave the room so she could have a few words with me alone. "I know this is frustrating," she said. "Dealing with the irrational feelings of teenagers is our cross to bear until the cerebral cortex is fully formed by their midtwenties."

I nodded with resignation. That was eight years away. Would I live that long?

"But whatever you do," Barbara added, "do *not* give in to her demand. You deserve happiness too, and for you to give that up for her would just launch a pattern of more demands. Stay strong."

I looked at her, gratitude beaming from my weary smile. Finally, someone who was on my side.

Meanwhile, communications with Steve were as frustrating as ever. He was relishing this, being the intermediary between Bronte and me. "I'll try to be part of the solution as best I can," he said in a voice of calm and reason. "I'd suggest you make your contact with Bronte as loving and understanding as possible." He was so happy to be the good, helpful father. Making me the unreliable, promiscuous mother.

"I agree," I said. "But understand this: I've kept my social life completely discreet from the kids for four years. I've often put it on the back burner completely just so Bronte can drop in at her convenience. I've told both Bronte and Amory that I don't plan to marry this guy or even introduce him to them for now. They're still number one in my priorities."

Steve made fake sympathetic noises.

"Clearly, this issue runs deeper and has, I think, a lot to do with her anger and fear about our moving on and new relationships," I continued. "Surely you know that your relationship with Mitzi is part of this."

"Hey, don't put this on me," Steve said, and I could hear his smile over the phone. "I don't think she's troubled by my relationship with Mitzi. But I appreciate your point about fear of new relationships. I'll do my part to minimize that from my end."

Hmmm. How will you do that when you've decided to marry my former close friend? I thought. The last I'd heard, they were still engaged. But through the black screen of my rage, I knew how futile it would be to make Bronte move back. Honestly, I didn't even want her back until her anger abated. It might be a bit of a relief to take a break. The next week I called Steve. "She can stay with you fulltime until the end of the school year," I said. "But Amory stays with me."

Eddie's Match profile had said he was sixty years old, and he looked damned good for his age. After he'd given me a gorgeous alpaca coat for my birthday, I wrote him a thank-you note. Since I'd forgotten his actual street address, I looked it up online. *Eddie Cabrera, 65 years old*, the listing read. I remembered the time, not long after we'd met, when he'd pulled out his driver's license as identification on some outing. I'd playfully reached for it, wanting to see his photo, and he grabbed it back as if his life had depended on it. Now I knew why.

The next time Eddie stayed over at my place, I went upstairs to fetch something while he sat reading the paper at the kitchen table. When I walked into my bedroom, I spotted his wallet lying nakedly on the nightstand. Of course I opened it and looked at the date. February 11, 1945, it read. Google had been right: He'd shaved five years off his age. What else might he be lying about?

When I confronted him, gently, I wasn't surprised when he reacted defensively. "How dare you stalk me on Google and look in my wallet!" he yelled.

"Eddie, it's bad enough for women to lie about their age," I insisted. "But on a man, it's like a bad comb-over. It's unseemly." He nodded grudgingly, and we didn't discuss it again.

Life continued to be a delicate balance, a pyramid scheme of my various lives—as a mom, a professional, and a woman with a social life. As long as I paid attention and took my vitamins, I told myself, I could carry it off.

This fantasy lasted until I called Bronte at Steve's one Thursday night in November and asked to speak to him. He owed me two months of shared expenses and wasn't answering my emails.

"He's not here," she said glumly. The very act of talking to me was depressing to her.

"Well, when will he be back?"

"Um, Sunday night?"

"Sunday? That's three days away! Where did he go?"

"He's at Mitzi's."

"In Southern California?"

"That's where she lives." The letters D-U-H were silent.

So my daughter was living by herself (or, more likely, with Sam) for days at a stretch while Steve visited his fiancée five hundred miles away. The man who had fought me tooth and nail for shared custody was now leaving one of our minor children to her own devices in a remote area. Who knew if she was even going to school?

On my call to Steve's cell phone, more yelling ensued. More impasses were reached. "She'll be eighteen in a year," he advised me. "She's almost an adult."

I wanted to kill the man. Again.

Between my fractured family and my dysfunctional workplace, I tried to focus on the small graces and minor achievements of each day. The collegial praise for a new Riordan ad. The sardonic company of our program team, a little island of camaraderie amid the unpredictable whims and demands of Tom Riordan. If I focused on each task, each hour, I could see the good fortune in my current life. But if I ever ventured into big-picture territory, it was all too obvious that the wheels were coming off.

I called Eddie every day from the car after work, as I was driving home from the ferry. I'd tell him about my day at Riordan, and he'd tell me about his workout and what he was making for dinner. Before too long, I began to mourn the predictable pattern of our conversations, but they were like placeholders until I could see him again. Driving to his apartment, or waiting for him to show up at my front door, I imagined the smell of his cologne and the feel of his warm neck against my lips. Once we were actually together, though, the room just seemed to get smaller and louder.

Once again, I had landed myself an alpha male. They were so attractive in the beginning—suave and smooth and in control. And then the polish wore off, and I was left with just the controlling part. I was a strong woman—why did I fall for this every time? And where was the line between compromise and passivity? Still, with Eddie I'd been aiming to be different. After twenty-two years of trying to be the voice of reason in the face of Steve's domineering stance, I was ready to push back when it felt like that line had been crossed. This time, there were no kids to worry about fighting in front of. For Eddie, who came from a more emotional and dramatic culture, this was normal conversation. But for me it was stressful and felt like failure.

Steve and I had agreed to start meeting with another local mediator to work out our disagreements about the loans—which still had my name on them, because Steve couldn't refinance and refused to sell. But even finding time to get together in the same room was nearly impossible, between my thirteen-hour days and his extended periods in Southern California. We emailed back and forth endlessly, trying to find a weekday or evening when we might be able to meet with the mediator. Then, as if adding that he'd just gotten his hair cut, he dropped the bombshell that he'd recently undergone emergency heart surgery and now had a pacemaker implanted. Our children had been staying with him at the time.

I sat in my office and gazed out at the ruby neon sign of the Palace Hotel, a few shredded clouds passing behind it in the late-afternoon sky. How had it come to this, leaving our kids alone as one parent was rushed into heart surgery while the other remained oblivious, just a few miles away?

In mid-December, I had just dropped Amory off at the high school gym for a basketball game. The plan had been for Steve to pick him up later and take him home for the weekend. As I pulled into the garage, my cell phone rang.

"I'm going to need you to keep Amory this week," Steve said. He was having trouble speaking. His words came out in little gasps.

"What's wrong?"

"I'm having a little intestinal problem," he whispered. "I've just checked myself into the ER."

I was used to Steve's physical crises. Our marriage had been full of trips to the ER, usually for problems that Steve had ignored until they became unbearable.

"You don't sound good," I said. "Is there anything I can do?"

"Just keep Amory until I can get home," Steve said, and his voice broke.

"Yeah, yeah, of course. But let me know when you can that everything's all right. Okay?"

"Yeah, sure. I gotta go."

The next morning Steve's daughter Samantha called. I hadn't spoken to her since the divorce.

"I'm at the hospital with Dad," she said.

Samantha lived in Grass Valley, three hours away. This was alarming.

"They admitted him last night. They're still doing a lot of tests, but I spoke with the doctor this morning. He said it's cancer."

Everything froze as I stood at the kitchen counter.

"You know, he had gastric bypass surgery a few years ago," I tried, "and he was supposed to eat only four ounces at a time. But he still consumes enormous quantities of food. He's probably just ruptured something."

"Kirsten," Samantha said. "It's stage four colon cancer."

"What?" I couldn't seem to get the words past my ears and into my brain.

"Listen, I've got to get back to his room. I'll call you later when I know more, okay?"

"Yes, okay. Thanks for letting me know."

I hung up the phone and stood there, blinking. I thought of all the times I'd wished Steve dead.

It was a Friday, so Eddie picked me up after work on the Vespa and we rode over to Union Square, where we bought mochas and pastries and sat and watched the skaters on the holiday ice rink. Amory would be staying at a friend's overnight, and Bronte was still living at Steve's. I had a day to figure out what to say to them.

"Holy Mother of God," Eddie said when I told him. "What are you going to do?"

"There's nothing I *can* do, except wait and see what happens," I said. "My least favorite thing in the world."

We drove back to Eddie's apartment and fell into bed. I can't say why—maybe it was some life force thing or maybe I am just a terrible person—but the sex was more passionate than it had been in weeks. I do know that there was a tiny voice buried deep in my brain that told me that the marathon race of my divorce would soon be over. And for one second, before I banished the thought from my mind with shame, I felt a twinge of relief that almost approached a sense of victory.

Part III

Chapter 22
Requiem and Raw Sewage

A few days later, Eddie broke up with me. Christmas was two weeks away. My chamber group was in final rehearsals for our holiday concert, putting the finishing touches on Fauré's *Requiem* and selections from *Messiah*. It wasn't lost on me that *Requiem* was part of the Catholic mass for the dead and that *Messiah* was about rebirth. That night I was sitting in my driveway, the phone to my ear, and Eddie was telling me that he didn't want to compete for my time anymore.

"You've got this monster job, and your kids, and then you even have to work on the weekends," he said. "I want to be with someone who can pick up and run away for the weekend, no questions asked."

I sat silent, processing.

"I mean, I admire how hard you're working, babe, I really do. I tell people about you all the time, and they can't believe all the things you handle. And now your ex's illness—I don't want to be one more thing fighting for your attention."

Long silence. Eddie's place on my priority list was not the most pressing issue in my mind at the moment. It was just one more thing to struggle with, to make sense of, to have feelings about. It exhausted me. Of course Eddie would see Steve's illness as competition.

"I totally understand," I finally said. And I did. I think he was surprised not to get even a little fight out of me. "I've got a lot of plates spinning right now. I get it that you don't want to live this way too."

We hung up, wishing each other well.

A big part of me was sad: no more Vespa rides or romps in the grad pad. But another part of me was relieved. I knew the relationship promised no long-term future, with our polar opposite lives, so why put off the inevitable? There was also the issue of pride: In my whole romantic history, I had never begged a man to take me back. My pattern was usually to leave them before they left me. Either way, my pride stayed intact.

By four o'clock the next afternoon, I had a text from Eddie. "I miss you already," it said. He called off the breakup. That's when I understood that he hadn't really intended to break up with me at all. He'd just wanted to fight about it.

Steve would remain in the hospital for a week. His eldest daughter, Lisa, had joined Samantha and, between the two girls, I got regular communiqués about his condition. Serendipitously, they both happened to have settled in the Grass Valley area, near the farm, but for now they were needed at Pope Valley. An oncologist had been brought in to discuss therapeutic options, and at first Steve had refused to consider chemotherapy. But by the end of the week he had relented—he wasn't ready to die. With the right therapies, the doctor told him, he could live another five to six years.

Bronte, who was seventeen and still living at Steve's, had to be told, of course. But with Amory, who was just fourteen and living fulltime with me, I softened the message. His dad was very sick, I said, but under the care of good doctors. Amory would eventually have to be told about the four stages—that there wasn't a stage after four—but I assumed that Steve would be doing that. Had our positions been reversed, I wouldn't have wanted Steve to tell him for me.

I called Bronte to see what she knew but, as usual, she didn't want to hear anything from me. She'd already learned the basics from Lisa and Samantha and had no interest in her mother's support. Within a few days, Julie, the youngest of Steve's first set of daughters, had flown down from Portland to join the group. They set up camp at Steve's tiny house in Pope Valley, and I was glad that Bronte would have three of her older sisters around. Michaela, the third eldest daughter, remained in Vancouver, Washington.

While Steve was still hospitalized, Lisa called to brief me. Steve would be going in for surgery—the first of several operations—but could be released on Saturday. Could I bring Amory up for a visit? Of course I could.

Then I asked the question I'd been afraid to ask. "Does he have health insurance?"

There was a pause. "I don't think so," Lisa said. I moaned slightly under my breath.

"There's something else," she said. "He and Mitzi have reconciled. The engagement's back on." Apparently, they'd broken up at some point, but of course no one had told me.

I almost laughed but restrained myself. I wanted to think that Mitzi chose to be by Steve's side in his hour of need but . . . no, I didn't. I could not imagine that her timing was related to anything but marrying a man with lots of property and retirement savings who had just been given a death sentence.

"What do *you* think of her?" Lisa said.

I thought she'd never ask.

"Hello?" Steve answered in a weak voice. Thank God. I had wanted to give him some time to settle in after returning from the hospital. Then, after a week, I'd started emailing him, and he'd never responded. Now he answered on the second ring.

I had been lying awake at night wondering about all the

unknowns—how, if he should die, I would be able to support two kids on my own. Was there life insurance? Would there be a trust? When we'd divorced, I knew he'd received the bulk of our ample retirement funds, but how much of that was left? Since then he had bought two motorcycles and an RV and taken both kids—plus Mitzi's family—to Club Med. Lying in the dark, I would fumble with the feeble abacus in my brain, but I had no idea what Steve's bank account looked like. I *did* know what my own bank account looked like, and it was definitely not enough to support a family of three for the next eight years. There were small college funds for both kids—maybe enough for two years of school for each of them—but what about living expenses, healthcare, keeping us in this expensive town until they were both launched? I was getting no spousal or child support, but at least Steve and I were splitting the kids' expenses. What would I do when that was gone too?

"I'm so glad I caught you," I said. "How are you feeling?"

He sighed. "I've been better."

"Well, um, I was thinking we should really sit down and talk about the kids, given your diagnosis."

"Talk about what?" he asked, his voice a dull gunmetal gray.

"Well, you know . . . um, planning for the future?" This was tricky. I didn't want to sound like I'd already buried him.

"What are you talking about?"

"Well, we both know how sick you are. It just makes sense to have a conversation about, uh, worst-case scenarios and . . . "

"Kirsten, I'm not going anywhere. I've already started chemotherapy. You're jumping ahead of yourself."

"Sure, of course. But, Steve, surely you understand how worried I am. I'd just like to know what the plan is, going forward. For the kids." I always needed a plan. We all knew this. Long silence.

"Okay, fine. I need to come into town on Saturday morning. I could be at your house around eleven."

Excellent. It had been so long since we'd had a face-to-face encounter. Maybe cancer would finally be the thing that would enable us to join the same team.

On Saturday morning, I went to my usual yoga class, then figured I had just enough time to run to Napa to drop off my old cable box at the Comcast office and be back in St. Helena by eleven. With my ridiculous work schedule, Saturdays were the only days I could run errands.

I walked into the office at a little strip mall on Jefferson Street, carrying the box and attendant cables. There was no one at the counter, and the sole clerk in the store was engaged with a customer at a side table. Two young girls were playing on the carpet. "I just want to drop this off," I told the clerk, gesturing with the box in my hands. "Can someone help me do that?"

"Ma'am? You'll need to wait your turn. I'm helping this customer now, and I'll assist you when I'm through." She went back to talking about bundled rates to the woman seated in front of her. I looked at my watch. It was already ten thirty-five. If someone helped me immediately, I could get back to St. Helena by eleven. If I was even five minutes late, I worried that Steve would just leave. I didn't want to lose my chance to see him in person for another whole week or longer.

"I'm in kind of a hurry," I said. "Isn't there anyone else who can help me?" I could see through the window of the door to the back room, where two people stood chatting.

"Ma'am? I'll help you when I'm done." She went back to her sales pitch.

I walked over to the door and poked my head in. "Excuse me," I said.

"Ma'am! Ma'am! You can*not* go in there." The woman at the table was standing up now, yelling. "Our safe is back there. You are not allowed in there! I told you to wait. You can't just go bothering our other employees. I can have you removed from the store!"

Inside me, something broke, like a jar of some rotten, foul-smelling liquid being dropped onto pavement. The cancer, the job, the commute, the money worries, the divorce, the betrayals, the manipulation. Everything that I had been sealing off behind a wall of control and composure and hope for four years suddenly burst forth like a flood of raw sewage.

I turned back to face the woman. "Don't. You. Fucking. Yell at me!" I yelled back, slamming the counter with my fist. "I am a Comcast customer, and I have to be back in St. Helena for an important meeting at eleven o'clock, and you're making me wait for no fucking reason. There are two employees behind that door! Tell one of them to come out and fucking help me!" Cumulatively, it was the most I'd used the F-word, ever. I felt like a fucking fool. But I was beyond caring. The sales girl stared, and the woman and her children gaped at me, their eyes wide with alarm.

Hearing the commotion, one of the employees came out and ran behind the counter. "Miss? I'm happy to help you now." She was a woman about my age. Instead of anger or righteousness, she looked at me with genuine concern and kindness. "What can I assist you with?"

It was the kindness that completely undid me. My face crumpled. I dropped my head into my hands and began to weep. "I'm just trying to return this box," I began. *May Day, May Day!* I had lost control in front of everyone. My plane was in a death spiral.

"Miss, don't worry about it! It's fine to return the box. Just let me look up your address."

"It's not about the box," I sobbed. Searching in my purse for a tissue. Pushing my hair out of my eyes. Completely humiliated. And yet, did it even matter anymore?

"I understand, miss." Of course she had no idea what was happening, but she pretended she did.

"Thank you," I cried. "I'm so sorry, I'm not usually like this." I managed to spit out my address, but I couldn't stop sobbing. She typed furiously into her computer, frantically searching for my client account page.

"Uh-huh, uh-huh. Okay then, all set," she said, and gave me a big smile as she handed me a receipt. "You have a good day now, okay?"

"Thanks. You too." My sobs were coming so hard, I could barely form the words. I stumbled through the double doors to my car parked just in front. I glanced over my shoulder through the plate-glass windows and could see everyone in the store staring back at me, mouths in little O's. Then I drove home, twenty minutes, and cried the entire way. By the time I got home, I was out of tears. I thought.

Steve looked terrible. His clothes hung on him like bedsheets. His face was gray. His hair stood up on the back of his head from lying on a pillow, and he was dwarfed as he sat in my big striped armchair. He looked about eighty years old.

We exchanged polite small talk. Rather, I offered it, and he absorbed it like a dry sponge. The man who had played the victim for the past few years was now actually deserving of my pity.

I angled toward the hard part. The real reason I needed to see him.

"Steve, I'm worried about what's going to happen should you . . . if your condition takes a turn for the worse," I began.

He made a laughing sound, but without a smile. "I should've known you'd be thinking about money at a time like this," he said.

"That's not fair," I said. "We have two children to support. It's only natural that I'd want to know how we're going to make this work going forward."

"You don't need to worry, Kirsten. The kids will be taken care of."

"How? Do you have life insurance? Will there be a trust?"

"I don't have to discuss the details with you. I love my kids, and I wouldn't leave them without resources."

"It would just help me to know what the plan is."

"Look. I'm not dying. The doctor has told me that, as long as I continue with the chemo, I can live to a ripe old age."

"Well, that's good news." *Also hard to believe.*

Suddenly his face crumpled, as mine had in the Comcast office. He put his head in his hands and silently wept. It's so hard to watch a man cry.

"Are you in pain?" I asked.

"No," he whispered. "I'm just scared."

"But I thought you said you aren't dying?"

"Well, we never know, do we?"

"So what should I say to the kids?"

"It's not really your place to say anything, Kirsten. Isn't that my job?"

"But Amory has questions."

"Then tell him to ask me."

We sat like that for a few minutes in silence, then Steve got up and made his way to the front door. As he turned to leave, I said, "Listen, Steve."

"Yeah?" His bony hands hung at his sides, like a marionette's. The lines from his mouth to his jaw, like a Charlie McCarthy puppet.

"I just want to say . . ." And now I was fighting back tears too. Again. "I'm just really sorry. I know I've hurt you in the past, and I'm sorry for any pain I've caused you." Justified or not, I *had* been the cause of at least some of his suffering since I'd ended the marriage.

He looked me in the eye. It was the perfect moment for a mutual absolution. I waited, hoping for his apology too.

"Thanks," he said. "I really appreciate that." Then he shuffled to his car.

More than ever, I felt like I was running a marathon. I'd remind myself how lucky I was to have a job, a good job, even though it was so far away—and find moments of beauty to sustain me every day. Hot air balloons rising in the fog as I passed through Yountville at dawn. San Francisco glinting in the sun as my ferry approached, white like the marble of ancient Rome. The smell of coffee and sugar as I passed the open door of a Starbucks. Most importantly, I was earning a regular salary, plus receiving income from my freelancing work on evenings and weekends. I had good benefits for the kids and me. I didn't have to worry how the mortgage would get paid each month. I was killing myself with overwork, but it was absolutely worth it.

Every day brought an unspoken agreement with myself that I would see the glass as half-full and find a source of gratitude. It felt as if I was being tested spiritually to rise above my circumstances. Or else I was just some sort of fragile Tennessee Williams character, walking a tightrope of fantasy. One thing was certain: I was afraid to look down. Lurking just behind my gratitude and moments-of-beauty rituals was a bottomless pit of despair and fear. As long as I kept my eyes on the road and my head in the clouds, I could maintain the balancing act. Or so I hoped.

Eddie used to tell me how, in the early sixties, he and his friends would go out all night salsa dancing in the clubs of Spanish Harlem. I pictured their skinny ties and sharkskin suits, and the girls all looking like the young Rita Moreno. Spring had arrived, and with it a feeling of flirty optimism. "We should try it sometime," he said. "There are clubs in the Mission where they give lessons and then you can stay for the live music." I was dying to go dancing with Eddie, but he had been born with salsa in his blood and, while I was a pretty good dancer, I knew I wouldn't be able to keep up on the first try. And I didn't want to embarrass both of us by looking like a novice in public.

On one of the Cuban CDs Eddie had given me, I found a song with a slow, steady beat that went on forever. It would be perfect for learning some basic steps, to find our rhythm together. I frequently mentioned it to Eddie, wanting to try a half hour of dancing around my living room. But he was never in the mood.

One day as Eddie and I were unloading groceries in his kitchen, a fast, frenetic salsa song came on the radio. He grabbed me by the small of my back and spun me around, his feet marking out a fancy pattern on the floor. I tried to follow, but within thirty seconds, he pulled away. "You're hopeless!" he laughed.

"Give me a break—that was thirty seconds! Nobody can learn to dance that fast."

"Nah, you flunked!"

"Come on, Eddie. Let's try again."

But Eddie was done. He never brought up salsa dancing again. I'd missed my chance.

And yet, no matter how often our words flew past each other without connecting midair, no matter how frustrated I felt when I hung up the phone, there was something that happened when we were in bed that kept me coming back for more. His smart-ass irascibility fell away. My judgment and perfectionism melted. And there we were, two people naked in body and soul, whispering intimacies and being kind to each other. The only way I can describe it is a heart connection. I actually felt as if our hearts were pulled together and touching, like magnets. I was addicted to the feeling. And I was willing to tolerate even Eddie's most insensitive behavior in the anticipation of more of it. Or was that just the by-product of good sex?

One evening I got a phone call from Bronte, in tears. "I can't do this anymore," she wailed. "Daddy's in the big bedroom so he can be near the bathroom, and Julie and I are squished in the tiny bedroom." Julie, in her late thirties, was Steve's youngest daughter from his first marriage. She'd graciously agreed to take a quarter off from school to come care for her dad and had moved into the Pope Valley house with Steve and Bronte.

"I feel like the maid around here," Bronte whined. "I'm doing all the grocery shopping, all the cleaning up, everything."

Welcome to my world, I wanted to say, but held my tongue. "But, sweetie, Julie's there," I said instead. "Isn't she taking care of things?"

"No!" came the pathetic voice again. "She's too busy dealing with the hospital and trying to get insurance. It's all on me!"

"Bronte, why are you sharing a tiny room with Julie when you've got your own bedroom here? Why don't you come home for a while?"

"That's what I want to do," she sniffed.

"Well, tell your dad you need a little break," I said. "Your room is here waiting for you."

By the time I got home the next evening, Bronte was on the couch watching TV, as if she'd never left. It had been nearly a year since she'd moved to Steve's fulltime. She still seemed as sullen as before, but I didn't care. Seeing her back home made my heart swell.

By Saturday, however, I'd heard from Steve. "Can I come over and talk to Bronte?" he asked. "It's important."

"Sure, okay." *What fresh hell is this?* I thought.

Once again, Steve sat in the big armchair looking small and frail, and once again he cried. Julie had driven him over, and she and Bronte sat on the sofa.

"I can't do this without Bronte," Steve half whispered. "Of all my daughters, I'm closest to her, and I need her with me right now."

Alarmed, I looked over at Julie, who nodded. "It's okay, Julie knows," Steve said. She knew that Steve preferred Bronte over his other daughters? This wasn't healthy.

Steve outlined all the ways that things would change around the house if Bronte would only come back. "Honey, I really need you there," he repeated, his voice still shaking.

Bronte sat with her arms crossed, her usual position of defense. But when I turned and looked over at her, there were tears rolling down her cheeks.

"Steve, this is a lot for a girl her age to deal with," I said. "A little break . . ."

"It's okay, Mom," Bronte said. "I'll go back."

"Are you sure?"

"Yep."

The next day, I watched my seventeen-year-old daughter pack up her duffel again and drive away. I felt as if I were sending her off to war.

Somehow, we'd managed to get through the holidays with no major collateral damage. After all the expensive hoopla of Christmas, New Year's always came to me like a relief. When the children were little, Steve and I had created a "grown-ups only" way to celebrate. We'd do confetti and noisemakers with the kids, and put them to bed. Then we'd lay out a feast of champagne, smoked salmon, and caviar and watch some preselected vintage movie. We'd be in bed well before eleven.

It was a tradition I kept even after I was single again—minus the caviar. And Eddie loved the idea. With both kids at Steve's, we bought two enormous cracked Dungeness crabs and a bottle of champagne and sat down to watch *The Lost City* on DVR, limbs entwined on my sofa. Eddie had seen it at least twice before, so he repeatedly paused the movie to give me his own narration. Sometimes he just talked over the dialogue.

"Babe," I finally said.

"What?"

"Would you rather just tell me the whole story yourself?"

"No, I'm just giving you background. You know, I've read a lot about Cuba in the fifties."

"It's very annoying."

"Fine. I'll keep my knowledge to myself." We watched the rest of the movie in relative silence.

When the movie was finally over, I told Eddie to stay put, and I scampered upstairs, where I'd arranged white votive candles on every windowsill, every cabinet, every table in my bedroom. It took me about ten minutes to light all hundred and fifty candles, but the room fell into a magnificent, flickering yellow glow. I couldn't believe how beautiful it looked.

I went downstairs and took Eddie by the hand and walked him upstairs. I opened the double doors to my bedroom, which, if you squinted a bit, looked like a lamplit opera set from the Baroque era. "Happy New Year, baby," I said. We kissed. Then Eddie excused himself to go brush his teeth, while I got under the covers.

When Eddie returned, he climbed into bed and rolled onto his side, away from me. I snuggled my naked body against his back and wrapped my arm around his ribs. Time passed. I began stroking his chest and kissing the back of his neck. All quiet on the Western front. Finally he said, "I'm just really tired."

Tired? A hundred and fifty votive candles, and you're too tired? I lay back, confused. In twenty-two years of marriage, I had been too tired many times. But Steve had never been. In my thirty-five plus years of sexual activity, no man had ever just turned over and ignored me. What felt like a blatant, personal rejection took me right back to the insecure pangs of middle school.

I lay there for a while, a hard lump in my throat, listening to the sound of Eddie's breathing, trying to determine if it was sleeping breath or just lying-there breath. He didn't seem angry from our exchange during the movie. He just seemed uninterested. Finally, I got up and blew out every candle, one by one by one, feeling more shame with each extinguished flame. It took about five minutes. Then I took my pillow and walked across the hall to Amory's empty room, where I bedded down for the night. The humiliation stung in my eyes, my ears, my heart.

The next morning, the door flew open with a bang. "Get in here,"

Eddie said, and pulled me back to my big bed. We lay there, snuggling, but it was clear nothing more would be happening.

"I've got to tell you," I finally said. "You really hurt my feelings last night."

"Well, if it makes you feel any better, I barely slept either," Eddie said.

No, it didn't make me feel better.

"Why were you so uninterested?" I asked.

"Babe, I was just tired."

"It was New Year's Eve. I spent a lot of time lighting those candles. I thought it would be really special."

The silence was so long, I thought he'd fallen asleep again. Finally he said, "I forgot my Levitra."

I'd known that Eddie took Levitra for, as they say in the ads, erectile dysfunction. As I'd long since learned, even the most robust man in his sixties usually needed a little help, and I was fine with that. But he'd always anticipated the event and made it a seamless transition. And who forgets their Levitra on New Year's Eve, anyway?

"All you had to do was tell me," I said. "Instead, you rejected me."

He rolled onto his back and stared at the ceiling. "Sometimes I shouldn't need to spell everything out," he said. Which was not the first time I suspected we were speaking in different codes.

Chapter 23
Indemnification

One day as I was sitting across from Monica's desk for our weekly check-in meeting, she asked me about a project she'd apparently described the week before. I looked at her blankly. I had absolutely no recollection of what she was talking about. I knew I was having short-term memory problems—wasn't every woman over fifty?—but lately whole conversations seemed to be evaporating. Monica stared back at me, her irritation palpable.

"Kirsten, if I have to repeat myself one more time for you, we're going to have a serious problem," she snapped. Monica didn't suffer fools gladly.

The following week, I was in my doctor's office for an annual checkup. She did the routine exams and asked endless questions about my diet, digestion, vices, and sleep habits. She finally sat back on her stool and crossed her legs. "Anything else going on?" she asked.

"Well, my short-term memory seems to be completely shot," I said. "Just one more benefit of menopause, I guess. But none of the over-the-counter or herbal remedies seem to help." She made a few notes on her clipboard. "Tell me about your lifestyle," she said.

I told her. The bitter divorce, the moving twice in ten months, the five-hour daily round-trip commute, the taxing job environment, the freelancing on weekends, the conflict with Bronte. Wow, it did sound like a lot.

"Kirsten, that's not menopause," she said. "That's stress. Your brain can't handle any more."

I laughed. "Any suggestions?" We talked about meditation, about where I might scale down my life (nowhere), about giving myself just a little more breathing room wherever I could find it. There were no real solutions, to be honest—what was I supposed to do, go work at a local winery for $15 an hour? But the fact that someone had just acknowledged the impossibility of my task—to support my kids and myself at a job sixty miles from home—made me feel infinitely better. And it made me realize just how much I *was* doing. Memory problems or no, it seemed I was kind of a badass.

It was just Amory and me at home now. At fourteen he had, by necessity, an incredible degree of independence. I'd wake him up on my way out the door in the mornings, but he had to get himself to and from school, make his own lunches, get to basketball practice, and get home again. I usually called in the afternoons to check in, but by the time I pulled into the garage at seven fifteen, he'd already made his own dinner—usually mac and cheese or pizza. He'd taken to eating most of his meals in his room, and even when we were both home, we seemed to live in separate universes. But he was still the sensitive, affectionate kid he'd always been.

Sometimes, I'd drag myself through the kitchen door after a bad commute and find Amory cooking, with the television on the counter tuned to the cartoon channel or Comedy Central. He'd see my tote bags and my tired expression and say, in a Stuart Smalley voice, "Does somebody need a hug?" Then he'd open his arms wide and give me a tight embrace, always waiting for me to let go first. How did he know how important that was, to hang on until I finally pulled away?

It was a strange, almost paternal gesture, and sometimes I worried that Amory was feeling too much pressure to be the man of the family. But I was so grateful to have him—he made me laugh, and he didn't push boundaries the way so many teenagers did. I actually looked forward to seeing him at the end of the day, and I suspected he felt the same about me. Some evenings we'd play Wii or watch the History Channel together, the dog gently snoring in the corner. They were among the happiest moments of my life in those days.

As the chinks in our communication began to deepen, it became more difficult to deny that my fondness for Eddie was rooted in physical attraction and great sex. Until now, the insensitive comments could usually be assuaged by an afternoon of lovemaking or even just walking down the street together, my arm tightly linked around his bicep.

One day I was standing on the corner at Union Square waiting to meet Eddie for lunch—the exact corner where he had texted he'd be waiting for me. I spotted him crossing the intersection diagonally, looking over his shoulder at the traffic stopped at the light. This had happened repeatedly—he'd tell me to meet him on one corner, but there he'd be on the corner opposite. It suddenly dawned on me: He always positioned me in a spot where I could watch him approaching, appreciating the view. I wondered if he was even aware of the conceit or if it was just another aspect of his lifelong machismo. It made me laugh, but I didn't let on. "When you go for the sizzle," the saying goes, "the steak might be tough." Why was it always a trade-off?

By April, my home phone had begun to ring. A lot. While I was at work, messages were being left from banks, informing me that the two Modesto rental properties that Steve and I owned were in default and were headed for foreclosure. Apparently Steve's return to Pope Valley from Southern California had been prompted by his return to unemployment, or at least underemployment. And since he'd been sick, he'd apparently stopped paying the mortgages altogether.

Thus began my third job: to try and extricate myself from the swamp of financial ruin that Steve was pulling us into. Because the bank statements and bills were being sent to him, I'd had no idea that he was defaulting on the payments, though he had continued to collect rent from the tenants. I also had no access to account numbers, contact info, anything. It had been nearly two years since our divorce—a year past the deadline at which Steve was supposed to sell or refinance the properties to remove my name from the loans. I'd already signed quitclaim deeds for all of them, but the banks didn't care. They just wanted their money, and my name was still on their records.

I frantically ordered an online credit report. My score, which had been in the B range when I'd last checked, was now in D territory. It was already happening—the house of cards was falling. Steve wasn't content to jump off the cliff himself; he was pulling me down with him.

"Don't worry, I'm working with the banks" was Steve's response to my shrill calls. "Besides, I read that it's really more advantageous to foreclose than short sell."

"So you're planning to foreclose? Are you kidding me?"

"Not necessarily. I'm just saying that it's not as bad as you think."

It was worse than I'd thought. And between the effects of chemo on Steve's memory and my already failing sense of recall, our communication skills were at an all-time low. His emails were full of typos and non sequiturs, and the facts constantly changed. It didn't really matter—I was dealing with a moving target. It had taken me too long to realize that I needed to document every conversation in writing.

Finally, I took matters into my own hands and started looking up Modesto real estate agents who specialized in short sales, hoping to sell our two properties there. Steve's furious reaction wasn't unexpected, but I didn't care. "I'm handling this!" he shouted. "*My* name is first on these loans. It's *my* responsibility to deal with it."

"But in the meantime, you're ruining my credit and possibly leaving me as the responsible party if you default."

One of the two properties soon went into foreclosure. Within a few weeks, Steve paid the minimum amount to bring it out of arrears, and the sale was called off. Meanwhile, I was spending every free moment on my lunch hours calling lenders and writing letters. I filed a "divorce alert" with the three credit bureaus, asking for leniency on my ratings. I received form letters in reply, essentially saying *we can't help you*. They didn't care about divorce. If my name was on the loans, I was financially liable. The only way to remove my name was by selling or refinancing the properties. And I couldn't do that without Steve's consent.

One day Monica called me into her office. "Close the door," she said, which was never a good sign. She sighed. I sat down in one of the fancy club chairs facing her desk. I could see that the constant capitulation to Tom Riordan was weighing her down too. The morale of the whole office was sagging.

"Doug seems to feel that you're not carrying your weight around here." Doug was the foundation's CEO, who appeared sporadically in the office, usually carrying several shopping bags.

I was expecting bad news, but this was beyond bad. It was ridiculous.

"Are you kidding me?"

"I know, I know. But apparently he was here at five the other day, and you'd already left."

"Monica, you know I leave at four forty-five to catch the ferry. Otherwise I have to stay for another hour before the next one. And I come in before nine—I'm often the first one here. Ethan and Nicole don't even get here until ten most days." Even I could hear the whine creeping into my voice.

"That's true," she said, "and I'm going to speak to them too. But Doug took particular notice of you. He said you didn't come in until almost nine thirty the other day."

"That's because I had to stop at Speedy Print on my way in to pick up the proofs of the *Riordan Report*!" I remembered that day—as I'd walked in, Doug had made a tsk-ing sound with his tongue, as if he'd caught me sneaking in.

"You've got to remember that appearances are what count around here," Monica said. "Doug said all you do is flit around the office and come and go as you please."

My jaw was hanging open. The unfairness of this statement—we all knew who it was who came and went and flitted around the office.

"I'm just saying that it wouldn't hurt for you to stay late once in a while, just to look good," Monica was saying. "It's not about the work. You're doing fine. But you've got to be more aware of"—she paused—"the optics."

The optics. I walked back to my office shaking my head. I was already away from the house thirteen hours a day, with a teenaged son at home. I felt like I was in some bizarre Kafka play, surrounded by foreign logic. I'd already begun browsing the job boards for new employment, but now I started looking in earnest.

For the next few weeks, I stayed late one night a week. Occasionally Ethan's light was still on, but for the most part, I was working in an empty office. Doug, of course, was long gone. So I went back to leaving at four forty-five again. Let them try to fire me.

As winter leafed into spring, I began to feel sharp edges emerging in all aspects of my life. Every day at Riordan seemed to hold the possibility of some new, unpleasant surprise. And Eddie was beginning to reveal a harder, less empathic side, as well.

Over the past few months I'd been helping Monica to plan a gala event—the annual luncheon at which we would present the Riordan Award to some celebrity philanthropist whose funding areas reflected our own and would bring us some media attention. This year it was former tennis star Andre Agassi and his foundation. After an elegant sit-down lunch, there was an interview with Agassi, who was endearing, soft-spoken, and self-deprecating. As the guests filed out, we handed them signed copies of his recent autobiography and autographed tennis balls.

I was delighted to bring home one of each for Eddie who, in a previous life, had been a tennis instructor in Golden Gate Park. He avidly watched every broadcast tennis match and still had a stack of expensive rackets in his closet—though knee injuries had ended his playing a few years before. It's hard to buy casual gifts for men, especially for Eddie, who was as picky as I was. So I was pleased to have something meaningful to give him.

"What's this?" he asked when I handed him the autographed book.

"I thought you'd like it," I said. "Look, it's signed."

"I can see that," he said, flipping through it. "What do I need this for? I already know Agassi's whole life story. I don't need to read a book on it." He handed it back to me.

"Okay, so here's an autographed tennis ball. How about that?"

Eddie bounced the ball on the floor and caught it. "Geez, they don't even use real balls," he sneered. He put the ball on his dresser and didn't look at it again.

"Wow, you're a tough customer," I managed, not trying to hide my disappointment. "When someone gives you a gift, it's customary to say thank you. At least pretend to like it."

"Aw, babe, I'm sorry. It was nice of you to think of me, anyway."

But I was already getting used to Eddie's tough side. He could be totally lacking in sensitivity when he felt embarrassed or threatened. Or any other day of the week.

—

The high school cafeteria was decorated in a western theme, and everyone sat at long tables covered in plastic blue-and-white ging-ham tablecloths. It was the final event of the year for FFA, at which students would be awarded prizes for service and distinction in their roles as officers. Steve and I sat awkwardly across from each other, eating our tri-tip, cornbread, and Caesar salad from paper plates. The speeches went on forever, but I reminded myself that FFA had kept Bronte from sinking this past year, her senior year in high school. Besides her horse, it was her passion, and I didn't want to think about what she would have done without it. All the FFA students had served their parents and then sat down to eat with them, each in their navy FFA corduroy jackets with the big red-and-yellow emblem embroi-dered on the back.

When Bronte got up to help clear tables, Steve looked across at me and said, "I should tell you, I'm going to have to file for bankruptcy."

I shook my head. "You do that, and I'll be completely liable for those loans. The loans *you* agreed to take on but never took my name off of. The loans *you* stopped paying. You can't do that to me, Steve."

"I'm sorry, but I have no choice. I just can't afford them anymore."

"Then you should have sold them."

"I've been a little busy having cancer."

"Steve, I've been asking you to sell all the properties for months now, but you didn't bother. Now, if they foreclose, it'll go on my credit report as well as yours."

"I have no choice, Kirsten."

Steve's color looked a little better than the last time I'd seen him. But something odd was happening with his shirt—it was inflating and deflating. There was something under his shirt—what was that, a colostomy bag? It was completely distracting.

Suddenly we heard Bronte on stage calling us up. Apparently all the FFA students were inviting their parents to the stage to thank them for their support, handing them a single rose.

Steve and I shuffled onstage and stood awkwardly as Bronte thanked us and handed me the rose. I felt like we were a complete fraud, trying to appear as a single happy unit when the family bus had been totaled years ago. I wondered what was going through Bronte's mind—was she angry, or sad, or just happy that we were there? Was this event as humiliating or melancholy for her as it was for me? I felt as if everyone in the room could see how tragic and false we were.

And then the crowd was spilling out the doors into the night, and I watched Steve hobble off in his cowboy boots to his truck. The man I'd loved for so many years, who was now ruining my life.

The phone calls from lenders continued. My letters to the banks and credit bureaus had no effect. My only hope was that Steve would be as apathetic and careless about filing for bankruptcy as he'd been about everything else. But sooner or later, everything would fall into my lap anyway. I began making some calls to bankruptcy attorneys.

As the months passed, I began to feel less like the most beautiful woman in the world and more like the fifty-six-year-old woman I really was. "You should use more moisturizer on your legs," Eddie told me one day. "Your skin is looking a little dry and crepey." Or "You'd do us both a favor if you gave those pants away. You've got a great ass, but they don't do anything for it." One evening as we sat across from each other at the dinner table, he plucked the glasses from my nose and started wiping the lenses on his T-shirt. "They're smudged," he said. "It's a bad look."

His tone was never mean, just matter-of-fact—as if he were just doing his duty as a good citizen to point out the simple truth. But it stung all the same. Now when Eddie spoke, I jumped to conclusions or got defensive. "You're too sensitive!" he'd yell. "I'm just being honest!" And he'd shrug his shoulders like a cartoon character. But whenever I'd give him the same treatment, his feelings were hurt also. "I'm just sensitive!" he'd say. Minus the "too."

"Have you ever heard of the Golden Rule?" I finally said one day. He'd just told me he'd like to see me use less product in my hair. We were standing in his tiny kitchen, surrounded by boxes on the floor filled with vitamins and protein powders, stacks of partially read newspapers on top of the refrigerator.

"Of course I have!" He was eating an orange and threw a bit of peel into the sink, as if he were disgusted by it.

"What is it?"

Eddie laughed. "What is this, a catechism test?"

"Just tell me."

"Do unto others as you would have them do unto you." He said it in a singsong voice, like a six-year-old.

"Exactly," I said. "My point is that you're so proud of the fact that you read scriptures every day. You kiss your Madonna medal every time you put it on or take it off. And yet you fail to observe the most basic premise of the Bible. That's all."

Eddie looked at me for a long time, like he was trying to remember ever feeling any fondness for me. Then he tossed the rest of his orange in the sink and said, "You'd better watch out, or you may find yourself without a boyfriend." And he went into the other room.

Yet within a half hour, we were back on the sofa, our legs woven together on the coffee table, with Eddie narrating the U.S. Open to me as it played on the huge flat-screen TV. I knew this wasn't a healthy pattern, the constant unresolved bickering, but I wasn't ready for it to end. So we'd just press the "reset" button to end the weekend on a high note.

By June, I'd found a bankruptcy attorney in Santa Rosa who had come highly recommended by a friend in the mortgage business. I took a day off work and found my way to his office in an industrial park just off the freeway. Martin Keplinger looked like something off a vintage "Most Wanted" poster, his gray muttonchop sideburns compensating for his thinning hair. His office décor was reminiscent of the seventies, with lots of overwrought cherry furniture and potted plants on every surface. His Wild West demeanor gave the impression that it had been a toss-up whether to go to law school or work on a cattle ranch.

Keplinger scanned the paperwork I'd brought, then looked up with a crooked smile and shook his head. "Another wine country divorce gone bad," he said. I wasn't sure if that made me feel better or worse. "The first step is to determine whether you need to file Chapter Seven or Chapter Thirteen," he continued, "and that depends on the value of the assets." He went on to explain the two approaches in detail, losing me after the second sentence. I nodded and tried to look engaged, but inside I was cursing Steve for leading me to this end. It was getting easier and easier to feel sorry for myself, just a victim of Steve's bad judgment and vindictive behavior. But then I'd pull back, refusing to go there. I would not let myself be victimized by Steve. I refused.

". . . but if you file Chapter Thirteen, you'll lose your home, because you have more than seventy-five thousand dollars in equity. Which is something I imagine you'd rather not do," Martin was saying.

Lose my home? *Lose my home?* The idea of filing for bankruptcy had been bad enough. The knowledge that my credit score would tank was unsettling. But those had all been on paper—events that would be inconvenient, sure, but not life-changing. But losing the house? The anger that had been bubbling inside me for the past few years was now coming to a rolling boil.

"However," Keplinger said, "you may be able to avoid losing your house by paying a fee to the trustee."

"The trustee? Who's the trustee?"

"Someone impartial appointed by the court."

"Why do I have to pay them money? Isn't the point of bankruptcy that there are no funds to pay off loans?"

"It's just part of the Chapter Thirteen process. You thought there was a free lunch?"

Martin did some calculations. "Without knowing all the numbers, I'd estimate that your fee would be in the fifty-five-thousand-dollar range."

I left Keplinger's office and drove home in a funk. I had thought that bankruptcy, while undesirable, would at least clear me of the roughly $1.5 million in loans that were headed for me like a runaway truck. Now it was going to cost me $55,000? I didn't have that kind of money, not even close, unless I raided my already meager retirement savings. To my knowledge, those funds were safe in a bankruptcy. But how was I going to pay off the trustee?

For once, my memory rose to the challenge, and somewhere on the mountain driving back from Santa Rosa, the answer came to me: During our divorce negotiations, my lawyer, Glen Fisher, had tried to convince me to keep the properties with Steve, to maintain them jointly until the real estate market improved and we could sell them together, then split the proceeds. I had refused. I knew that several more years of having to manage anything together with Steve would drive me headlong into insanity. I chose instead to risk having my name stay on the loans. And really, I had been right. If I'd kept the properties with Steve, I'd be in the exact same position I was in today, except I wouldn't have received the proceeds from the Mee Lane house and, as a result, I wouldn't have a house of my own.

At the final hour, Glen had said, "Well, if you insist on doing it your way, at least let's include a clause that stipulates that Steve must put one hundred thousand dollars into an escrow account, to indemnify you in the event he defaults on the loans."

God bless Glen. He had just saved my hide. As soon as I got home,

I pulled out the locked file box holding all our divorce documents. I leafed through the marital settlement agreement until I found the relevant page:

> In order to provide WIFE with security to enforce HUSBAND's indemnification of the secured encumbrances, HUSBAND hereby agrees that he shall maintain assets having a value of no less than $100,000 in the Bank of America SEP IRA standing in HUSBAND'S name, or a substitute Account with assets worth no less than $100,000 which HUSBAND may delegate with advance notice to WIFE.

Kneeling on the rug next to the file box, I actually bowed my forehead to the floor in a posture of gratitude. I had found a way out. The only trick now would be to get Steve to agree to release the funds. Of course, they'd never been put into an escrow account. But Steve did have generous retirement savings. Still, every time I had called to discuss a bankruptcy plan, he had yelled about me being "critical and accusatory." I could no longer distinguish between Steve's normal irrational anger and his chemo-induced mental incapacity.

In July, I hosted an Independence Day dinner with my neighbor, Jane, for our bocce team and a few others. We set up a long table in the driveway between our two houses, and people brought platters of food and craft beers. We sat around talking and laughing until it got dark, and then walked over to a nearby vineyard, where we watched the fireworks display from Martini Winery. Eddie usually refused when I asked him to join me with a group of friends, but this time he had agreed to come. He seemed unusually quiet, even though my friends made efforts to include him in the conversation. "It was interesting to see you in your milieu," he said later, correctly pronouncing the French word. "I'd never seen that side of you before."

"What side is that?"

"Oh, just the party girl, the hostess. You know: See and be seen."

"That sounds like a backhanded compliment," I said.

"No, you're fine."

I laughed. "Yes, I *am* fine."

The next weekend, Eddie came to my place again. The traffic had been dreadful all the way up Highway 29, and he burst through the door complaining and waving his arms. "I'm never coming up on a Saturday afternoon again! That was ridiculous, all those freakin' yahoo tourists!"

That night, I made steamed mussels for dinner—perhaps an unintentionally nostalgic reference to our first meal of clams. Everything felt a little weighted with meaning, but I couldn't say why.

After we'd loaded the dishwasher, we assumed our now habitual place on the sofa in front of the TV. We couldn't find any movies we could agree on, so Eddie flipped to HGTV and turned on one of his favorite shows, *House Hunters International.* The show ended, and Eddie started watching a second episode, so I got up and fetched a book and lay on the couch reading—my feet in his lap—while he periodically filled me in. Before long, I was dozing. Then he led me upstairs to bed, where we both fell asleep immediately.

I awoke to the sound of shuffling—in the half light of the early morning, Eddie was getting dressed. By the time I had both eyes open, he was starting to close the bedroom door quietly behind him.

"Are you leaving?" I asked.

"Babe, I'm just going to get an early start. Get a good workout in," he said.

"But we were going to spend Sunday together." I leaned on one elbow, squinting at the sight of him.

"Look, you've got work, and you're tired."

"Who says I'm tired? And I finished my work yesterday so I could be with you today."

"You fell asleep watching TV last night."

"So? Come on, Eddie. Don't go."

"Go back to sleep. You won't even notice I'm gone."

"Are you mad about something?"

"No, no! I just want to get home. I've got stuff to do, and so do you."

I fell back on the pillow with a loud moan. It was becoming more and more difficult to remember how great he looked in jeans.

I used the morning to get caught up on some more freelance work. I cleaned out the refrigerator and did three loads of laundry. At four o'clock I picked up the phone and called Eddie, not even sure of what I was going to say.

"Hey, babe," he answered, on the second ring.

"How was your day?" I asked.

"It was great. I hit the weights, then went for a great bike ride in the Presidio."

"So you had fun, then."

"Yeah, it was a good day. How about you? Did you get some more work done?"

I didn't answer.

"Babe? What's wrong?" He was starting to sound nervous.

"Everything's wrong."

"Aw, come on, *mi amor*. . . ."

"We both know it. We're not even trying anymore. We're like some old married couple, and I already did that once."

"Okay," he said. His tone was softer, concerned. "We can take a break, then."

"Not a break. It's too late for a break."

There was a long silence on his end. I didn't try to fill the void. Finally, he said, "I think I left my toilet kit in your bathroom. Could you mail it back to me?"

I said, "Listen, you've got some other stuff here too—some T-shirts and shampoo, and your extra saxophone. I'll drop them off next weekend."

"And I'll leave your stuff in a bag by my front door." We hung up, the silence of hurt feelings muffling the click.

The following weekend, I let myself in with the code to the iron gate of Eddie's apartment building and walked up the sad, squishy stairs to the fourth floor for the last time. In front of his door was a brown grocery bag with a note stapled to it: "Here is all your stuff, including your WINE and your ALCOHOL. Have fun." So now I was an alcoholic. Leave it to Eddie to slap me on the way out.

So this, clearly, was my pattern: to find attractive but controlling men, try to change them, fail, and then put up with them until I could no longer stand it. Then be the one to walk away, somehow vaguely victorious, my ego intact.

I had been attracted to Eddie because he seemed to be the polar opposite of Steve. So why did leaving him arouse in me the same emotions—frustration, outrage, self-righteousness—that I felt when I left Steve? Why could I not see the pattern of my own behavior that accommodated narcissists?

Weeks after I split from Eddie, I realized that I didn't miss him as much as I missed the woman I had been with him. With Eddie, I'd been sexy and spontaneous, urban and a little hip.

Maybe I'd just have to be that woman on my own.

Chapter 24

A Shakespearean Tragedy

My newest mantra, as I lay awake in bed, was this:

It's only money.
This too shall pass.
The kids are healthy.
You'll be fine.

And I'd remind myself that there were so many worse things that could happen. I thought of the people on the street who truly were homeless. Of the parents of children with fatal diseases. Of the millions of people living in war-torn countries. Those images put me in my place, and I would eventually drift off to sleep. But it was an exercise I had to go through every single night.

August arrived, the hills golden brown and everyone's front lawns parched. It was finally time to take Bronte to college—a day I'd long been hoping for. Things were still tense and angry between us, and I looked forward to the time when she wouldn't be living with Steve. She'd set her sights on Iowa State University, which had an excellent pre-veterinary degree and the oldest agricultural program in the country. It was what she wanted, but I had to force myself to keep an open mind about the flyover state with its Midwestern values and horrible winters. Steve, Bronte, and I flew to Des Moines, then drove onto the campus—which I had to admit was lovely. Old brick buildings set on rolling lawns with lush foliage that would surely turn brilliant colors later in the fall. A dining commons that was as good as any local restaurant. And a charming bell tower, the campanile, which the locals called "the Campan-*eel*."

We spent the first day unpacking the countless items that Bronte had previously shipped to her dorm—monogrammed sheets and towels from Pottery Barn that she and her new roommate had color-coordinated. Then we made no fewer than three trips to the local Target to pick up additional items. Her dorm, Helser Hall, was a fifties-era brick fortress that hadn't been renovated since its original construction and didn't include such basic amenities as air conditioning—we later learned its nickname was Hell Hall. But Bronte didn't notice. She was so thrilled to be starting this new chapter and, I could only assume, saying goodbye to the last few difficult years with her family in St. Helena.

On the second day, the three of us took a road trip east to the Amana colonies—seven historic communal villages that now specialized in selling homespun kitschy crafts. With her collegiate future on solid ground, Bronte seemed to be letting the frozen ice cap between us thaw, and the two of us talked and laughed in the front seat like old times. After passing Freedom Rock—a twelve-foot boulder painted with patriotic slogans and scenes—we giddily pointed out other possible tourist attractions, making up names for them as we went.

"There's the Telephone Poll of Nations," I said.

"There's the Grain Silo of the Gods," Bronte added.

Before long we were bent with laughter, and at one point I had to pull over to catch my breath, tears streaming down my cheeks. It felt so good to be friends again.

Steve sat in the back seat, saying nothing. I occasionally found his face in the rearview mirror and saw him gazing out the window, his haggard expression devoid of emotion. After all these years, when he and Bronte had been so close, excluding me, now he was the one who was left out. Despite everything he had done to deserve my anger and hatred, now I could feel only pity and sadness.

We raced back from Amana to the hotel that evening, already late for the dinner we'd scheduled with the family of Bronte's new room-mate. Steve was too tired to join us. But when we got to the hotel, he said, "I just want to run to the grocery store to pick up a few things for dinner."

"But we need the car to get to the restaurant."

"I'll be ten minutes. I'll be back by the time you're ready."

We quickly changed and ran down to the lobby. Steve wasn't there. We waited for another fifteen minutes, Bronte madly texting him that he was making us later. When he finally pulled up, I waited to see what her reaction would be. If it had been me, Bronte would have barked and whined, loudly complaining about my lack of con-sideration. But with Steve she said nothing. She just swallowed her anger and got in the car.

Dinner was at Hickory Farms—an Ames institution. Formerly a train station, the rambling restaurant was packed with tourists and families in a series of small rooms. The menu featured a wide array of massive meat dishes, breaded and fried side dishes, and a full ice cream fountain. Everything came on enormous platters—it was Middle America in all its greasy, deep-fried glory. I ordered a quarter barbecued chicken and a salad, but by the end of the meal, I had finished only half of it. So I asked for it to be boxed—rather than waste the food, I'd take it back to Steve. I know, I know—he was consistently horrible and the source of all of my problems, but it just felt like the right thing to do. I wasn't going to be finishing it.

When we got back to the hotel, I knocked on the door to Steve's room. I heard his muffled voice saying wait a minute, but it was a full four minutes before he came to the door. His head poked out, and I could see him bent at the waist, as if he were half-dressed. And then the smell hit me—like raw sewage. I reflexively took a step back into the hallway. What was going on in there?

"Here, I brought you some leftovers," I said, extending the box. "I figured you might be hungry."

The look on Steve's face nearly broke my heart. "Well, thanks," he said weakly. "That was really nice of you."

"My pleasure," I said, but the door had already closed. Since arriving in Iowa, I'd been trying to find the right moment to bring up the $100,000. But it never arrived. And I knew that if I brought it up at the wrong time, I'd never get the chance again.

On the third day in Ames, Steve and I met for breakfast in the lobby restaurant. Bronte had stayed overnight in her dorm, and we were going to spend the morning with her before catching our flight back to California later that afternoon.

But at the table, Steve just sat and looked at his food, his hands in his lap.

"Are you feeling okay?" I asked, cutting into my home fries. His face was gray again, and some of his teeth had broken off—a result, no doubt, of the heavy chemo. He looked terrible.

"I can't feel my hands," he whispered.

"You can't? Not at all?" I put my fork down.

"No. They said this isn't uncommon after chemo," he said.

"Well, what can I do?"

"Nothing."

We sat in silence for a few minutes. "Look," I said finally. "Why don't you just go back to the room? We don't have any big plans, so just rest. Bronte will understand." He didn't argue the point.

I spent the morning with Bronte, running last-minute errands since she wouldn't have a car on campus. After our gaiety of the day before, she was back to her old self—ready to argue or snipe at me at the drop of a hat.

Finally, I helped her carry the last few things to her room. We stood awkwardly in the doorway. "I guess this is it," I said.

"I guess so," she said. I could tell she was trying to seem nonchalant, but I heard a slight break in her voice. I gave her my best smile. And then I saw the tears gathering at the rims of her eyes.

We fell into a hug. It was the first time Bronte had let me touch her in at least three years, and now she was holding on for dear life. On the outside, so fearless and angry. But on the inside, just a quivering young soul perched on the flight deck, not sure if she could make the jump.

"Sweetie, you're going to be just fine," I said.

"I know," she sobbed.

"You're going to have the *best* year of your life! I know it feels unfamiliar now, but you are going to have *so* much fun," I said.

"I don't want you to go," Bronte said, between sobs.

"I know, sweetie. But in ten minutes, you'll have forgotten I was even here. Remember all those activities they have planned for the freshmen all week?"

"Uh-huh."

I slowly, reluctantly pulled away. After all the anger and alienation of the past few years, this emotion felt overwhelming. At the same time, I knew that the only thing that would heal our relationship would be for Bronte to leave home. And me.

I stroked her hair off her face. "I love you, sweetie. Call me tomorrow night, okay?"

"Okay."

Then I turned and walked toward the parking lot. I didn't look back.

I returned home from Iowa to Amory—who'd been staying at a friend's—the ongoing drama at Riordan, and the continuing holy war with Steve. During the trip, I hadn't found the right moment to discuss the $100,000 indemnity funds. Instead, I appealed to Martin Keplinger to do it for me. "He's more likely to listen to you," I said. "You're an attorney, even if you're *my* attorney." Martin agreed, and I gave him Steve's phone numbers as well as a list of talking points. "Mention the kids," I said. "Remind him that if I lose my house, they lose their house too."

Meanwhile, Steve and I were in regular contact. He wrote that his cancer wouldn't be cured but could be controlled and that his numbers looked very good.

A week later, Martin called to report back. "We had a nice long chat," he said. "He couldn't have been nicer. But he won't give you the money. He told me that he's a very sick man, he doesn't know how long he has to live, and he needs all his money for his medical expenses."

So, with me, he was totally optimistic about his prognosis. With Keplinger, he was at death's door. The games would never end. And it came as no surprise to learn that Steve had never had the funds put into an escrow account. So now I would have to fight to get the money directly from his own funds.

It was beginning to dawn on me that—beyond the bankruptcy—I needed serious legal help. My friend and neighbor, Jane, recommended a woman attorney in Napa who'd done a great job with some issues surrounding her divorce, and I gave her a call. Unlike Glen Fisher, Mimi Chang had a modest office in an unpretentious part of town. She seemed to operate more from instinct than software and spreadsheets. She was canny, strategic, and had gone through her own divorce. I liked her immediately.

I told Mimi the background on Martin Keplinger and my looming bankruptcy, and she was immediately suspicious. After months of my back-and-forth with Keplinger on filing Chapter 13, she smelled something funny in his proposal that I give him the $55,000 to hold in a trust account before paying the trustee. So she contacted a different bankruptcy attorney on my behalf.

"I've just gotten off the phone with him," she said now. "What Keplinger told you to do is not only fraudulent, it's illegal."

I gasped.

"Yeah," Mimi said. "Since you have a claim against Steve for the one-hundred-thousand-dollar indemnification, that's listed as an asset in your bankruptcy. In other words, if you file for bankruptcy, you'll lose the one hundred thousand dollars *plus* your house. This other attorney suggested another solution—to have the money paid directly to you to pay creditors as they pursue you after Steve's death. You don't lose your house, you don't lose the one hundred thousand dollars. The only problem left is your damaged credit."

"I've already got one foreclosure on my record," I said, "with a second one likely. My credit is ruined anyway."

"Well, he's painted us into a corner," Mimi said. "The only option now is family court."

"You mean suing him for the funds?"

"I'm afraid so."

My head fell into my hands, which seemed to be a regular pose for me these days. I thought about the cost of preparing for a trial and going to court, the days of missed work, the furious phone calls from Steve.

"Let's do it," I said. Not only did I desperately need the money, but I was *not* going to let him win by manipulation and intimidation. Mimi told me the amount of her retainer to get started, and I gave her my credit card number. There I was, spending the money already.

Three days later, Mimi's assistant called to tell me that my credit card had been declined. Obviously a mistake, I said. I had paid the balance just the month before. "Well, you'll have to call them to work that out," she said. "In the meantime, do you have another card you can use?"

I called Chase to learn that they had closed my account, with no notification, because of the activity on Steve's Visa card—also with Chase—that retained my name. I had stupidly not closed the card years before because Steve and I were fighting about how to split the frequent-flyer miles. Then, even more stupidly, I had forgotten about it and opened a card in my own name. In the meantime, Steve had happily been using the joint card, had maxed it out, and now left me to deal with the damage.

I couldn't wait to see his pathetic face in court. I had the clause from the marital settlement agreement, I had the bankruptcy documents, and now I had further evidence of Steve's misdeeds. It was a slam dunk. Our court date was set for October 24.

I was at war now. I would take this bastard to court, and I would win.

As I drove to work in the early morning hours, I counted the white snowy egrets made brighter by the rising sun in the wetlands of south Napa. Now it was still light by the time I arrived home again after seven in the evenings. But such serendipity hardly made an impression. By now, Chris Markle, the Modesto real estate agent Steve had hired, was contacting me. Steve wasn't returning his phone calls or emails and wasn't sending the documents he'd promised so that Chris could sell the properties. "The tenants of both houses are ready and willing to buy," Chris said. "But I couldn't get Steve to respond. Now the first property has foreclosed, and the second one is due to go to auction next week."

With Chris's direction, I began calling the lender several times a day, but all my calls were answered with an automated menu, and I couldn't find a way to break the chain of robots. I faxed letters. Nothing. Finally, the date of the second auction arrived.

Chris called in a panic. "Sometimes if you call the day of the sale and agree to pay a portion of the overdue funds, you can get a reprieve," he said.

As soon as I got on the seven o'clock ferry the next morning, I called the number he'd given me. I listened to the repetitious hold music for the full hour as we sailed from Vallejo to San Francisco. But as we pulled in at the Ferry Building, I finally hung up, disgusted. The foreclosure meant that everybody lost: the tenants and potential buyers, the real estate agent who had hoped to make the sale, even the neighbors, who would now have a foreclosure lower their own property values. And, of course, me. I couldn't wait to see my next credit report. The only person who seemed unaffected—or at least didn't care—was Steve.

From September until December 2011, the San Francisco branch of the Occupy Wall Street movement had been camping in the five blocks along Market Street from the Embarcadero to First Street. At first I was amazed to see the community of dissidents emerging from their tents and sitting around in their camp chairs as I walked to and from the Riordan Foundation, then watch the same folks on the local news each night. But soon I started seeing their encampment more personally as I wondered if I would lose my own home in the months ahead. There was still no guarantee that I wouldn't go bankrupt.

It's true what they say: The nights are the worst. During the day I furiously focused on what needed to get done, but at night I just lay there, and all the demons of fear and failure crept out from under the bed. I couldn't stop them, the vivid images of packing up my house and moving to some depressing, dark apartment. I tried to imagine how the conversation would go as I told Amory we'd have to move, that I'd lost the very house he lived in. And then I'd remind myself that it hadn't happened yet, that tonight we were sleeping—or not sleeping—in our comfy beds, with our own roof overhead. For now, we were okay. It was only money.

—

On October 23, the day before we were due at the Napa County Courthouse, Mimi called. "I just got a call from Steve's lawyer," she said. "Steve's too ill to appear."

Of course he was. And his illness was that I had an airtight case against him.

"I've filed a continuance," she said. "Our next court date is November 15."

But on November 13, my fifty-seventh birthday, Steve's lawyer called again with the same news. Steve wouldn't be able to make it.

"Can't we just meet without him?" I asked.

"We could, but if he's too ill to appear, that would just make the judge more sympathetic to his side," Mimi said. "I think it's better to wait." We postponed again until December 12.

"You know, there *is* one other thing we can do to get Steve's attention," Mimi added.

"I'm listening."

"We can put a freeze on all his retirement accounts. That's where the funds would be coming from, so it's within our rights."

Why hadn't we thought of this sooner? "Absolutely!" I said. "Let's smoke him out!"

"What's going on up there? I keep getting troubling images of Steve." It was Bonnie Fournier, my old psychic friend from UC Berkeley. She had an uncanny intuitive sense, and she tended to call out of the blue when things were going sideways. I hadn't spoken to Bonnie in over a year—it was just like her to call at a time like this. I told her about Steve's condition, how out of control things were with his health and our finances. "Would it be okay with you if I called him?" she asked. "You know I've always liked Steve, and it sounds like he needs a friend."

"Well, he's a different person than the one you used to know," I said.

"He's the same person under very different circumstances."

"Whatever. I'm sure he'd be happy to hear from you. He doesn't have any other friends."

Bonnie called back a few days later. "I had a good long talk with Steve," she began.

"Uh-huh."

"That is one frightened hush puppy." Bonnie was originally from New Orleans and was fond of the colorful Southern turn of phrase. "He told me how scared he was of dying. That spirit is the one thing he never found time for. And now he's worried that he'll pay the price for it."

"We're all paying the price for it," I said.

"Kirsten, he was blubbering like a baby," Bonnie said. "He's truly scared that he might be going to hell."

"Well, at the moment, I think that might be a suitable place for him."

"Kirsten Mickelwait, don't you go casting stones, now. Don't forget, we choose our lessons and the people who can teach them to us. Stephen Beckwith is suffering a lot more right now even than you."

And that was Bonnie's gift: When she said it, I knew it was true.

On December 12, I eagerly drove to the Superior Courthouse in Napa. I'd been playing this scene in my head for weeks—presenting my slam dunk case to the judge—and I practically danced from the car to the lobby. Waiting to meet me were Mimi and Steve's attorney, Taylor Addison. Both women looked grim.

"Taylor got a call from Steve this morning," Mimi began.

"You're kidding me. Right?"

Taylor shook her head. "I'm afraid not. He's too ill to appear."

Although Steve had kept both the rental house in Pope Valley and the farm in Nevada City, he was apparently living up at the farm nearly fulltime. He'd even switched to a medical team at the small regional hospital up there, instead of St. Helena's state-of-the-art cancer center.

We sat down on a wooden bench in the echoing marble hall. "Taylor and I have been talking about work-arounds," Mimi said. "It doesn't look like we're going to get our day in court."

I slammed down my briefcase. "Damn it!"

"Taylor's been talking to Steve's eldest daughter, Lisa," Mimi said. "He's already given her power of attorney, but she can't go against his wishes. He's agreed to pay twenty-five thousand dollars to each of the lenders, but he refuses to give the money directly to you."

I laughed. "Giving twenty-five thousand dollars to each lender, when the total owed is one and a half million dollars, does nothing. It's just throwing the money away." My hands were fluttering around my face in a pantomime of frustration. "If he gave it to me, I could use it to pay off creditors in a more strategic way. Or if I did face bankruptcy, I'd have that money at my disposal."

Taylor nodded. "I know."

"Can you believe how vindictive this man is? He just wants to take me down with him!"

She nodded again. "It's a Shakespearean tragedy," she said. "It's *King Lear* without the redemption."

"So even you, as his lawyer, agree that he's in the wrong?"

Now she shook her head. "That man is a tortured soul," she said. "I don't know how to get him out of the dark place he's in."

I returned home and picked up the phone. When Steve's second eldest daughter, Samantha, answered, I asked, "So how's your dad today?" I expected a detailed account of his current symptoms with a coda of diminishing hope.

But instead she said, "The ambulance came to pick him up this morning. His body's just shutting down, even after the colostomy operation."

Not what I expected to hear. So, at least this time, he hadn't been faking.

"The doctor has told him he has six to twelve months," she said. "For some reason, this came as a shock to him."

"Wow. He's been telling all of us that as long as he takes the drugs, he's cured."

"Yeah. All he does is take the drugs and listen to the doctors. Kirsten, I don't think he's even Googled his disease. It's like he's a child."

I thought back to the previous February, when Steve and I had taken Amory out to dinner for his birthday. I'd watched as Steve ordered the biggest piece of steak on the menu and thought about all the times I'd read that red meat is like fertilizer for cancer. It was as if he actually had a death wish.

"So, what's next?"

"I've found him a smaller house at Lake of the Pines, which is a lot closer to Lisa and me. Once he's discharged from the hospital, we'll take him there."

I was about to hang up when Samantha said, "Listen, Kirsten, I know it's a long drive for you, but he's been asking for Amory. Would you be able to bring him up to Nevada City to visit Dad in the hospital?"

Of course I could. We made plans for me to drive Amory up on Saturday morning. Then I started doing some math. I recalled that Steve's last colonoscopy during our marriage was soon after his gastric bypass surgery. I remembered it because he'd had a difficult recovery from the procedure, which his gastroenterologist said was probably due to the surgery. That had been in 2005, just six years before, and most doctors advised a colonoscopy every ten years. I got on Google myself and read from the *Surgery News of the American College of Surgeons* that "the risk of colorectal cancer was significantly increased among people who had undergone obesity surgery in a retrospective cohort study of more than 77,000 obese patients enrolled in a Swedish registry."

So why hadn't he gotten in to see a doctor as soon as he'd started having symptoms? I already knew the answer: Because he hadn't bothered to get health insurance.

On December 21, Chris Markle called. "The bank decided to proceed with the foreclosure sale, eliminating our chances of getting a short sale offer accepted," he said. "It was held on Monday the nineteenth with no bidders, so the property reverted back to the bank and ultimately will be sold as a 'bank-owned' property. The short sale on the other property is still alive and moving along, but it's in 'preforeclosure.'"

We had tenants in that house who had been ready and willing to buy it. Now they'd be evicted, and I had a foreclosure on my credit report.

After a week, Steve was still in the hospital with a very low white blood cell count from his impaired immune system. "I don't want to be an ambulance chaser," I told Mimi, "but I'm really worried that he'll die suddenly without agreeing to turn over the funds."

"Can you talk again to Lisa?" she asked. "There's nothing more we can do from a legal standpoint."

From the time of our separation, in 2006, to 2010 when Steve had been diagnosed, I'd had minimal contact with his four daughters from his first marriage. I'd suspected that he was probably speaking ill of me, and I didn't want to put them in an awkward situation. Now we were on the phone regularly, discussing game plans. Lisa was handling all the financial and insurance issues, while Samantha was taking care of the medical side. Michaela lived much farther away and had less involvement. And Julie, who had been helping to care for him, had left his house in the middle of the night saying she wanted nothing more to do with him. Now Bronte had returned from Iowa for Christmas break and was staying mostly in Nevada City at Steve's or with Lisa in nearby Auburn.

"Kirsten, I've tried talking to him from every angle, and he just won't budge." Lisa was on the phone and, as usual, the subject was the indemnity funds that Steve refused to sign over to me. "I've told him it's the right thing to do, that now is the time for forgiveness. But his mind's made up. He's also refusing to give you power of attorney on the kids' college funds."

Steve had managed the college funds since we'd opened them when both kids were babies. And since we'd split, we'd both been contributing to them equally. For two years I'd been asking Steve to put my name jointly on the accounts, and he'd always had some excuse for not doing it right away. Now it was clear—he didn't want to give me access to them at all.

Once Steve died, Lisa would lose her power of attorney, and it would be nearly impossible to gain access to any of the money. My biggest fear was that he'd die before we'd straightened it out. Lisa was my only hope. "I'll keep trying" was all she said.

I had a new mantra. I was too tired to remember any of the old ones. Now, as I lay in bed each night, I simply asked, *Did I do my best today?* If the answer was yes, and it always was, that was enough. It had to be. It was all I had.

On Saturday I drove Amory up to Nevada City to visit his dad in the hospital. There was no snow in the foothills, leaving the winter land-scape dull and gray. We found the hospital just off the highway—a small, squat rural building that clearly wasn't the place you'd choose to save your life. As we walked out of the elevator onto the third floor, Samantha came out to greet us. I sent Amory into his dad's room to visit—from the hallway, I could see Steve's blanket-covered feet at the foot of the bed, but I willed myself not to look any farther. Instead, Samantha and I found a small waiting room down the hall, where we could sit and talk.

"How's it going?" I asked.

"He can be such a son of a bitch," she said. "You'd think he'd be grateful that we're here for him, but he sure doesn't see it that way."

"I'm sure he's grateful, Samantha," I said. "He's just too wrapped up in his own pain to realize it." She'd had some pretty rough years with her dad—they all had—and I knew that down the road she'd be grateful to have had the chance to care for him at the end.

"What's the status of the house?" I asked.

"We've moved him to Lake of the Pines. It'll take weeks to clean his old place out. I don't even go over there without a pair of rubber gloves."

After the past six years, I didn't think I could be surprised anymore at Steve's behavior. But the idea that he'd been living in such isolated squalor did shock me. The man who had swept me off my feet with his élan and charm had become a sad, filthy hermit. And yet my future still lay at his feet.

Chapter 25

The Whole World in His Hands

On Sunday morning, I made the kids help me decorate the Christmas tree. It felt like an obligation, anything but joyful. But I also knew that if I didn't bother, we'd all be depressed and resentful. As usual, Bronte's sullen presence was creating unspoken tension, and Amory was rarely seen outside of his room. The low point came when Bronte moved a chair so carelessly that she knocked over two other pieces of furniture, causing a favorite ornament to drop and shatter on the hardwood floor. Amory stomped up to his room, and Bronte then happily decorated the tree with just me—clearly, she'd gotten what she wanted. Happy holidays, one and all!

January 2012 arrived, cold and dry. On New Year's Day I was performing my annual ritual of sweeping the front walk. But instead of a sense of rebirth and anticipation, this year I felt only dread as I swept up the dead crepe myrtle blossoms that had blown across the small yard.

On Wednesday, January 4, Lisa called. "He's in and out of

consciousness," she said. "I'm not sure how much longer he has." Bronte had returned to Nevada City to be with her dad and her sisters, while Amory had stayed with me.

Lisa still hadn't been able to get Steve to agree to pay me the $100,000 he legally owed me, and the moment he died, she would lose her power of attorney. It would be a lost cause, Mimi said.

"Listen," Lisa said, lowering her voice. "It's just not right that you should lose that money because of Dad's poor behavior. It's clearly stated in your marital agreement." She took a breath. I waited. "I have power of attorney. I'm going to sign it over to you. It's the right thing to do. I'm also going to give you power of attorney on the college funds."

When I finally found my voice, I simply said, "Thank you, Lisa." *Deus ex machina.* Divine intervention.

"There's only one problem. Mimi put a freeze on all his accounts. We need to lift the freeze in order for me to write you a check."

I promptly hung up the phone and called Mimi's office. Carol, her assistant, answered, and I gave her the good news. "That's wonderful," she said. "I'll tell Mimi as soon as she gets back from vacation."

"What? When did she go on vacation?"

"She's out all week, until next Monday."

"Well, call her! He may not live until Monday."

"She left strict instructions not to bother her. Besides, she's on Kauai. I'm not sure if she even has cell reception."

I pictured Mimi lounging on a beach as I lost the one chance I had to dig myself out of financial ruin. She probably had a piña colada in one hand and a trashy novel in the other. God certainly had a sense of humor. I appealed to Carol's good nature and common sense to at least try calling Mimi, explaining that, if I lost this money because she couldn't be bothered, I would not be a good sport about it.

"I'll do my best," she said. The rest of Wednesday passed with no word. Thursday. Friday morning. For that entire week, my feelings about Steve's imminent death were no longer personal—they were financial. This man held my future in his dying hands.

After lunch on Friday, I called Carol in a panic.

"Don't worry, I just reached her," she said. "She's going to call in a release of the hold to Steve's investment company this afternoon."

"Remembering that Hawaii is two hours behind mainland time, right?"

"Right," Carol said. "It's handled."

I let out a long, slow breath of relief and gratitude. It was done. That evening on the ferry ride home, I ordered a Bloody Mary and bought a packet of Cheez-Its—my usual Friday evening commute celebration. Now I sat by a window facing west, watching the January sun slip quickly behind the Golden Gate Bridge. I knew that there were still years of struggle ahead to get myself out of this mess. But this was a substantial victory. Steve was probably beyond caring now.

The very next day, in the middle of the night, I awoke—or thought I did—to a strange sensation. It wasn't a dream. It was a half-conscious experience. I felt myself in a strange room with people whispering and bustling around in the dark. A commotion. The only light was a pale blue illumination, as if from a cell phone or a video camera. And in that light I could make out a bed, a beige blanket, and people moving around the bed. The only detail I could see of the person in the bed was a left arm with some kind of bright blue plastic bracelet. I fell back asleep, but the moment I awoke the next morning, I knew what I'd seen. "Uh-oh" was all I could think.

I went downstairs around nine and found the red message light blinking on the phone, which I hadn't heard when it rang at six eighteen. I looked at it a long time before hitting "Play." I knew it must have big news for me, and I was trying to sort out my feelings about what it would mean.

Kirsten, it's Lisa. Dad passed this morning around three. We're waiting for the ambulance to come pick up his body. Bronte's in pretty bad shape, but we're all here, so we'll get through it together. Call me when you can.

I dialed Lisa's cell number. "How's she doing?" were my first words when she picked up the phone.

"She's a mess, but she'll be fine. She sat with Dad from the time he died until the ambulance came—about five hours."

I thought about my eighteen-year-old daughter and what she'd just been through. I'd never been present with someone when they died. Even at my dad's death, he waited until everyone had left the room and snuck out of his body on his own terms. Now Bronte had experienced something I couldn't navigate for her. It was a lot for a teenaged girl.

"Is she ready to talk to me?" I asked. I didn't know what I'd say. I just wanted to put my arms around her.

"I'll have her call you later," Lisa said. "She's still pretty upset."

"Okay," I said. Then, "How did he go? Was it easy?" It was then I realized that I had been hoping for a fourth-quarter epiphany, that Steve would see the error of his ways in his final hours and have a moment or two of actual grace.

"He struggled up until the end," Lisa said. "He was really afraid about what was waiting for him on the other side."

I've never really believed in a traditional version of heaven or hell. In all the reading I've done on near-death experiences, almost everyone described the moment of death in a similar way. All shared the phenomenon of seeing their entire lives presented to them like a movie—the good, the bad, the ugly. They were forced to relive all the love, all the hurt, everything they had directed toward others during their lifetimes. I wanted to believe this idea, that "Judgment Day" was that personal—it fulfilled my desire for divine justice. And now I deeply, deeply hoped that Steve had had such a supreme, fore-head-slapping moment, when he'd suddenly understood how much he had hurt me and damaged our family.

"Well, I'd better get back to it," Lisa said. "There's a lot to do here."

"Just one more thing," I said. "Did your dad have some kind of blue plastic bracelet on his left wrist?"

"His hospital ID tag," Lisa said. "How did you know?"

When the Maharishi Mahesh Yogi died in 2008, it was said by his followers that he "dropped his body." I liked the expression. It supported my belief that our souls are part of a larger continuum and that our bodies are just our "earth suits," to be discarded when we've finished our course of study in a single lifetime, like a snake sheds its skin.

In the days and weeks that followed, I couldn't stop thinking about the arc of Steve's story, his tortured final years, and his choice to punish me until his dying breath. His death quickly became a marker of time for me, with a before and an after. Now I could start a new way of life, one in which I could advance without constant fear of being pulled down by Steve.

I thought back to the very first time I'd had to think about death. I was in the sixth grade, and on the cover of *Life* magazine was a full-color photo of a blood-spattered nurse's cap. I turned to the story inside and read the whole thing, barely blinking. The eight student nurses. The remorseless criminal who'd raped and killed each one as the others lay bound, helpless, and terrified in the other room. I pored through the article, memorizing the nurses' names and the details of their girlish bedrooms.

For several years after that, I was fascinated by death. So mysterious, so final, so out of our control. It was the first time I really understood that our stories don't last forever, and how we die is rarely up to us.

When my dad was dying, the hospice worker had advised our family that it would be a matter of days. He was comatose. I'd gone to Palo Alto and spent a week there, waiting for the final moment, writing his obituary as I sat by his bed, thanking him for his love and care and telling him it was okay to go. But he wasn't going. On July 17, my sister and I spoke with the woman from hospice again. The next day would be my seventeenth wedding anniversary. I hadn't seen my kids in a week. But I was afraid to leave my dad for fear that he would die while I was away.

"All families feel that way," she told me. "They think it's of utmost importance that they be there, holding a hand, when the moment comes. But very often we're tying them to this earth. They can't leave while we're in the room. After days at the bedside, you'll leave to get a cup of coffee, and that's when they'll pass. Don't worry about it. Go home for a couple of days. See your kids, celebrate your anniversary. Everything will happen as it's meant to."

Gratefully, I'd returned home with plans to go back the next day. Steve and I celebrated our anniversary with our bocce team at the park. It was a sweet reminder of how good life can be, after a week of waiting for death.

Early the next morning, I decided to swim laps in the pool before packing up and returning to Palo Alto. As I swam, I gazed at the puffy summer clouds, the pure blue sky. Suddenly, in the middle of the pool, I stood up. Sobs came out of nowhere. Something had passed through me that filled me with emotion—completely unbidden, out of my control. I figured it was the exhaustion and grief of the previous week, suddenly surfacing in a moment of relaxation. I finished my laps, grabbed a towel, and went inside. The first thing I saw was the blinking light of the message machine.

"He's gone," my sister sobbed into the phone. "I literally went out for coffee, just like hospice said. He left in the ten minutes I was away."

I checked the time on the machine. It coincided with the moment of emotion I'd experienced in the pool. Clearly, my father had passed through, saying goodbye to me on my way to the great beyond.

—

On Monday morning, I called the office and explained that I needed to take some bereavement leave. Amory was staying home from school, and Bronte was due back from Lisa's that afternoon. I would play no role in planning the funeral or dealing with Steve's things, so I wasn't sure exactly what to do. But clearly I needed to be home with the kids.

"Of course, take all the time you need," Monica said. "Do what you need to do." But what I needed to do was get a commemorative Riordan book to the printer by Wednesday. If I didn't, there would be no books at Tom's gala event in two weeks. So, between checking in with Bronte and Amory, who were numb with shock, I was on the phone with the designer and printer to make sure the final edits were made to the proofs.

Bronte came home and set up camp on the living room sofa. She had every possible device activated—the TV, her laptop, her iPad, and her phone—and she appeared to be in a fugue state. She got up only to pour a bowl of cereal or use the bathroom; otherwise, she was immobile on her couch of misery.

Amory dealt with his grief in the opposite way. "I'm not doing anything here, and all my friends are at school," he said. "I don't want to have to make up schoolwork later. I just want to get back to normal." I insisted that both kids see the same therapist I'd made them see after my separation from Steve, and they both fought me on it. I just didn't know what else to do. Where were the guidelines for this situation? Two children dealing with the loss of their father, and a mother who felt nothing but relief at his death. I guess I was in my own form of shock. And rage: His financial abandonment had been bad enough, but now he had abandoned all of his children in the most permanent way. How would this materialize years down the road, as their sense of loss and anger rose to the surface?

I made my own appointment with the therapist. "I know that forgiveness is the ultimate goal," I told her. "But I also know that's simply not going to happen until I'm out from under this shitstorm he left me."

"Don't even try to forgive him right now," she said. "Just focus on letting him go."

That, too, felt like a challenge. But at least it was a small step forward.

The Saturday morning after Steve's death I went to yoga class, as I did every weekend. It was the first class since the new year, and the teacher, Faith, led us through a long meditation, reflecting on what we were grateful for from the previous year. I sat in lotus position, back straight, eyes closed, flipping through the pages of the past year like a worn magazine of bad karma.

I remembered how many times Faith had invoked the name of Ganesh, the Hindu god credited with the removing of obstacles. How many times I had pictured Steve's face as the sole obstacle I wished to remove. He'd felt like the one thing standing between me and financial solvency. Me and peace of mind. Me and happiness. He was practically all I had focused on for six years, but especially in the most recent one. And now the obstacle had been removed, finally and completely. Praise Ganesh. Gone. It would be years, of course, before I would be done with his legacy of damage. But when that was finally over, how would I structure my life? Who would I be then? Without Steve's chaos and anger to struggle against, the world seemed vast and unorganized.

"Gratitude." Faith's voice brought my thoughts back to the current assignment. "Deepak Chopra says that it opens the door to the universe—to creativity and wisdom. We know that it's not happy people who are thankful, but thankful people who are happy. It literally has the power to change our world, and to change us."

I thought of all the things that had kept me afloat. Bronte and Amory—if not for them, I wouldn't have found the motivation or ferocity to fight. My friends and family, who had listened tirelessly as I ranted and complained, then had given me the best advice they had. My bocce team and my choral group, who had reminded me how to be joyful in the midst of panic and despair. And this yoga class, which had given me balance and calm on my mat every Saturday morning.

As Faith guided us to close our meditation, I realized that tears were spilling down my cheeks. Two warm hands appeared on my shoulders, and Faith began to gently knead the back of my neck and my skull. Then she wrapped her arms around me and gave me a big squeeze as I wiped my face with the heels of my palms. So much kindness. So many people who loved me. I couldn't respond with failure.

The funeral was held the following day in the little stone chapel at the St. Helena Catholic cemetery. All six of Steve's children stood at the altar next to an enlarged photo of him from a few years before, back when he was healthy and happy. Lisa, Julie, and Amory spoke, but all the kids had helped in some way to organize the service. Apparently it had been announced in the *Napa Register,* and a few friends showed up to pay their respects—including Steve's old law firm colleagues and his Alaska fishing and camping buddies from farther afield.

I had assumed that I wouldn't attend the funeral. At that point, I had no respects to pay, and I didn't think I could stand hearing Steve being eulogized. But Bronte made it clear she wanted me there, so I called Lisa to ask if it would be okay if I came.

"Of course you should come. We're expecting you," she said.

"Then I'll be the one in the back pew with the duct tape over my mouth," I joked. Lisa laughed. "You won't be alone. My mom will be sitting back there with you."

Listening to Steve's kids remember him, I'd never been prouder of them. They spoke about their love for him without sugarcoating who he was. After the memorial, the tiny congregation moved outside to the burial plot where Steve's ashes would be interred. Lisa had arranged for a military honor guard to perform taps and do the flag-folding ceremony in recognition of Steve's years in the army. I watched as his camping buddies, also veterans, stood at attention and saluted, and thought about how much that would have meant to Steve.

There was a reception and luncheon after the service. The family and a few core friends met at a brewing company just north of town to toast Steve's memory, tell a few endearing stories about him, and shake our heads over his sudden departure. I hadn't seen Beth, Steve's first wife, in a long time, but we'd become friendly at family reunions. I waited until I saw her sitting alone, then walked over to her table and sat down. "So tell me," I said. "Who was this guy we were married to? After all that's happened in the past six years, I feel like I hardly knew him."

"Steve was the golden child," Beth told me. "He was the example the other three kids were held up to. He did well in school, and he was a star athlete in every sport. The family didn't have much money, but after every one of his games, his mom would cook a big steak just for him. She'd even cut his meat for him." We both shook our heads and laughed. The grooming of a narcissist.

"Here's another example," Beth said. "Before we got together, Steve was invited to the junior prom by a girl he was dating. He told his mother, 'I wouldn't dream of going to the prom in that old jalopy of ours.' She bought a new car, just so he could drive it to the prom without embarrassment."

"Wow," I said. "That's extreme."

"He was the prince of the family," Beth said. "He could do no wrong in his mother's eyes."

So that's where he got his appetite for the finer things, and his sense of entitlement. But there was something else at work. I thought

back to how easily he had slipped into playing the victim, how insecure he could be when things didn't go his way. And in that moment
I understood Steve in a way I never had. Now I saw how he expected
the royal treatment, but inside, he didn't believe he deserved it. He
probably saw how unfair it was to his siblings and even felt guilty
about it. I left the luncheon and drove home with a sense of peace I
hadn't felt in years. It was as if a missing piece of the story had been
slipped into place, enabling me to make more sense of all the anger
and hurt.

Part IV

Chapter 26
Earth Is Forgiveness School

It was the middle of January, and Bronte was due back at Iowa State the following week after the long holiday break. But the day after the funeral, she informed me that she wanted to take the next semester off to deal with her grief.

"Are you sure?" I asked. "It's going to set you back on your academic schedule, and you may even lose your financial aid. If it were me, I'd want to stay busy."

"If I go back now, I feel like I'll just flunk out," Bronte said. "It's my life, Mom. I just can't go back right now."

She was eighteen—old enough to make such decisions for herself. Despite my own misgivings, I agreed. And, as the weeks passed, it was clear that Bronte was in a full-blown depression. She rarely left the living room couch. She was a tightly wound lump of despair—an emotion that, when it surfaced and mixed with oxygen, turned into fierce anger. Her hair remained unwashed, and she never got out of her pajamas. After a couple of sessions with the therapist, she refused to return for another visit. I decided to let her grieve in her own way, but it was hard having her installed in the main living area. When Amory or I wanted some TV time, she stomped upstairs and hibernated in her room.

Meanwhile, I had my own troubles. Lisa had arranged for Steve's mail to be forwarded to my address, and I was suddenly bombarded with the full force of his negligence. One of the rental properties had already foreclosed, with a second one headed there very soon if I couldn't get the bank to postpone the auction to allow me to short sell the property. Every other day I would receive a notice from another collection agency concerning a bill, a credit card, a loan. Equipped with copies of our divorce decree and Steve's death certificate, I made a list of the injured parties and began making calls during breaks at work.

One of the first was to Chase Visa, the credit card I'd canceled back in September after learning that Steve had continued using it without my knowledge. Now Chase informed me that I was responsible for the remaining balance of more than $58,000. My name was still on the card. "He was making pretty regular payments until this one to Jimmy Vasser Chevrolet," the representative told me.

"Jimmy Vasser?" I asked. That was the dealer who'd sold him Bronte's truck several years before. "How much was the charge?"

"Sixteen thousand, five hundred dollars," the rep said. "On July twenty-first, 2009."

My mouth fell open. "That bastard!" I said aloud. Steve had told me that he would finance the truck himself, and I could make monthly payments to him to split the cost. I'd paid him $250 a month for two years, until Bronte went to college, when he'd agreed to take over the payments himself, like he was doing me a big favor.

Instead, he'd charged the truck's full cost to a credit card under both our names, knowing he could just leave the whole amount to me. With twenty percent interest, the cost of that truck had now risen to more than $20,000. Just weeks before his death, Steve had signed title on the truck over to Bronte, so she now owned it free and clear. And he'd known full well that I would be left holding the bag for the entire balance.

Any compassion or sympathy I might have felt for Steve on the day of his funeral now went up in smoke, leaving nothing but charred ashes and fumes. How brilliantly he had duped and manipulated me. As he had lain dying, fearing what might await him on the other side, he had good reason to worry.

It wasn't long before I received another notice in the mail from a collection agency representing St. Helena Hospital. *This is your final notice,* it read. *This delinquent payment will now be reported to the credit agencies and be reflected on your credit report.* The amount was $126,000. I called the phone number listed on the notice and finally got a live voice, a harried-sounding woman who was clearly regretting her decision to work at a collection agency.

"Reference number?" she asked wearily. I gave it to her.

"So how can I help you?"

"This isn't my bill," I began. "There's clearly been a mistake."

"This bill is for the treatment of Stephen M. Beckwith at St. Helena Hospital from December nineteenth to December twenty-sixth, 2010, correct?" Those were the dates that Steve had been hospitalized and diagnosed after his trip to the emergency room.

"It may be, but I'm not the responsible party."

"This is your fourth notice. We've been sending you notices of delinquency since July."

"But they were being sent to my ex-husband's address. This is the first notice I've seen." I wondered how many conversations she had like this every day. Outside the window, dark clouds looked on the verge of tears.

"Okay, but it says here you were the responsible party."

"We were divorced in June of 2009. He wasn't covered by my health insurance."

She was silent while she read through the file. "He claimed your divorce wasn't yet final."

The sound that came out of my mouth was a kind of hybrid thing, between a laugh and a cough. A hysterical choking sound. He had lied to the hospital a year before his death. He had given my name as the responsible party, fully conscious that it was a lie. He had received countless notices of delinquent payment, knowing that it would negatively affect my credit score. He'd had daily reminders of the harm he was doing.

Again I thought of the plate of food I had delivered to his hotel room in Iowa. The apology I had offered, unreciprocated. The full year he had known what he had done and still gladly received my kindnesses. Had he felt even a glimmer of remorse?

Of all the damage Steve had inflicted on my financial status, this one was the most easily corrected. I submitted copies of our divorce decree and his death certificate, and the negative item was soon removed from my credit report. But the audacity of the act stayed with me. I simply couldn't comprehend how one person could be so vindictive toward another, especially one who had mothered his children. It would be years before I'd understand the term "narcissistic personality disorder."

A week or two after Steve's death, I came downstairs to the customary sight of Bronte on the couch watching television. "What's wrong with the TV?" she asked in a weary voice.

"Nothing that I know of. Why?"

"It keeps switching channels. I'm not even touching the remote."

"Is it switching to another show that the DVR's recording?"

"No! It just keeps switching to this other program on Channel 760."

"Well, what's the program?" I asked.

"It's this survivalist show I used to watch with Daddy," she said.

I stopped as I passed behind the sofa. I had read many accounts of how the recently departed often tried to communicate through electromagnetic energy, such as flickering light bulbs. When my dad had died, fourteen separate light bulbs had burned out in our house within two weeks.

"Honey, I think that's your dad telling you he's still here," I said, and I meant it. It had to be more than a silly coincidence. The very same show?

"That's what I thought," Bronte said. She didn't seem shocked, or upset, or pleased. Just matter-of-fact.

I walked into the kitchen and turned on the faucet. Not that I wanted to communicate with him, I thought, as I rolled an apple under the tap. But if I did, what would the sign be? What could he do to let me know he was still around?

For some reason, the first thing that came to mind was a car we had leased soon after we were married. As a partner in his law firm, Steve was given an automobile allowance for a leased vehicle, and he wasted no time in shopping for luxury cars. We finally settled on a light brown Mercedes sedan, with a custom-ordered chocolate-brown leather interior. It was a beautiful car, and we drove it for four years, until Bronte was born and we traded it in on an SUV. But for years afterward, every time I saw a brown Mercedes on the street or freeway, I'd check to see if it had the chocolate interior, since that would clearly identify it as our former car. In twenty years, I had never seen the exact car. All the others had beige interiors.

Then I corrected myself. Twenty-two years of marriage, and all I could think of as a symbol was a fancy car? Shame on me. I changed my symbol instead to a joke that Steve and I used to tell each other early in our marriage, based on a Peter Sellers movie. The joke's punch line was "Carabinieri," the Italian military police force. *If I see or hear the word* Carabinieri *in the next week, I'll consider it a sign from Steve*, I thought. Then I forgot about it.

Roughly a week later, I was making breakfast before work, the small television on the counter tuned to the early morning news. Normally I listened to the news as I raced to eat breakfast and get out the door, but this morning I had stopped to watch a story that had horrified me—the shipwreck of the Costa Concordia cruise ship off the coast of Italy, which had taken thirty-two lives. I stood a few feet from the TV, transfixed at the report that the captain had allegedly abandoned his ship in distress.

Suddenly, apropos of nothing specific in the narrative, the entire screen filled up with a sign: CARABINIERI, it read, in letters about two inches high. Yes, it was a story set in Italy. But the reporter hadn't even mentioned the military police. *Okay, Steve,* I said in my head. *I get it. You're still here with us. Nicely done.*

A few days later, I was walking the dog on her usual route around the block. As we approached the house just before our driveway, I saw it: a light brown Mercedes parked at the curb. *Not the same one,* I told myself. *Of course not.* As I approached, I tried to make out the color of the interior, but the windows' reflection made it difficult. I walked up alongside the car and peered in. Chocolate-brown leather. Unbelievable. Twenty years of not seeing this exact car, and now, two weeks after I thought of it, it was sitting directly in front of my house?

"Oh no, you didn't," I said aloud. "Come *on*! How did you do that?" I circled the car, taking it in from all angles. It seemed impossible, and yet it just confirmed what I had believed all along. The veil between this life and the other side was thinner than we thought. Our loved ones—and our hated ones—were gone only in the physical sense. Then I took a photo of the car with my phone to serve as a reminder, just in case I forgot or doubted myself later.

I walked back inside, still shaking my head. *Don't think this means we're speaking again,* I told Steve in my head. *I'm not ready to forgive you yet. Not by a long shot.*

Several weeks after Steve's funeral, I received an email from a real estate agent claiming to represent a man named Peter Michelakis, who had been renting the Oakland loft from Steve for the past year.

Michelakis had apparently been receiving notices of foreclosure on the property and was justifiably alarmed. He'd been paying Steve $2,300 a month to rent the two-bedroom condo and didn't want to be evicted. I wrote back to the agent to tell him of Steve's death, providing documentation that I was now the full owner of the property and explaining my intention to sell the loft as soon as possible. In the meantime, Michelakis should begin paying rent to me. I agreed to call him directly to iron out the details.

Finally, a break! The guy was a commercial real estate developer who had rented the unit from Steve after going through a divorce himself. His manner on the phone was calm, professional, and charming. When I told him of my intention to sell the property immediately, he expressed his interest in buying it. At least here was one problem quickly solved. I said a prayer of thanks to the gods of real estate.

After I got off the phone, I Googled Peter Michelakis. He had made the cover of the *San Francisco Business Times* not once but twice, for his golden touch with East Bay live/work conversion properties. In the most recent photo, he was leaning against a late-model red Jaguar convertible, his arms crossed in the manner of highly successful men.

By now I had hired a real estate agent in Nevada City, who specialized in short selling properties, to handle the sale of the farm. Justin Kaplan was a no-bullshit, straight-talking guy who clearly knew his way around the massive bureaucracy of the banks and the reporting agencies. Because a short sale is less about marketing a property and more about wrangling documents, he convinced me to let him sell the Oakland loft as well. I put him in touch with Michelakis's real estate agent, and we were on our way.

By January 31, we had a contract to sell Michelakis the condo for $50,000 under market price. I had learned from the bank that, because the property wasn't a primary residence, I was not actually liable on it. But a foreclosure would have negatively impacted the property values of the building's other residents. And, as a conversion loft in a rapidly gentrifying neighborhood, it was a desirable piece of real estate. I would make no money on the deal, but it seemed worthwhile to do the right thing.

Lisa called one day and asked me to meet her in Sacramento to offload some things Steve had willed to the kids. There was his extensive knife collection—I had never found the receipts, and Steve didn't include the collection in our marital settlement. There were a few really nice watches and rings. There was the largest flat-screen TV I'd ever seen, which he'd bought just weeks before his death. And there was a big bag of clothing he was giving to Amory. When I got home, we went through the clothes together. His fringed and beaded leather vests. His full-body buckskins. All the embarrassing cowboy outfits he'd worn in the waning days of our marriage.

"You know, these'll bring a lot of money on Craigslist or eBay," I told Amory. I couldn't wait to get rid of them.

"I'm going to keep them," he said.

"All of them?"

"Yes, all of them. I don't have many things from Dad."

I could almost hear Steve laughing from the great beyond. I put everything in a big plastic bin, labeled it "Dad's Leathers," and stashed the box on a shelf in the garage. The following year, when the high school was having a "Seventies Day," Amory wore one of the fringed buckskin shirts to school. He'd been growing a beard and shaved it into a Tom Selleck–style mustache with long sideburns, just for the day. He got scads of compliments.

By April, I realized that I hadn't yet actually received a rent check from Peter Michelakis, who had been living rent-free in the loft for four months. He had initially claimed that he didn't want to pay me until I'd proven that I was the legal owner of the condo, but I'd done that months ago. Now I contacted him again, reminding him that he owed me $9,200. He knew my circumstances and how much I needed the money. But when I emailed him a reminder, he had a new reason. He had no intention of paying me rent, he explained, until I completed the repairs that Steve had promised. He attached an estimate from a handyman—no doubt one of his contractor friends—for $9,200, exactly the amount he owed me in back rent.

I had recently received an estimate from an actual painter that came to $3,000 for my whole two-story house. And we were under contract for a short sale, in which I was selling him the loft for $50,000 under market price. I pointed out that he was buying the property "as is" and that I was not liable for repairs promised by someone else under completely different circumstances. But Michelakis held fast, returning to the refrain that he was going through a painful divorce and had never been able to feel that the loft was a real home since he'd been living under threat of eviction should it go to foreclosure.

And that was when I realized I was dealing with yet another charming, manipulative, unreliable man. It was as if Michelakis had been created from the same mold as Steve Beckwith.

Thank God for Justin, the Nevada City realtor, who worked directly with Michelakis's lawyer and negotiated a deal—Michelakis would make a partial payment on the rent, I would give him a reduced rate for the unrepaired items, and he would pay me a lump sum of $5,000 at the time of closing.

"The only difference between guys like that and people like us," Justin told me, "is that we owe hundreds or thousands of dollars. They owe millions."

Wednesday morning, February 29. Of course I remembered what day it was. Steve was a leap year baby, and every four years we had celebrated in some special way. I had thrown him surprise parties for his fortieth/tenth birthday and his fifty-second/thirteenth birthday.

Today he would have been sixty-four/sixteen. *Don't expect me to wish you a happy birthday this year*, I told him in my head. *That's not going to happen.*

I was cleaning out the stack of papers that had piled in my inbox at Riordan when I got a call from my psychic friend, Bonnie.

"Hey!" I answered. "Something must be up for you to call me at work." I loved hearing from Bonnie—she always had a spiritual message to deliver. And she always called me one of many endearing nicknames.

"I just had to call, Pumpkin. Steve's been following me around all morning. He wants me to remind you it's his birthday."

"I remember," I said. "But aren't they done with that kind of stuff on the other side?"

"He just wants to be remembered by you. He's asking me to tell you that he loves you. He always has." We'd seen a lot of Bonnie during our early marriage. She'd been a remarkable source of love and higher wisdom during my three miscarriages, and we even asked her to be Bronte's godmother. In truth, I felt like she was *my* godmother.

"That man loved you so much," she said now. "I know he had a strange way of showing it toward the end. But that doesn't mean he didn't feel it."

"Yeah, yeah," I said. "I'm still recovering from all his 'love' of the past few years. Bankruptcy, fraud, nearly marrying my close friend, trying to set the kids against me. I think I'm better off without his love, thanks."

"Kirsten, try not to judge him for his earthly behavior. The picture is bigger than what you can see."

I sighed. "I know you're right, theoretically, but . . ."

"I'm just right," Bonnie said. She was always impossible to argue with.

I told her about the sightings of *Carabinieri* and the brown

Mercedes, apologizing for the cheesiness of choosing something so material as a luxury automobile. "That car represented a time when you were both happy," Bonnie said. "Did you ever think of it that way?" I hadn't.

With the phone still to my ear, I heard a distinct phrase in my head. It wasn't my voice and it wasn't Bonnie's. It said: *Isn't it time to stop telling stories—to others and to yourself—about all the bad times?* I knew I hadn't created that thought myself.

"I've got to go," I told Bonnie, and the minute I hung up the phone, I put my head down on my desk and sobbed. It seemed to come out of nowhere. In that moment I felt something flutter in my chest. I could feel myself forgiving Steve.

This wasn't according to the plan. My schedule for forgiving Steve had conditions. I needed to feel as if I'd landed safely. I had to clean up my credit score. I wanted to get refinanced. Forgiveness was supposed to be years down the road. And yet, the voice was clear. I already knew that conditional forgiveness is like conditional love: It's not the real thing. Anne Lamott wrote, "Earth is Forgiveness School. You might as well start at the dinner table."

With my head still facedown on my desk, I sighed.

"I forgive you, Steve," I said.

Chapter 27
All the Things He Didn't Do

In the weeks that followed, I found it was a little easier to forget, if only for a few minutes or an hour, all the damage Steve had wrought in my life. I began to consider how it must have felt to be him, particularly in his last year—to realize on some unconscious level all the mistakes he'd made and everything that he'd lost. His profession. His fortune. His wife. His reputation. His health. How frightening it must have been to witness his own body sprinting toward a premature death. And I suddenly realized: No revenge I could have dreamed up would have been remotely as bad as what he'd inflicted upon himself.

Every week brought a slight improvement in Bronte's outlook. Despite her best intentions, the fear and anger seemed to be lessening. She'd been texting and calling her best friend in Ames around the clock, and after a few weeks, she was even making plans to see her St. Helena friends in person.

Amory had no interest in his father's ashes, but the five daughters had agreed to split Steve's "cre-mains"—what hadn't been buried—and Bronte came up with a novel way to honor her dad. She'd found a tattoo artist in Sacramento who would incorporate the loved one's ashes into a permanent memorial of body art.

"You're not serious," I said, unable to censor myself. I'd forbidden both kids to get any tattoos or piercings until they were legal adults. Now Bronte was eighteen and could do whatever she wanted.

"Totally serious."

"Is it safe?"

"Completely safe."

I shook my head. "Well, what kind of tattoo are you thinking of?"

She showed me a picture of a small Christian cross. "Because Daddy was a Catholic," she said.

I could feel my teeth clench. *Not a very good one!* said the silent thought bubble over my head. Steve hadn't set foot in a single church of any persuasion in the twenty-plus years I'd known him, except to attend weddings or funerals.

"You know," I said, struggling to keep my voice light and thoughtful, "I think it would be much more meaningful to your dad if you inscribed something unique to your relationship. What about his nickname for you as a child?" My own father had called me "Buglet," like a little bug. We had then called Bronte "Bugletina," a further diminutive of the term.

Bronte cocked her head. "I'll think about it," she said.

A week later, she proudly showed me her new tattoo: Bugletina, written in tiny script in a vertical line behind her anklebone. "Don't worry, it won't show in a job interview or in a wedding dress," she told me proudly. I loved her pragmatism, which she obviously got from me.

Thank you, sounded a faint voice in my head. Pretty sure it was Steve.

Justin, the Nevada City realtor, was like my new husband. Every day brought another series of phone calls, either about the Nevada City or the Oakland property. We no longer bothered with greetings or introductions; we just kept the conversation going as if we'd never hung up on the previous call. As with the Oakland loft, I hadn't seen the Nevada City house for several years. Samantha had said that it was uninhabitable when they finally moved Steve to a smaller place near them for his final days. But somehow a renter had been found—a young woman, Lucy, and her boyfriend, Adam, who'd had some kind of relationship with Steve while he lived there—and they'd been renting and maintaining the place since December.

Once again there were issues of neglected rent, of repairs and unpaid bills. But Justin was running interference for me and only told me things on a need-to-know basis.

One day he called to tell me that there'd been a showing, and the couple had seemed interested in the property.

"Well, that's good news!" I said. We were still under threat of foreclosure if we didn't sell the place before the scheduled auction in June.

"Yeah, they just had one concern. About the greenhouse."

"What greenhouse?"

"There's a greenhouse now. Lucy and Adam have been, shall we say, running a little business on the side."

"A business?"

"A commercial marijuana grow. We need to shut it down before we have any more showings."

"Good God. They actually built a greenhouse?"

"No, the greenhouse has been there since last year sometime. Apparently Steve was in business with them."

Long silence. Finally, "You're kidding me."

"No, I'm not."

"Steve was a marijuana dealer?"

"Apparently so. It's extremely common up in these hills."

I thought back to the last time I'd visited the farm, in 2008, when

I'd found five tiny marijuana plants in pots in the dining room and had confronted Steve. Clearly, his interest had deepened. Was he supporting himself this way? What kind of people were coming and going from the property? And, my biggest question: Did the kids know about this? I didn't want to be the one to bring it up, in case they were unaware. But how likely was that?

To be learning of the chaos of my children's father's life piecemeal like this was heartbreaking. I'd known things were bad, but I still thought he'd been trying to keep it together when he had custody of the kids. Now I knew differently. How much had they seen? And how much of a fool was I, in their eyes, to have been completely ignorant of the whole mess?

Bronte was still living at home, still largely camped out on the living room sofa. One day, she decided she'd go through her childhood photos and pick out the ones she wanted to reprint. Of course it became a massive endeavor, with her calling me over to relive certain shots or identify them for her. When she'd finished a few hours later, I came down to see a pile of selected photos on the table next to the box. I riffled through them, glimpses into the wilderness of Bronte's emotional state. They were almost exclusively shots of Bronte with Steve—as a baby, as a toddler, as a child. I'd be lying if I said I wasn't hurt. But it was also terribly clear that Bronte was deep in mourning for her dad, trying to make sense of the loss. At least it was a step up from the couch.

One weekend in June, I took the kids up to Auburn for a visit with Lisa and Samantha and their families. It had been six months since Steve's funeral, and the time seemed right for a reunion. I wanted to remind them that they had a larger family, and a lifelong connection to their dad, with their half sisters. As we stood around the kitchen—a roomful of people talking baseball and motocross and rodeos—I was struck by how foreign I was to this family. What an odd fit it had been when Steve married me, and how strange that must have felt to his girls. Although they'd never lived with us, I had done my best to love them and support them through their dad. Still, I felt a lot like that effete character Diane from the sitcom *Cheers*, always invoking literary references and making dishes they'd never heard of.

Now I felt that foreignness more keenly than ever. I simply had nothing to contribute to the conversation—I had no idea who was headed for the World Series or when the Nevada County Fair would be held. I smiled and nodded but felt like the wallflower at a middle school dance.

Later, Lisa and I peeled off from the group and talked quietly about Steve. I'd always admired her, with her pragmatic intelligence, her professional ambition, her fierce love of her family. It was hard to believe that she was now forty-five—she'd been just nineteen on our wedding day, and now she was thirteen years older than I'd been when I married Steve.

Lisa told me about how each of Steve's older daughters was dealing with the aftermath of his death—one had turned him into a martyr, one didn't even want to hear his name, and another seesawed between extreme anger and extreme grief. He had never fully reconciled with any of them, and now they seemed to be the walking wounded. For her part, Lisa said, she chose to think back on Steve as an uncle or family friend. "Otherwise, the disappointment in his behavior is just too great," she said. "I know he wasn't capable of anything more. But if I think of him as my dad, I can only remember all the things he didn't do."

Lisa also confided how Steve had divided his remaining estate among his six kids, particularly Bronte and Amory—the two youngest, who still needed support through school. Still, he'd left all their inheritances tied up in his own IRAs so that if they made any withdrawals before the age of fifty-nine, they'd pay high tax penalties.

"He definitely used money to punish and reward people right up to the end," she said. She paused. "And when it came to you, he was determined to punish you until his dying breath."

"I know," I said. "He made that pretty clear."

Driving back to the hotel that night, I mentioned to Amory my earlier discomfort in the kitchen, how aware I'd been of the cultural differences between me and the older Beckwith girls.

"I could see that," he said. "You just wanted to be back on the bocce court wearing your quilted vest and a big scarf, passing around plates of nuts and figs."

I laughed so hard, I snorted. "You know me too well" was all I could say. Fifteen years old and, in just a few swift strokes, he'd painted my exact likeness. My heart swelled a little with gratitude and pride.

July 5 was one day before we were scheduled to close escrow on the sale of the loft to Michelakis. I had just arrived at work, dropped my backpack onto my desk, and was changing from my walking shoes into my suede flats when my cell phone rang, Justin's number lighting up the screen.

"Good morning," I answered. "I'm hoping you're calling to tell me he's ready to sign."

There was a long pause on the other end. Not a good one.

"He's backing out," Justin said. "He couldn't get financed."

"Backing out?" I wailed. "*One day* before the close of escrow?"

"Yep," Justin said. In his line of work, Justin had seen it all. But even he seemed incredulous. "This guy is such an asshole, Kirsten. I'm blown away."

I sank into my chair. I could have walked away from this property, but I'd chosen to stick around and do the right thing by selling it. And once again I'd been thwarted by some egotistical man with no integrity. Why was this evil archetype haunting me from every angle?

I looked around my tiny office, the family photos, the color-coordinated file boxes, the framed prints on the walls. Why was I working so damned hard when the bastards of the world were out to get me no matter what I did?

"So what next?" I finally asked.

"It goes to auction in less than two weeks," Justin said. "I don't think there's any chance that we can sell it in that time."

So after all the emails, the phone calls, the strategizing and negotiating, after all the nights of lying awake and worrying about this property, it would go to auction anyway.

"He'll be out of the condo by the end of the month," Justin finally said.

"How do I get the five thousand dollars from him?" I asked. It had been attached to the close of escrow.

"I'm afraid there's nothing I can do from my end," he said. "If it were me, I'd take him to small claims court."

Like I had nothing better to do.

But July turned out to be the month of my deliverance from real estate hell. Despite Michelakis's last-minute default, Justin soon pulled yet another rabbit out of his hat and arranged a sale with a young woman whose father could pay cash for the loft with very few questions asked. We closed escrow the day before the condo was to go to auction.

We also closed on the Nevada City farm in a short sale. My credit report was branded with an F, and that would take years to repair—but the relief of unloading the last two properties was immense. Now all I had to worry about was my job.

Chapter 28
These Men Don't Like You

In April our office hosted the quarterly board meeting, and afterward, as board directors and staff were milling around gathering their things, Tom Riordan turned to me.

"Kirsten, my dear," he said, with a degree of interest he rarely showed me. "Are you in a relationship?"

I've never been able to lie on the spot.

"Um, not at the moment," I said. This wasn't going to be good.

"Well, I don't know if you're aware of this, but I happen to be a pretty good matchmaker," Tom said.

No one had ever made an offer like this to me before, let alone my employer. What was the protocol?

I laughed and decided to treat it as a joke. "I'll bet you are! That is so sweet of you! I'll definitely let you know if I ever need your services."

"You do that, Kirsten," Tom said. "You're an attractive woman, and I know a lot of very wealthy men who're looking for someone like you."

The next few times I saw Tom, he made a point of mentioning his matchmaking talents again. Each time, I deflected the comments with feigned gratitude and humor.

But one day in late May, Tom flagged me down again.

"I have a friend," he began, and went on to describe a gentleman who happened to be single. The two of us would get along great—what if I just went to lunch with him?

Tom was in his eighties. I assumed his friend was too.

"Tom, I couldn't be more flattered. But I'm just so busy right now with work and my commute," I began weakly.

"Fred's the kind of guy who could take you to London for the weekend," Tom said. "He has his own venture capital firm. He's loaded."

I laughed. "I have a teenage son at home," I said. "I can't go to London for the weekend."

"You'd take your son along!" Tom said. It was clear he felt benevolent, opening the door to such opportunity for me, a simple working girl.

I sighed, still grinning.

"Just lunch," Tom said. "If you don't like him, no problem. Just spend an hour with him and see what you think."

I'd run out of excuses. "Okay," I finally said. It felt like making a deal with the devil.

"Terrific!" Tom said. Then, "Just one caveat," he added. "He's on the short side. But if you stood him on top of all his money, he could play basketball."

I faked a laugh. I had just been pimped by Tom Riordan.

On the appointed day at the appointed hour, I walked into Yank Sing restaurant and scanned the room for Fred Nowak, whose face I would recognize from having Googled his company website. He looked like a hobbit, but his bio was impressive. Born Friedrich Novosky in Poland, he'd barely escaped the Holocaust in 1945 at the age of eleven and had come to the U.S. with no resources. He made his way to Harvard Business School and now, decades later, was cofounder of a wildly successful VC firm in San Francisco.

I found Fred at a corner table, already eating an appetizer.

"I'm sorry, am I late?" I took off my jacket and hung it on the back of the chair.

"No, no, I just got here a little early," Fred said. "Please, sit down. Take a look at the menu."

He was wearing a salmon-colored corduroy jacket that matched the thinning, copper-colored hair circling his head like a nest. Once he'd flagged down our waiter and I'd ordered enough food to catch up with him, we did the dance of pleasantries. Fred had been married twice and had two grown, very successful children. He had a hilltop villa in West Marin, with views of the ocean. He was personally very involved in his charities, which spanned the globe, from the Tenderloin district in San Francisco to remote villages in Nepal. He really sounded like a good man. He was smart and funny and kind. But he was also about twenty years older than me, and I still didn't like the circumstances of our meeting.

We were thirty minutes into our meal when Fred said, "Well? What do you think? Are we a match?" I frantically calculated how I could make this work without losing either my self-respect or my job. I needed to phrase this as delicately and diplomatically as I could.

"Fred," I began, "I can tell that you're a lovely man." I was well into listing all my obligations—the fulltime job, the freelance work on weekends, the two children, the long commute—when Fred interrupted.

"But I can help you with all that," he said, and laid his hand on mine.

I froze. With that one statement, he confirmed that this was indeed an arrangement. I looked down at my pot stickers and my eyes began to fill. My chin quivered. Life suddenly seemed comically cruel and overwhelming. All of it. I had reached yet another breaking point.

I pulled my hand away and looked straight ahead, past Fred's concerned face, past the other diners to the large aquarium of tropical fish built into the wall. "Regardless of what Tom may have told you," I said coolly, "my affection is not for sale." Suddenly, my voice sounded like steel.

"No, no, of course I didn't mean *that*," Fred stammered.

"What did you mean, then?"

"I meant . . . I meant that I could provide some emotional support." He was backpedaling. We both knew it. "It sounds as if you could use a good friend."

"I have plenty of good friends," I said.

We sat in awkward silence. Finally I laid down my napkin, thanked Fred for the meal, and left the restaurant as quickly as I could.

The minute the fresh air hit my face, I burst into tears and cried all the way back to Riordan. I returned to my office and shut the door, where I tried to compose myself and wipe the mascara from my cheeks. Within minutes my phone rang, with "Riordan, Tom" on the caller ID screen.

"Kirsten! Tom here. My sources tell me that your lunch with Fred went very well! How do *you* feel it went?"

"Thanks again for introducing me to Fred," I began. "He's obviously charming and successful. I'm so flattered you thought of me."

"Well, apparently he likes you very much," Tom said. "Now I want to know what you felt about Fred."

"Well, like I said, he seemed really lovely."

"And?"

"And I really appreciate your thinking of me."

"But do you want to see him again? Toss me a bone here, honey."

"Okay. Tom, he was really a great guy. . . ."

"But . . . ?"

"But he's a little out of my age range. It's not really what I'm looking for."

There was a pause. Then Tom said, "Listen, sweetie. Sex comes and goes, but money is forever. This is a guy who could take care of you for the rest of your life."

"I appreciate that, Tom, I really do, but for me it's not about the money."

Another long pause as I squeezed my eyes tight, dreading his response. Then Tom said, "Well, sweetheart, that's to your credit."

I exhaled. "Thanks, Tom," I said. "Thanks for understanding."

"You have a good day, now." And he hung up.

Every day that passed, I breathed a little easier that I hadn't insulted Tom Riordan to a punishable degree. But then, two weeks later, I dealt myself a death blow. Rather than print an ad with twelve-year-old data from the internet, as Tom had requested, I meticulously updated the facts. I thought he'd be pleased—his credibility protected. I was mistaken.

When Tom read the copy and called my office, I could practically hear his anger before the phone had even stopped ringing.

"What the hell have you done? This isn't the ad I gave you!"

"You'd wanted Consul General Maher to sign the ad, but he said he couldn't sign without it being updated," I stammered.

"To hell with him!" Tom roared. "Did I tell you to fact-check? I sure as hell didn't!"

"I'm sorry, Tom," I said. "I just assumed you wanted the most up-to-date—"

"Don't *ever* assume!" Tom said. "It makes an *ass* of *you* and *me*!"

"I'm so sorry."

"Now, change that ad back to exactly the language I sent you. And I want it in Saturday's *Chronicle*!" He slammed down the receiver.

My head fell forward into my hands. The yoga pose for *I am fucked*.

A week later, Monica called me into her office and gestured for me to close the door. I'd been in negotiations with her for weeks requesting a salary increase based on my proven deliverables.

She sighed. "Kirsten, these men don't like you," she began. "They just don't. I've gone to Doug three times about a raise for you, and he won't budge. He keeps saying that you've got to show more commitment to Riordan before he'll even consider a salary increase."

"*More commitment*?" I gasped. "I commute five hours a day, five days a week! I've worked weekends and holidays and sick days and even bereavement days after my children lost their father, and he wants to see more commitment?" I was practically hissing.

"I know, it makes no sense. And now you've pissed Tom off, not once but twice. You've really painted yourself into a corner."

I was fighting back tears, but they came anyway.

"You really need to find another job," Monica was saying. "They can't fire you—there's no rational cause. But I can negotiate a nice severance package for you, something that will give you a few months to find something else."

I sat there sniffling and shaking my head.

"Look at you: You're a wreck. Let's call it a day."

I wiped my eyes and walked back to my office, where I gathered my things and left early. Never before had I been asked to leave a job. And I'd never left a job before lining up another one. I made my way home filled with humiliation and confusion, but also a kind of relief.

The next day Riordan's CFO called me into her office and read me the terms of my severance—three months' salary, including benefits—and asked if I would accept them. I nodded. It seemed fair. Only later would I realize I could have negotiated for much more.

Between the stress of the past six years, the trauma of Riordan, and now the bleak outlook for future employment, I felt shipwrecked. Had there been a husband, or better financial reserves, it would have been a great time to just take a break and recoup. But once again I was on my own. For all the dysfunction and anxiety at Riordan, the security of benefits and a regular paycheck had made it all worthwhile. Now I was unmoored, back in the Gulf Stream of an uncertain financial future.

Chapter 29
O Magnum Mysterium

My friend and neighbor Jane had long spoken of her "spiritual life coach," Arjuna, whom she'd been seeing weekly for a couple of years. From what I could tell, Arjuna's program was based on common sense mixed with tools for a spiritual practice that didn't so much change your life as change the way you felt about your life. In the time she'd been seeing him, I'd watched Jane transform from an anxious divorcée with low self-esteem to a confident woman unafraid of going after what she wanted. I knew several other women who had lost weight, battled serious illness, and just become happier people after working with Arjuna. I shot him an email, and the following Monday, he appeared on my doorstep for the first session of what would become two years of weekly therapy.

From the name Arjuna, I'd expected someone who looked like Gandhi. Instead, I opened the door to a white man in his sixties, with an athlete's build and long silver hair. I later learned that in younger days he'd been a model. He wore a white cotton kurtha and blue jeans with flip-flops and a wool scarf around his neck. "*Namaste*," he said, bowing.

Our first session consisted of my telling Arjuna about my rocky recent past, my disastrous career story, and my need to land a high-paying job in the city.

"Sounds like you need an awful lot," he said, smiling.

"Look, I'm a one-man band," I said. "I have two kids to support. And a mortgage. I can't waste any time gazing at my navel. But I also know I'm seriously out of whack here."

"You can rev your engine and spin your wheels all you like," Arjuna said. "But until you're ready to get quiet and find your inner guidance, I can't promise you're going to get very far."

I knew he was right. But what he was proposing sounded so hard.

We agreed to meet for an hour every Monday for as long as necessary. I figured it would be a few months. That's all I had.

In August, I wrote to Peter Michelakis, giving him a last chance to pay me $5,000 before I took him to court. Sure, I needed the money. But more than that, I needed to not let this jerk win. I felt as if I were fighting against the legions of unscrupulous, controlling men who thought they could roll over me with their legal loopholes, their street-smart savvy, and their fake charm. The idea of going to small claims court exhausted me, but the idea of letting Peter Michelakis off the hook woke me up in the middle of the night. He never responded to my letter, so I filed the paperwork. The court date was set for January 8, 2013, the one-year anniversary of Steve's death. That seemed like a good sign.

I prepared a package, including an itemized statement of facts and a stack of supporting correspondence and real estate documents, and sent it to the Superior Court.

In addition to working with Arjuna, I made an appointment with an astrologer. Astrology wasn't my thing, but my friend Nancy had sworn this woman was jaw-dropping. In a little cottage behind her house on the Silverado Trail, she pulled up my chart on her laptop, as well as the charts of Bronte, Amory, and Steve. As with the psychic, I was careful not to tell her anything about myself that would affect her reading.

"Yours is the sign of the Phoenix rising from the ashes," she said. "This process of resurrection is due to begin on January 8 of the new year." Wow. That was impressive.

"You have the chart of a teacher," she added. "Others will always be interested in what you have to say."

"No, that's not me," I jumped in. "I'm a terrible teacher. Once I learn something, I want to move on and learn something new, not turn around and teach it to someone else."

"Ah, but you're a writer, yes?"

"Yes."

"That's your method of teaching. Don't write about the past but about what you're feeling and observing in the present moment. Your life is rife with contemporary satire and fiction."

"Ha, really?" That was the last thing on my mind.

"You need to dust off the cobwebs and start writing creatively again," she said. "Do it in your spare time."

Spare time. Hilarious.

Two months passed. I spent my days scouring online job boards, writing thoughtful but witty cover letters, and tailoring my résumé to each new position. I was a marketing expert! I was a publicity whiz! I was a deeply experienced content provider! With all my experience, I thought, I could easily fit in as a copywriter at a creative agency. But most of my digital submissions went ignored; if I received even a form email in response, acknowledging my letter, I was elated. In the few interviews I was called for, I learned they were looking for a communications expert who would do everything from marketing strategy to social media, including publications, public relations, even design. And for a fraction of the salary I'd been making. Suddenly the job market seemed intended only for millennials who were willing to work around the clock for a pittance. How had I gone from being a seasoned communications professional to a has-been?

It wasn't long before I began looking forward to Monday mornings. I relied on Arjuna's weekly pep talks to get me through another week of professional rejection and financial shrinkage.

Our sessions usually followed a predictable pattern: In a whiny voice, I'd recount the disappointments of the previous week. Then Arjuna would remind me of the importance of self-love, letting go of the fear, surrendering to the schedule of the universe, having faith in the outcomes, believing in my ultimate success.

"You're being tested," he said. "All your life, you've been rewarded for your intelligence and hard work. You've been laboring under the misimpression that it's all under your control. Your lesson now is to let go of that control and have faith in God, or the universe, or spirit, or whatever you want to call it." He always sat in the big striped armchair, his legs tucked under him, a shawl around his shoulders. Dolce, the dog, would usually curl at his feet.

"I get that," I said. "But one day in the not too distant future, I'm going to run out of money. Does the universe have a checkbook?"

Arjuna laughed his deep laugh. "That's the point of faith," he said. "It doesn't work with guarantees. Once you relinquish control, you'll be amazed at how God provides. Let go of all your conditions. Just try it."

In between spiritual therapy and the job search, there were the kids. Bronte had returned to school in Iowa, where she seemed to be doing okay after her six months of depression on the couch. She called me every Sunday evening but only because I insisted on it. Amory was still putting on his "everything's good" routine, but his grades were in the toilet, and I suspected he'd discovered the pleasures of cannabis.

In hindsight, I can see the benefits of being forced to stay at home just then, but at the time all I wanted to do was get back into the grind of a daily job. I needed to feel like I was moving forward.

One Friday night in October, I got a phone call every mother dreads. It was the coach of Amory's junior varsity football team, which was playing that night in Lakeport.

"I'm afraid I'm calling with some bad news," he said.

I tried to suppress thoughts of worst-case scenarios and quickly asked, "How bad?"

"Amory took a big hit, and he seems to have broken his collarbone," the coach said.

"Where is he?" I asked. "Are you taking him to the nearest hospital?"

"Well, unfortunately they don't have medical staff on the field here," he said. "All we have is the team doctor. You can either come get him yourself, or we can bring him home with us on the bus."

"On the bus? You mean in two hours when the game is over?"

"It'd probably be more like three hours, once we get the team loaded back on."

"And you're telling me that no one is available to give him medical care until I can drive there, over an hour from now?"

"Yes, ma'am."

"You are fucking kidding me."

"I'm afraid not, ma'am."

"I'm on my way. Have you given him any painkillers?"

"All we have is Tylenol. State law."

I jumped in the car and raced through the dark, up the winding mountain road and through the strange town, until I saw the lights of the stadium ahead. I found Amory sitting on a bench, a varsity jacket over his shoulders, shivering from the cold and pain and shock.

The coach ran over and tried to be helpful getting my injured son into the passenger seat of my Prius. Amory winced and groaned with every move. "If it were my son, I'd take him directly to St. Helena Hospital," he offered. "The ER here in Lakeport isn't very good."

I scowled at him. "I honestly expected better from St. Helena High," I said, and slammed the door.

Amory began moaning louder as soon as I started the engine, and I drove gingerly back over the mountain and into the parking bay of St. Helena Hospital's ER. The doctor there taped him up and recommended that we see the orthopedic surgeon first thing the next day—the same guy who had set Amory's two broken arms. Then he gave us a week's supply of Vicodin.

Five days later I walked into the recovery area and watched my son, still knocked out from the surgery, lying like a slain soldier on the bed. In his collarbone were a new titanium plate and six screws. Steve had been thrilled when Amory had decided to try out for football; "He should play *two* sports," he'd said. That's what Steve had done, so he expected the same for our son.

I had adamantly protested, but I'd given in. Now, once again, my child was injured. And once again, I blamed myself.

A week before we were due to appear in small claims court, I received a copy of Michelakis's response to the court, including a similarly thick stack of documents. His defense was the by-now familiar refrain that I hadn't made the promised repairs, and he was caused personal distress by the threat of foreclosure. "I was going through a devastating divorce, and I was never able to make this unit a home for my sons when they visited. I did not have quiet enjoyment of the premises during the entire time of my stay." He didn't mention that his sons were in their late twenties, with lives of their own.

Our court date was a week away. I couldn't wait to see his smug face in the presence of a judge. On Tuesday, January 8, I waited in line to be let into the courtroom. When the doors opened, I found a seat in the second row and a minute later watched a dark-haired man sit down directly in front of me. I'd never met Peter Michelakis, but I knew his face from having Googled him. He was dressed in a fancy but rumpled brown suit. His thick head of hair looked hastily combed, and his face was that of a man who had been getting little sleep. *Good*, I thought.

The bailiff called everyone in the courtroom to rise, and Judge Emily Yu—a small, graying Asian woman about my age—entered and took the bench. We sat through several cases, and in each case Judge Yu asked the plaintiff and respondent each to state their case, then instructed them to meet out in the hallway to see if they could reach a last-minute settlement before turning the decision over to the court.

Eventually our names were called, and we rose to face the judge. It was clear that I would not be allowed the time to read my full two-page statement, so I nervously recounted my key points against my tenant—failing to pay rent for five months, holding up the property in contract until a day before it was to close escrow, failing to qualify for a loan, being evicted in August for lack of payment.

Michelakis then voiced his rebuttal: the fact that I didn't legally own the property, my unwillingness to make the requested repairs, his devastating divorce, his emotional distress at not being able to call the loft his home, his poor sons. I tried not to smile. How quickly these successful, powerful men resorted to playing the victim card.

We were then dismissed to the lobby, where I summoned my nerve to face Michelakis at close range. Both of us were clearly feeling the awkwardness of the moment.

He began with the now tired song about his bad year, his terrible divorce, his "lack of comfort" living in my unit. I held up a hand, traffic cop style.

"Peter, I've been there. I've seen much worse than you—I was almost forced into bankruptcy by my ex-husband. And at no time did I fail to make my monthly mortgage payments. You don't just stop paying your rent because of a bad lighting fixture. Especially when you're in contract to buy the place."

"Look, I'll very likely win this case," Michelakis said. "You're the one in the wrong here. But I'm willing to pay you a thousand dollars just to make this go away."

I laughed. "No thanks." Then we were called back into the courtroom.

"Were you able to reach an agreement?" Judge Yu asked.

"No, Your Honor, we were not," Michelakis said, sending a dark look my way.

"Very well, I'll review your case, and you'll receive my decision by mail in about a week." The gavel sounded and I raced out. On the BART ride home, I laid my head back and closed my eyes. If she ruled in his favor, I'd just have to put it behind me. I'd done everything I could. *It's a lawsuit*, I told myself. *Not leukemia.*

Among Arjuna's prescriptions for healing my soul was to spend time creatively, so after a hiatus of several years, I began writing fiction again and formed a writing group with several other local writers. I started taking a drawing class. And I was in my sixth year of my beloved chamber-singing group. I once read that to recover after a heart attack it helps to take up knitting, that the act of tying yarn together with two needles can literally knit the cardiac tissues back together again. That's the way I felt each Monday night when I joined seventy others to rehearse for one of our semiannual concerts.

On one such night, we were rehearsing "O Magnum Mysterium" by Morten Lauridsen, a slow, melodic piece that felt inspired by Gregorian chants. We ended with the basses singing the final resonant note like an old cello, a transcendent moment that filled the rehearsal room. After a moment of complete silence, one of the altos let out a moan of pleasure, and the whole group laughed. "I'll have what she's having," one of the sopranos quipped. It made me realize, once again, what a soul-saving gift this group was to me. The fact that I was part of it felt like another little blessing. Piece by piece, I was taking off my rusty armor.

On January 15, I opened my mailbox to find an envelope from the County of Alameda Superior Court. I studied the official seal as I brought it in and laid it on the counter. I made a silent, fourth-quarter plea to Steve. *Last chance to help me with this*, I told him. *Are you in my corner?* Then I slit open the envelope and took out the Notice of Entry of Judgment.

"Defendant Peter Michelakis shall pay Plaintiff Kirsten B. Mickelwait $5,000.00 principal and $60.00 court costs on Plaintiff's claim," it read. "Principal and costs are payable forthwith. Enforcement of the judgment is automatically postponed for 30 days or, if an appeal is filed, until the appeal is decided."

And then, on January 29, I sorted my mail to find an envelope from Parthenon Properties—Michelakis's real estate development firm. I ripped it open, and there was a check for $5,060—the full amount awarded by the court. I quickly endorsed the check and deposited it on my phone. Then I proudly signed the Acknowledgment of Satisfaction of Judgment form to the clerk of the court and put it in the pre-addressed envelope. It was done. I had won.

Thanks, Steve, I said again. I didn't know how he'd done it, but this time I was sure he'd played a role in my salvation.

Chapter 30
Despair Is a Spiritual State

Over the next few months, I told Arjuna my history, my anxieties, my frustrations. I whined and cried and listened like a desperado in church. Every Monday he greeted me with a dazzling grin and a hug, and after our hour was up, I said goodbye feeling like a completely different person than the one who had opened the door. It would be no exaggeration to say that he sustained me from week to week. Despite all my fierce independence and fortitude, I felt like a child waiting for her parent to pick her up from school. "Despair is a spiritual state too," he'd say.

Like my own personal Yoda, Arjuna would sit cross-legged in the big striped chair and dispense pithy advice that sounded cliché but also felt entirely true. "Everything is happening as it should, with perfect timing," he would say. "Let go of all those expectations. Surrender, surrender, surrender. And, above all, you must open your heart."

I thought of how I loved my children, how I loved my mother and sister and friends. "But my heart *is* open," I'd wailed.

"Yes, to everyone but yourself," Arjuna said.

—

Before long, Arjuna taught me how to meditate. For years, I'd only dabbled in meditation. Now he coached me on the breath, the mantra, the visualizations. I began setting the morning alarm fifteen minutes earlier than usual and using that time to meditate. Most days, my mind raced and wandered like an errant puppy.

"Thoughts are the breath of the mind," Arjuna said.

Some days, if I hadn't slept well the night before, I would doze off. But every once in a while, I would feel peaceful and transcendent—a perfect stillness humming like the echo of a gong. Once or twice I came out of my meditation in tears.

Over a period of months, I began to notice small changes. I was able to focus more easily during the day. I had better balance. Most of all, my daily fear about the future went from a high boil to a low simmer.

Meanwhile, the employment situation remained bleak. Every week I would give Arjuna a report on the cover letters sent out, the LinkedIn connections pursued, the new versions of my résumé created. And every week, Arjuna would say, "I don't know, I keep seeing you doing your own thing. Working from home. Freelancing."

I sat in doubting silence.

"All you have to do is stay open to the *possibility*," he said. "Try it on, and if it doesn't feel right, take it off."

I felt I had failed at freelancing once and insisted that I didn't have the nerve or the resources to try it again. But I had retained a few small clients, for whom I had worked on evenings and weekends. I began to consider fully jumping back into freelance.

Gradually, I returned to Match. Online I found the usual assortment of eager, "easygoing" men. Javier was originally from Mexico and had assimilated well into life in the East Bay, where he worked as a social worker and junior college administrator. He had the leathery good looks of Julio Iglesias. I agreed to meet him at a pizza place just two blocks from my house.

On my bike ride over, I found myself praying that he was truly the five foot eleven inches he had advertised. But as I sat on a bench outside the restaurant and watched him emerge from his car, I saw that he was at least an inch shorter than me, and—despite the thinning hair on top—a thin ponytail hung at the back of his skull.

Javier greeted me with a long bear hug. Too much, too soon. And from the moment we sat down, he began reaching across the table and grabbing my arm, hard, as if marking his territory. I found myself pulling away, shrinking back, wanting the time to figure out how much I liked him. *Slow down*, my body language said. *Give me a chance.*

I thought back to my first date with Eddie, how it had been such a graceful dance. There was eye contact, and laughter, and me gently touching his hand to let him know the door was open. When he told me to take his arm as we walked along the Embarcadero, he knew I was ready to do just that.

But with Javier, it was a one-way conversation. As we stood on the sidewalk saying goodbye, he leaned in for a kiss on the mouth, uninvited. I swiftly turned my head to offer my cheek instead, and his kiss landed awkwardly on my ear.

One morning in February, Bronte called to discuss the possibility of a new apartment for spring semester with two other girls, which would save her more than $100 a month. As usual, I was on a deadline and didn't really want to spend the time on the phone, but I put my work down and really tried to listen. Bronte's tone was calm. She was interested in my viewpoint. She was actually asking for my input and approval. And of course she had thought through all the logistics—the cost, transportation to and from campus, the personalities of her potential roommates. I was proud of her. It was the first time in a long while that I felt we were just two rational people having a conversation. It felt like the first faint rays of a weak spring sun.

"Why are you so afraid of men?" It was March, still chilly, and Arjuna had his bare feet extended by the fire in my fireplace, the dog sleeping in her usual position at his ankles.

"I'm not afraid of men," I said. "Why would you say that?"

"You can't wait to get rid of them. You would rather send them away than find out more about them. Because you're afraid you might find something you like."

I made a scoffing noise. "I just have certain standards and boundaries," I said. "I can usually tell pretty quickly if they're right for me or not." Arjuna smiled and said nothing.

"Okay, maybe I am just the teensiest bit defensive," I said.

"I want you to close your eyes and get still," he said. "I want you to visualize an open heart and an open mind."

I sat for a few minutes in silence, breathing deeply, eyes closed.

"Now tell me," he said. "What are you afraid of?"

"I'm afraid of being trapped again," came a voice from my mouth. "I'm afraid of having to settle. I'm afraid of being stuck with a man I don't love."

"Good," Arjuna said. "Now tell me. When was the last time you felt that way?"

"With Eddie," I said. "But mostly with Steve."

"Right. And what did you do when you felt that way?"

"I put up with it until I couldn't stand it anymore. And then I left."

"Right. You left. Are you trapped now?"

"No."

"Did you have a choice to leave?"

"Yes."

"So it seems that being trapped isn't the problem. Why do you pick such controlling men?"

Whoa. I'd never looked at it that way before.

"Well, I guess that with both Steve and Eddie, I was attracted to their charisma, their swagger, their command of the world. Physical chemistry was important to me. But after a while it felt like they were commanding me too."

"Uh-huh." There was another long silence. Then Arjuna said, "Could it be that what you're really afraid of is your own bad judgment with men?"

I laughed. "Could be." I got up to let the dog out. I was suddenly restless. Circling the couch, I said, "But if our purpose here is to feel love and joy, why doesn't God send me someone to love in a healthy way? Why do I meet nothing but inappropriate guys?"

"That's what everyone wants," Arjuna said, smiling. "We all say, give me a great guy and a great job and a beautiful life, and I'll be happy. We always place conditions on our happiness. That's not the way it works. You need to learn to be happy *without* the conditions. And when you do, you'll find that you receive the things you want."

I nodded, silent.

"Sometimes God doesn't change your situation, because he's trying to change your heart."

For a moment, I felt a pang of sympathy for Arjuna's wife. What would it be like to be married to someone who's so right all the time?

"You are meant to write a book," Arjuna kept saying. "And to do that, you can't be spending half your day getting to and from your job. You need to create some space in your life to let the magic in."

Hearing his aspirational words always lifted my spirits, but it was hard to sustain the high when, during the rest of the week, I felt isolated and broke. Soon enough, though, I sensed a little movement. Several people called me out of the blue to offer freelance work, just enough to make me think that perhaps I could actually make a go of it again. Despite my earlier adamant refusals, I finally caved.

"Fine!" I told Arjuna one Monday in May. "Have it your way! I'll try going independent again. Nobody else is making me any better offers anyway." Arjuna beamed. "The universe is on your side," he said, for the hundredth time. "It wants you to succeed as much as you do. It just wants your undivided attention right now."

"It's got my attention," I said.

At Riordan, there had been an on-call IT team for tech problems, and the admin, Heather, had handled the social media. Now I had to put my head down, confront my technophobia, and master the internet. For three full months I worked on a few small client projects but focused most of my energy on setting up shop. I created my own website, built its search-engine optimization, curated an online port-folio of past work, set up an e-blast program, started a blog, designed and produced my business cards, established my own domain, migrated my email to Outlook, created a business Facebook page, started Tweeting, and became somewhat addicted to my iPhone. I developed my "brand," carefully considering everything I posted on social media. I networked on LinkedIn and made lists of nonprofit organizations that I knew were undertaking fundraising campaigns.

In hindsight, it sounds as if all this was linear and effortless. In truth, it was probably the most frustrating, humiliating three months of my life. I found that many tech companies don't have telephone customer service, so I spent days in online chats and leaving irate emails asking for help. I got halfway through building my website with one platform before giving up and moving to another one. Once a week, I was reduced to tears. I kept reminding myself what I'd seen younger workers do when they faced a roadblock online: They didn't panic or think they'd break the computer if they hit the wrong key. Instead, they read the directions again and tried other menus and click-throughs to see what was behind each door. I changed my theme song from "I can't do this!" to "I'm going to figure this out."

When I'd finally finished building my infrastructure, I was amazed that clients actually started finding me. A creative agency in Pennsylvania hired me to help them with fundraising brochures for several universities and flew me to Detroit and Columbus to meet with the stakeholders. A food manufacturer retained me to write a series of monthly print ads. And a tech company sent me several assignments to write about "big data" for their online blog.

These jobs weren't enough to support the kids and me, but it was more new business than I'd gotten in my previous three years of freelancing. It seemed like, with a little hustle and a lot of patience, I might actually be able to make a go of it.

Chapter 31

A Meatball at the Mouth of a Cave

Another new year. One morning in mid-January, Bronte lifted the last box into her truck, ready to leave for spring semester in Iowa. I'd lobbied hard against her making the trip alone, especially in winter, but she was both determined and excited.

She'd had her tires rotated; bought a plastic bin and filled it with emergency supplies; calculated costs of gas, food, and lodging; and researched hotels and figured out a driving schedule. And now that it was time for her to get on the road, she was positively giddy. I just had to let her go.

Bronte called me each night and reported on the day. And it turned out to be a fun road adventure—she stopped at shops and museums and took pictures for her Instagram. She bought an elk sandwich at Cabela's in Reno. She went to the Buffalo Bill Cody Museum in North Platte, Nebraska. She got the idea to work at a dude ranch in Wyoming after college graduation. She even ate in a restaurant by herself.

I ended up being quite proud of her. She was showing an

independent streak and a sense of adventure—and she had planned
and executed the trip with great common sense. I had to remind
myself that, at her age, I was traveling around Europe alone, staying
in hostels, taking trains, and even hitchhiking with friends. Could it
be that she was just like me?

Later that week, Bonnie Fournier called in a chatty mood. As usual,
she mentioned Steve and said how sorry he was now for all the trouble he had inflicted on me. He seemed to visit her regularly.

"I know," I said. "I realize he's no longer that person who hurt
me so much. But I'm still working on letting go of everything he did
while he was on this side."

Bonnie asked me if I'd ever sold the loft, and I told her the story of
the miracle, the way Michelakis had finally paid me.

"That was Stephen Beckwith," Bonnie said. "He did that."

"I wondered if he'd played a role in it," I said.

"Oh, yes! I see his face right now, and he's laughing and nodding."

"Really?"

"Really. Is there anything else you want him to do? Because he's
standing right here in front of me."

"Sure," I said. "Tell him to bring me lots of work."

Bonnie was silent for a minute. Then, "I'm feeling like it'll be
coming around the second week or so in March."

I hung up and sighed. The second week in March was just three
weeks away. I scribbled a note in my calendar to see what actually
happened when the time came. But there had been another little shift
as Bonnie had talked. I absolutely did believe that Steve was now
sorry, and even willing to help.

Then I heard from Kelly, a copywriter friend who had recently
gone to work fulltime for an online cosmetics company. "Can I just
say how awkward and shitty I feel at my new job?" she said. "It's a
room full of mean girls. One of my employees hates me. I'm afraid

these aren't my people." It felt like Kelly was the messenger sent from the road not taken.

That week, during my morning meditation, I had a spontaneous vision—like a little movie playing on the screen of my eyelids—of being in a dark cave. Suddenly a ray of light pierced the darkness, and I could see a large, perfectly round stone being rolled away from the mouth of the cave. It looked like an enormous meatball. The Biblical imagery wasn't lost on me, but I wasn't the Bible type. It just felt like a message of hope and optimism.

The second week of March arrived. On Tuesday, I had a meeting in Oakland with a small branding firm with several prestigious Napa Valley winery clients; they were looking for a copywriter. On Thursday I got a call from a woman with a digital communications company who needed a writer for two of her data storage clients. On Friday morning I had coffee with a woman who offered to connect me with a friend who did freelance tech copywriting for two ad agencies in the city. That night I received an email from the local vintners' association, offering to hire me to write its annual report. And on the following Monday I received an email from a creative staffing agency interested in hiring me to write a newsletter for the Port of Stockton. That was five job connections in a week, after months of almost no movement at all. And it all happened in the exact week that Bonnie had predicted.

The following Monday, when I told Arjuna about my eventful week, he laughed. "All your hard work is paying off—not just your pragmatic efforts, but your spiritual work. And your forgiveness of Steve has been like rolling the stone away from the mouth of a cave."

I stared at him in awe. "What made you use that image?" I asked.

"That's just what I saw in my mind's eye," Arjuna said. "These past seven months have been like your own little Himalayan cave, where you've retreated to contemplate and deal with your demons.

And now you're emerging back into the world. You've finally opened the door to let the abundance in."

July 18 marked twenty-six years since our wedding day. That morning I walked to the cemetery and wished Steve a happy anniversary. I had begun visiting his grave on important dates, like his birthday and Father's Day. At first, I'd stood at the gravesite with my arms crossed and told him, "I'm not ready to forgive you, but I'm working on it." With each visit, I could chat with him more easily. I've never been a fan of the faded fake flowers that adorn so many graves. Instead, I followed the Jewish tradition of leaving a stone at the grave marker, a simple gesture to show that the deceased was remembered. After a while, a neat little pile of stones had accumulated.

I asked Steve for his help with Bronte: Let her be more open to help from others, particularly me. Let her open her heart enough to let some light in, to help with her fear, her anger, her self-doubt. I also reminded him that I still needed plenty of help myself with work—especially with the challenging stuff, like the highly technical project I'd just received to write about data integration. Perhaps his total lack of support during his last six years could be redeemed by some support from beyond the grave.

About ten years earlier, I'd watched an episode of *Oprah* that changed my worldview. Oprah's guest was a woman named Carolyn Myss, a former journalist who had worked with Elisabeth Kübler-Ross and earned a master's degree in theology. Myss had developed skills as a medical intuitive and became a pioneer in the field of holistic and energy medicine. Her newest book, *Sacred Contracts*, described "a set of assignments that our souls formed before incarnation."

I already believed in reincarnation, and I readily processed this new information. Myss used principles developed by Plato, Jung, and others to create a new theory based on spiritual archetypes and explained how we could each find our higher purpose on earth by identifying our own archetype or energy. Before being born onto the earthly plane, she explained, we drafted agreements with soul partners on the other side. We agreed to help each other learn lessons during our earthly lives, lessons like abundance, forgiveness, and unconditional love.

When I'd read her book, I was still happily married and ensconced in my cozy life. But what she said made sense to me: that our biggest adversaries were often our greatest teachers, that there was an agreement behind our sometimes tedious and annoying lives. If we learned the lessons we had chosen to learn, we could move on to others. But if we refused to grow through the challenges, that lesson would continue to haunt us until we learned it. Our contractual partners were not only our immediate family members but also the passive-aggressive friend, the unreasonable boss, the needy colleague.

I had long accepted that Steve and I had some sort of contract—clearly, we were meant to teach each other some big lessons. But even after Steve died, this felt like an abstract concept. I wanted to believe that, although he'd been difficult and hurtful when he was in his earthly incarnation, he was his higher self now that he was on the other side.

One night, in the middle of a dead sleep, I awoke to the alarming sensation of another body in the bed. Someone—it felt like a man—was snuggling up next to me, spooning against me, his knees tucked right behind mine. With heart pounding, I imagined an intruder, someone who might have a gun or a knife, making himself known before he killed me. I felt the body move and then sensed a hand reaching up to massage my neck and shoulder muscles. As I struggled to emerge fully from sleep, I could still feel the body shifting on the mattress next to me. I was afraid to turn and confront him. But as I continued to lie there, dreading what came next, the movement stopped. Now fully awake, with gasping breaths, I realized that the specter behind me—so completely authentic a moment ago—had disappeared.

It hadn't been a dream. It had been a real, physical sensation. It wasn't until later that morning that it occurred to me: It had been Steve. Over the next year, it happened again several times. Each time I awoke with terror that a real man was actually in my bed. And each time it felt clear to me that it could only have been the ghost of my ex-husband.

In time, I gained several new clients. The communications agency in Pennsylvania wanted me to work with them on several new projects for a healthcare system. A design agency in Emeryville hired me to do a year-round series of monthly ads. And at UC Berkeley, the College of Engineering chose me to write sixty-five pages of content for its new website. That project alone would pay more than I'd made in a year during my previous freelance career. All told, I was juggling about fifteen projects. *More work than you can handle* had been Arjuna's prediction.

But now I faced a new problem: I was every bit as stressed out as when I hadn't known where the next job was coming from. I felt guilty for not feeling happier, but I was now worried about my ability to keep up with the workflow and not burn out or drop one of the many spinning plates. I found myself procrastinating, especially at the beginning of projects for new clients.

One morning, during my daily walk, I had an epiphany: The beginning of any project, especially with new clients, was always filled with an element of chaos. Unknown expectations. Conflicting ideas from different sources. Piles of unorganized material that somehow had to be tamed into a single, brilliant document. And often, it involved a steep learning curve in a field with which I was completely unfamiliar, like data integration or molecular biology.

I had never liked chaos. I had charted my life as a series of habits and systems designed to tame disorder wherever I found it, from my calendar to my closets to my children's toys. And now I was faced with it, again and again—often from people I'd never even met. So, with every new job or client, I put up a wall of fear and dread and spent time procrastinating or spinning my wheels. Once I forced myself to get into the project, though, I felt better and tended to lose myself in the work. And the closer I got to completion, the better I felt about myself and the more confidence I had in the work. Job after job, I had performed well, I had met my deadlines, and I had given the client what they'd asked for—if not more.

Seeing this pattern became enormously empowering. With the launch of each new project, instead of feeling worried and over- whelmed and doomed for failure, I simply reminded myself, *This is just chaos again. You hate chaos. Put your head down and move through it, and happiness awaits you on the other side.* It's a practice I maintain to this day with every unpleasant or arduous task. It was life-changing.

I began to augment Arjuna's teachings with additional reading. The book *Buddha's Brain: The Practical Neuroscience of Happiness, Love and Wisdom* by Rick Hanson built a perfect bridge between spirit and science. We'd evolved as a species to pay greater attention to unpleas- ant experiences, Hanson writes. This negativity bias overlooks good news, highlights bad news, and creates anxiety and pessimism. Every time we notice the good, we build a little bit more neural structure, and doing this regularly will actually change the brain and how we feel.

After all the years of stalwart discipline and fighting to survive financially, I felt parched and calcified, and my heart began to soak up this new, hopeful language. I was hungry for a new way to feel. A way out.

Chapter 32
Lifting the Veil

Yet another January rolled around. Impossible to believe that it was already 2015, three full years since Steve's death. With all of my work around forgiveness, I finally felt ready to face him, beyond just talking to him in my head. So I called the intuitive Karen Peterson's office and booked a private reading for a date around his sixty-sixth birthday.

Karen greeted me warmly. We settled in, and she sat silent for a few minutes, eyes closed, breathing deeply. Finally she spoke.

"It's a male energy. A father figure. Has your dad passed?"

My dad had been the primary spirit to come through in my previous reading with Karen. I'd wondered if he'd be in control again this time.

"Yep," I said.

She nodded but then cocked her head. "Where is your dad buried?"

"His ashes are scattered at the base of a tree in Yosemite."

"No, this isn't him. This spirit is showing me a cremation but also a burial in a cemetery."

"Ah. That would be my ex-husband, Steve," I said. "I figured he'd show up today."

"Yes, he's being very clear about being buried in the cemetery. It looks like you visit him often?"

"Fairly often."

"He's showing me you visiting his grave. And every time you do, he's right there with you."

I nodded.

"A name that's coming up is Michael."

"That was Steve's middle name."

"So he's right here. Is there anything you want to ask him?"

"Here's what I keep struggling with," I said. "I know that Steve was some kind of teacher for me. But specifically, what was the lesson I was supposed to learn from him?" I felt like he was standing right there but behind a wall. I couldn't see him to read his lips.

Karen listened, then said, "To persevere. To still be strong despite challenges. To be a good role model for your children."

"Well, I've certainly tried to do that," I said.

"He's nodding," Karen said. "He's so proud of the way you've done that."

Finally, it seemed, I had the rational Steve back. The partner who wanted me to succeed, who saw my best self. He was on the other side of the veil, but he was an ally again. I felt a dark cloud lift from somewhere deep inside. The oppressive weight of his disapproval peeled off my shoulders and back.

Karen spoke again. "He's showing me an antique key, and keys usually symbolize cars. Did you recently buy a car? Do you need a car?"

I chuckled. "Ask him if it's a brown Mercedes."

"He's laughing! What's that about?"

I told her the story of the Mercedes with the chocolate-brown interior, parked outside my house.

"Honestly?" Karen said. "I have *no* idea how they do that. But I hear stories like this all the time."

We talked about each of the kids, Karen accurately describing the issues I was having with each of them. There were also some past-life issues with Bronte, she said. That explained a lot.

Then she returned to Steve. "He's showing me a contract and a pen," she said. "Did you two sign some sort of agreement together?"

I laughed. "You name it. There was a marriage license. A lot of property purchases. A divorce decree. Deeds, liens, trusts, the works."

Karen nodded. "This is bigger than that. He's showing me an agreement you signed before you each incarnated into this lifetime. A soul contract."

I suddenly remembered the Myss book, *Sacred Contracts*.

"You need to ask yourself, why did I write this out for myself?" Karen said. "Steve says he played his role perfectly. You wrote the script, and he was your teacher. Everything he did *to* you, he did *for* you."

"Wow." I sat back and tried to reimagine the past eight years as a positive thing.

"You should be feeling grateful toward Steve. He's been helping you advance toward your own enlightenment. And he did so at considerable cost to himself."

We sat in silence for a moment. "One thing I'm being shown," Karen said. "Have you ever seen that movie *Grizzly Man*?"

I'd definitely seen it. The Werner Herzog documentary about Timothy Treadwell, who thought he was soul mates with Alaskan grizzly bears and ended up being eaten by one. "That was Steve," I said, "dressing in buckskin, going to Alaska every summer."

Karen said, "Actually, when I was watching that movie last summer, I knew Tim Treadwell had passed, so I mentally asked him, 'Why did you choose to be eaten by the bear? What was the purpose of that?' He told me that in a prior lifetime he had killed grizzlies for sport. So he wanted to give his whole life to the bears this time around."

I nodded. "Steve went through this whole personality change. He became a completely different person that involved guns and motorcycles and tattoos. He'd been a really successful attorney, and he turned into a kind of hillbilly."

"Are you kidding me?" Karen asked.

"He was dressing in costume, basically. By the time our marriage dissolved, he'd become someone else."

"Interesting," Karen said. "So this is what he's saying. If we look at ourselves as two people, there's the essence of who we are, and also what our soul signed up to do. There's the I, the me. I'm the attorney, I'm the husband. But there's also what the soul needs to experience. Perhaps he made an extreme amount of money in a past life and made fun of the homeless or uneducated people, so in order for him to feel that karma, he had to make a lot of money and then later experience what it's like to be the opposite."

"He basically lived those two lives in the one life," I said. "But in doing so, he abandoned his family. He left his job. He spent money he didn't have. He turned into a different man."

"So when these moments come up for you, try looking at the bigger picture," Karen said. "There are *so* many blessings coming from Steve's life. It's all in the way we interpret it. Yes, he did so well, then he did so much harm. But what if we say he did so well, then even better as your great teacher? Really, he's given such a gift to you all. I would say thank you, Steve!"

Karen was beaming, her hands lifted to the invisible presence. I was smiling and shaking my head. To thank someone for pushing you to the brink of bankruptcy? To leave you scrambling to earn a living and support your children alone? But if I squinted hard enough to see the bigger picture, I could start to comprehend it.

"I'm clearly seeing this as a gift," Karen was saying. "I'm telling you, he's laughing. He's saying, 'Finally, she got in here so I can turn this thing around! I think she's going to get it now.' You need to remember that this isn't the same Steve who caused you so much pain. We return to our higher selves on the other side."

I felt tears welling up. It was a generic message, but in that moment I could feel Steve's love. It had always been there, but his own bad judgment had so often gotten in the way. Now the love was there without the damage.

We sat for a few more minutes. Karen went on to describe my house, my neighborhood, the streets where I walked the dog. She gave me specific details about my life with Steve that she couldn't have guessed at.

She smiled. "He's not holding on to anything. I usually deal with huge heaviness in these readings. If he were holding on to it, he would have given it to me."

"Well, I figured he's all well and good on the other side," I laughed. "Now that he's his higher self."

"No, that's not always the case," she said. "At our moment of death, we all go through a life review. As he passed, he saw a kind of movie of his life, and he became his own judge. His energy was a lot heavier right after he passed, because of the pain he'd caused."

Here was the end-of-life movie again. "Can I interpret that to mean that I'm clearing that lesson from my karma?" I asked.

"Oh yes, absolutely," Karen said. "You've fulfilled your agreement with him. You had to go through it and understand it. He gave you a gift. So that's the finishing of the karmic relationship."

I suddenly felt a snap of revelation, like the tumbler of a lock falling into place.

"You know, for most of my adult life, I've felt like my true life's work would be to write something big. To express something in writing that would give my whole life meaning. I've been feeling so frustrated because life has gotten in the way of that."

Karen nodded. "Writing is a big gift for you."

"I feel like I've been waiting all along for my life's work, but it sounds as if *this* is my life's work—the struggle, the perseverance, the forgiveness."

"That's exactly right," she said. "You don't even realize what you've already done for people. The spirit guides are telling me that you've already done a lot, just walking your own path. Understand the growth you're getting from this life. You're not seeing the light you're achieving. You're only seeing the struggle. Let go of your expectations!"

I drove home in a fugue state. Several years of therapy had done less to lighten my soul than the past three hours with Karen. The visitation from Steve had completed my arc of understanding and forgiveness. Thank you, Steve.

A couple of months later, our St. Helena Chamber Chorus was performing Fauré's *Requiem* again, this time the full work for an Easter celebration. Because it was a traditional funeral work, one of the members suggested that we list an "In Memoriam" dedication to our lost loved ones in the program. It felt like a challenge laid personally at my feet. Was I finally ready to publicly declare my forgiveness? Turns out I was.

Remembering Stephen Beckwith, who lived life large and left the party too soon, I wrote. I could feel the last sliver of ice falling away from my heart, like the calving of a glacier.

Chapter 33
Disembarkation

My words of thanks to Steve that day offered a demarcation point in my thinking. I'd finally released him from blame for everything that was wrong in my life. And that allowed me to welcome him back as an ally.

My life doesn't look like I thought it would when I imagined being able to finally forgive him. I still have years of trying to improve my credit score ahead, and I've been waging a long fight to refinance my home. I still endure the financial uncertainty of being a fulltime freelancer. I'm still going on lots of first dates and very few second dates. In some ways, it feels as if nothing has changed.

But things *have* changed. In May 2015, I traveled to Iowa to attend Bronte's graduation from Iowa State University. Our relationship had been gradually thawing, but the young woman who greeted me at the Des Moines airport had truly evolved. The tension and anger were miraculously replaced by reasonableness, thoughtfulness, humor, and even kindness.

In my Ames hotel room, Bronte had left a gift basket of things she knew I'd like—travel amenities; dark chocolate with almonds; hand cream in mandarin orange, my favorite scent. *Thanks for being here*, read the card. She persuaded me to stay an extra day so we could spend time together, just the two of us, and we drove around Madison County to see the famous covered bridges. Bronte returned home the following week to start work as a veterinary technician on the Peninsula, and we began spending weekends together. It feels like a miracle.

That summer was Amory's last at home. Unlike Bronte, whose tires practically squealed in her eagerness to leave, Amory's excitement was tempered by uncertainty. Not yet ready to face a four-year school, he decided to attend Santa Barbara City College—six hours down the coast—for two years before transferring somewhere else. The decision felt sound. He'd be rooming with three buddies from high school, and he could ease into the academic load.

When Bronte and Amory were little, I'd always hated it when older mothers had said, "Enjoy every minute! It goes so fast!" Most days, it usually didn't seem fast enough. And now, whoosh. All gone. My chance to make it right was over.

I would walk past Amory's open bedroom door and sigh. He'd gone off to work out at the gym or to hang with his friends as the mounting piles of junk grew higher on the floor. With just two days left before departure, I couldn't even see the carpet for the clothes, the computer games, the sports equipment. It took my every ounce of restraint not to start shrieking in frustration.

And then, suddenly, Amory's teenage clutter magically formed itself into three piles—to keep, to give away, and to throw away—and his SUV was packed to the roof. The plan was for him to drive us both down to Santa Barbara on Friday; I would stay a couple of days to help him get settled and then take the train back on Sunday morning.

On Saturday, we moved him into his new Santa Barbara apartment, ran some last-minute errands, and went to dinner on State Street. An ocean breeze blew up from the beach, the palm trees swayed gently, and everyone looked gorgeous and tanned against the backdrop of faux-Spanish architecture. *How easy it would be to live here*, I thought, *to find a small house and simply move here myself.* It wasn't just the idea of proximity to Amory I liked; it was the beauty of the new life he had chosen. I realized that I was actually a little envious. The excitement of seeing the future materialize. The pure beauty of the unknown world.

All day, the finality of saying goodbye to my younger child had been growing like a lump in my throat. We got in the car. "Where to next?" Amory asked.

"My hotel's just a few blocks on the right, Ammo," I said.

"Wait, Mom!" he said with a rising panic in his voice. "I still need groceries!"

I pointed out that we'd driven around that afternoon and I'd shown him where the grocery store was, the Rite-Aid, the post office, the bike shop. I had given him his grocery money for the month; all he had to do was drive himself there. He'd been doing that for years in St. Helena.

"But I thought . . ."

The lump was so big now, I was afraid I couldn't speak. Bronte and I had been warriors at the end. I'd known that the distance would do us both good. But Ammo and I had been real buddies in those last few years. He was my last child. I couldn't imagine life without him.

"You should get an early night tonight, and so should I," I said. "I have an early train tomorrow." We'd driven the few blocks to my hotel, and I got out. Amory cut the engine and joined me on the sidewalk. He circled his long arms around me and pulled me in for a hug that went on and on. I was doing my Lamaze breathing now, willing myself not to let the sobs surface onto his big, beefy shoulder. Through his skin I could feel the edge of the titanium plate that had mended his collarbone. He muttered something into my hair.

"What was that?" I sniffled.

"You're my rock," Amory whispered. "I can't thank you enough."

I'm sure it wasn't the first time that the good people of Santa Barbara had seen a weepy mother saying goodbye to her college-bound child. But I cried and cried. And I cried some more.

The following year passed quickly, and I got used to the quieter, emptier house. Then that spring our beloved yellow lab, Dolce, died. As much as I mourned her passing, it also felt like a liberation. The future suddenly loomed broad and uncharted. There was nothing to tie me to this house or this town anymore. My clients were mostly in the Bay Area. The traffic along Highway 29 had become noticeably worse, making it a full day's round trip to the city and back. I was feeling stifled and trapped.

I walked around the house and scrutinized the walls, the furniture, the views from the windows. I suddenly saw this place as a container for all the drama and Dharma that had happened over the past seven years. Divorce, death, broken bones, broken hearts, financial ruin, recovery, healing, forgiveness, salvation. This house was the ship we'd sailed on through so many stormy seas. Now I was ready to dock that ship and climb ashore, to find a new boat, a new sea.

I began to investigate where else I might want to live. After months of exploration, I settled on Sonoma, another wine-country town roughly twice the size of St. Helena in another valley just an hour away. Only forty-five minutes to San Francisco and still close enough that I could return to see my friends and continue to play bocce and sing with my chamber group. It had a beautiful historic plaza in the center of town, a lively arts community, a Whole Foods market. It was small enough that I could still ride my blue Amsterdam bike everywhere I needed to go.

I moved to Sonoma in the middle of a July heat wave. I'd reluctantly given up our membership to the pricey Meadowood country club. It had been the last vestige of my Napa Valley marriage, and

I wasn't that person anymore. I joined the local gym, which had a functional lap pool. Instead of rolling lawns and uniformed waiters, there were mismatched lounge chairs and an always-closed "Snack Shack."

Now I stretched out on a chair, feeling the sun's heat on my wet suit and skin. Before I began this journey, I'd believed that we earned our good fortune, like recess or time off for good behavior, that if our life wasn't easy and successful and full of pleasures, we had done something wrong, perhaps in a past life. I had worked extremely hard to achieve professional success, to have a great marriage, to be a good mother. So why, I wondered, was I being punished with one catastrophe after another? It must have been my karma, I thought. I was playing an unfair game of dodgeball in which the universe was hurling misfortune at me faster than I could duck.

I see things differently now. I've learned that life on this earth isn't a vacation. It's a university. It's where we come to learn specific lessons, and we choose partners and families and friends to help us learn those lessons. One of the universal lessons for all of us, I've discovered, is to experience love and joy. Not conditionally—when everyone's behaving and the bank account is full. But unconditionally—when people disappoint us, or when we barely have enough money to cover next month's mortgage. Our adversaries are often our greatest teachers, and sooner or later we must learn to bless them.

But here's something else I've figured out: Until this all happened, I'd thought of myself as an incredibly lucky person. Great parents. Raised in an affluent, educated town with plenty of options. A first-class education. A stimulating career. And, for many years, a happy marriage to an extraordinary man, with two beautiful, healthy children.

When that luck seemed to run out, I fought back. I chose not to give up but to survive and to protect my children. Now I look back and realize that I actually engineered most of that earlier good luck myself. The common denominator in my whole lifetime of positive experiences, it turns out, was me.

My marriage was a strong wind that blew across that path, scattering challenges and blessings in its wake. A murmuration of starlings. The sunlight in blinding shards across a bay. A circle of clasped hands around a table. A world of messy, confounding chaos. I can see every memory, hear every voice, and hold them close in equal measure.

Book Group Discussion Questions

1. As a memoir, *The Ghost Marriage* tells the story of one woman's overcoming a seemingly impossible series of obstacles. Are there other comparable memoirs that come to mind? What distinguishes this book from those?

2. Kirsten opens the book telling the reader about Steve's funeral. How did knowing that he would die affect your feelings about his character?

3. Kirsten ends up forgiving Steve a lot sooner than she expected. How did you feel about her spontaneous moment of forgiveness? Would you have been able to forgive Steve?

4. Kirsten blames herself for not seeing Steve's dysfunction sooner and standing up to it more strongly. How would you have handled his increasingly negative behavior?

5. How did you feel about Kirsten's decision to leave her marriage? What would you have done in her place?

6. Do you consider Steve a narcissist? What does that make Kirsten?

7. How did you feel about Kirsten's relationship to her children? Would you have handled them differently?

8. How credible did you find Kirsten's experiences with Steve's paranormal communications?

9. In the end, how did you feel about Steve's character?

10. Have you received similar messages in your own life?

11. Did Kirsten's experiences with the medium change the way you feel about spiritual energy or life after death?

12. What do you feel is the lesson of this book?

ACKNOWLEDGMENTS

I didn't want to write this book. After living this story for nearly a decade, I had absolutely no desire to relive it in detail, let alone spend nearly four years documenting it. But every friend to whom I told my saga said, almost verbatim: "You have to write a book about that." Then the spirits started weighing in, through psychics, astrologers, and my life coach: "You're meant to write a book about this."

Fine. Are y'all happy now? Of course, during the writing process, I began to realize how therapeutic and healing it was to dig deep into my story and put words to those events, those feelings, those relationships that previously had made no sense. The writing itself was a gift of clarity, regardless of whether my words would ever see the daylight of publication.

Along the way, there were so many who cheered me on, who gave feedback, and who provided much-needed expertise. At many annual workshops of the Napa Valley Writers' Conference, Lan Samantha Chang taught me the basics of story structure. My writers' group—Rachelle Newbold, Jack Stuart, Allie Timar, and Greg Williams—provided early critiques and encouragement. Friend, mentor, and editor Anne Matlack Evans helped me to shape the story from a rambling diatribe into a more cohesive narrative. The two Robins—McMillan and Allen—gave me some fresh, objective eyes. Editor par excellence Jodi Fodor helped me to "kill my kittens" and made cutting thirty-four thousand words a lot less painful than expected. And Brooke Warner and her excellent team at She Writes Press brought this baby into the world.

This story of forgiveness would not have happened at all without the spiritual guidance of Arjuna Elkins, Karen Peterson, and Karen Watkins. Thank you for ushering me toward the light.

Finally, to my two children—whom I hope won't be reading this book for many years, until they're ready to understand it—thank you for your love and patience. If it weren't for you, this story would have been very, very different.

ABOUT THE AUTHOR

© Françoise Peschon

Kirsten Mickelwait is a professional copywriter and editor by day and a writer of fiction and creative nonfiction by night. She's an alumna of the Squaw Valley Community of Writers, the Napa Valley Writers' Conference, the Paris Writers' Conference, and the San Francisco Writers' Conference. Her short story, "Parting with Nina," won first prize in *The Ledge*'s 2004 Fiction Awards Competition. She lives in the San Francisco Bay Area, where she's at work on a new novel.

SELECTED TITLES FROM SHE WRITES PRESS

She Writes Press is an independent publishing company founded to serve women writers everywhere. Visit us at www.shewritespress.com.

The Buddha at My Table: How I Found Peace in Betrayal and Divorce by Tammy Letherer $16.95, 978-1631524257

On a Tuesday night, just before Christmas, after he had put their three children in bed, Tammy Letherer's husband shattered her world and destroyed every assumption she'd ever made about love, friendship, and faithfulness. In the aftermath of this betrayal, however, she finds unexpected blessings—and, ultimately, the path to freedom.

Seeing Red: A Woman's Quest for Truth, Power, and the Sacred by Lone Morch $16.95, 978-1-938314-12-4

One woman's journey over inner and outer mountains—a quest that takes her to the holy Mt. Kailas in Tibet, through a seven-year marriage, and into the arms of the fierce goddess Kali, where she discovers her powerful, feminine self.

Lost in the Reflecting Pool: A Memoir by Diane Pomerantz $16.95, 978-1-63152-268-0

A psychological story about Diane, a highly trained child psychologist, who falls in love with Charles, a brilliant and charming psychiatrist—ignoring all the red flags that will later come back to haunt her.

Not Exactly Love: A Memoir by Betty Hafner $16.95, 978-1-63152-149-2

At twenty-five, Betty Hafner thought she'd found the man to make her dream of a family and cozy home come true—but after they married, his rages turned the dream into a nightmare, and Betty had to decide: stay with the man she loved, or find a way to leave?

Letting Go into Perfect Love: Discovering the Extraordinary After Abuse by Gwendolyn M. Plano $16.95, 978-1-938314-74-2

After staying in an abusive marriage for twenty-five years, Gwen Plano finally broke free—and started down the long road toward healing.

Loveyoubye: Holding Fast, Letting Go, And Then There's The Dog by Rossandra White $16.95, 978-1-938314-50-6

A soul-searching memoir detailing the painful, but ultimately liberating, disintegration of a twenty-five-year marriage.

CPSIA information can be obtained
at www.ICGtesting.com
Printed in the USA
JSHW030935020721
16463JS00001B/1

9 781647 420307